CRUSH
YOUR NEXT
VIRTUAL
PRESENTATION

A modern guide for the modern communicator

RICK ALTMAN

Crush Your Next Virtual Presentation
A Modern Guide for the Modern Communicator
by Rick Altman

October 2025: First Edition

Published by:
Harvest Books
1423 Harvest Rd.
Pleasanton CA 94566
925.398.6210
www.CrushYourNext.pro

Copyright ©2025 Rick Altman. All rights reserved. No part of this book may be reproduced or transmitted in any form or by any means, electronic or mechanical, including photocopying, recording, or by an information storage or retrieval system. To seek permission for reprints and excerpts, contact the Publisher above.

Library of Congress Control Number
2025910875

ISBN
978-0-9906331-2-9

Printed in the United States of America

To my favorite copy editors: beloved wife Becky and devoted daughter Jamie. Keep reading to meet the rest of the uber-talented editing team...

Contents

Thanks to. i
Foreword. iii
Introduction v

Get Visual

Chp 1   Designing for Distraction. 2
Chp 2   The Triad of Good Presentation Design 11
Chp 3   The Three-Word Challenge. 14
Chp 4   Avoiding Handout Hell 28
Chp 5   Better Breadcrumbs 36
Chp 6   Fun with Fonts. 45

Get Personal

Chp 7   Flex Your Engagement Muscle. 56
Chp 8   Everything in Moderation. 72
Chp 9   The Eyes Have it 83
Chp 10 Please Read to Us...Said No One Ever 89
Chp 11 Notes to Self 95
Chp 12 The Paradox of the Gallery 106

Get Physical

Chp 13 Fighting Nerves 116
Chp 14 Sit Tall, Stand Strong 123
Chp 15 Talk Human to Me. 137
Chp 16 Fake it 'Til You Make it 156

Get Technical

Chp 17 The Sound of Trust 160
Chp 18 Get Your Shot Together 168
Chp 19 Lighting 101 183
Chp 20 Real Rooms, Fake Rooms, and Chroma Dreams 196
Chp 21 Zoom and the Art of Not Losing Your Mind . . 207

Be Intentional

Chp 22 The Choice to be Seen. 226
Chp 23 Showing Up, by Design 229
Chp 24 The Touch of a Button 244
Chp 25 Presenting in the Era of AI. 253
Chp   Postscript 274

Thanks to...

If it takes a village to write a book on virtual presenting, the Presentation Summit is the perfect breeding ground for it. For nearly 25 years, our annual conference has been cultivating a community of presentation experts, slide junkies, and Zoom jockeys. From this pool, it was not difficult to hand-pick a great team of technology editors. They join the two copyeditors/grammarians in the family, Becky and daughter Jamie, in providing this book with several thorough and diligent reads.

♦

As a longtime presentation evangelist, **Marsh Makstein** initiated the concept that would become the presentation design agency eSlide. Marsh believes that presentations are a critical corporate communication tool and that effective PowerPoint can actually bring life to ideas and organizations. In his 35+ years in the industry, he has seen great presentations motivate firms to survive tough challenges and has witnessed stock prices soar after a strong presentation by company leadership teams.

♦

Lori Manton opened her first presentation design and desktop publishing business in 1992, back when clip art was cutting-edge. While the tools have changed since those early days, the heart of it remains: clear messaging and compelling stories. At Manton Design, Lori specializes in PowerPoint slide design and custom templates for clients ranging from Fortune 100 companies to one-person shops. Her superpower? Teaching clever tricks that make clients say, "Wait, PowerPoint can do that?"

♦

Christiane Pusch has been working with PowerPoint for over 30 years. She has a master of arts degree in musicology, literature, and pedagogy and started her career organizing festivals and concerts, before she changed to an office job. Once there, PowerPoint soon became her true calling. Being creative is an essential part of her life—whether it's reading for hours on end, crafting, or making music. She is an alto in choir (in person and virtual), in a Renaissance lute duo with her husband and solo. She enjoys playing music from all periods on her instruments, her favorite being Irish trad on the mandolin.

♦

John Rahmlow is an internationally recognized authority on virtual presentations. Using his extensive experience, John has designed and delivered high-impact virtual presentations for some of the largest companies in the world. He served for three years on the Board of Directors of the Presentation Guild, including two years as Board Secretary. John was also a contributor to the Presentation Guild's influential white paper, The Future of Presentations in a Virtual World, and has delivered and led multiple sessions on virtual presenting at the Presentation Summit.

♦

And finally, a shoutout to my good friend and brilliant sketch artist **Mike Parkinson**, for his creative work on the cover. Mike showed off his talents years ago when he saw the crazy team names for the conference's trivia contest ("Fade, Wipe, and Flush"..."Morph Me Baby One More Time"..."Slippery Decks"). He found a white board and marker, and in about five minutes, whipped up the most clever sketches any game show host could ask for.

I asked him for the same five-minute treatment on the cover. He politely declined and provided me with something much more thoughtful.

Foreword

In a world where face-to-face interaction has shifted to face-to-screen, the art of presenting has undergone a radical transformation. And if you're holding this book, you've just made one of the smartest moves a modern communicator can make.

Rick Altman is one of the most trusted voices in presentation design and delivery. He doesn't just teach PowerPoint—he lives the power of the point. And in this book, he delivers what we all need: a clear, engaging, and practical guide to showing up with impact on virtual platforms like Zoom, Teams, or Webex.

Having spent thousands of hours engaging people through a webcam —whether emceeing a global summit, training Fortune 100 leaders, or turning bored employees into active collaborators—I know as well as anyone that virtual presenting is not just about technology. It's about connection.

Rick gets this. His best practices go beyond software tips. They are built for real human beings—from Nairobi to New York, from presenters in Manila to engineers in Munich. They are inclusive, actionable, and rooted in empathy.

Rick and I have collaborated on five virtual and hybrid conferences. I appreciate his thoughtful design and deep and decisive decision making to make his conference one of the best virtual events in the world.

Over these past five years, my presentations have improved. From modern features such as Morph to techniques of better design, I now consult and improve the slide decks of top speakers in the world, such as National Speakers Association Hall of Famers. This is due to Rick's dedication that *you* are the presentation and his sharing of his best techniques developed over the years.

This book answers the call for those who want to stop sharing screens and start sharing stories. For those who don't want to just talk online, but transform online. Follow what Rick shares with you and you can be the top speaker at your next presentation.

So, whether you're a speaker, educator, marketer, or anyone who wants to be unforgettable on a screen, you're in the right hands.

Read this. Use it. Enjoy it. And get ready to present like never before.

John Chen, CSP
Founder, Engaging Virtual Meetings
Keynote Speaker | Community Leader | Digital Diplomat
Seattle, WA

Introduction

The memories are vivid, if not always pleasant. The first was from 2009 when I was introduced to the Webex interface and shown how an audience of 150 could all see my screen as I performed various mouse tricks on it. If I had a camera attached to my computer, I could even show my face to my audience, but nobody had USB cameras back then.

Still, this was nothing short of remarkable. People from all over the world could watch over my virtual shoulder as I purported to cast off pearls of wisdom. These were not called virtual presentations; they were webinars. Or we referred to them by a noun culled from the predominant platform in use: We would deliver a Webex. Just like how we Zoom today…only this was 16 years ago. I probably used Skype to back-channel with my producer, too.

The second memory was much more recent, when we were all sent to our own silos to combat a disease in 2020. Suddenly, our webcam was like our lifeline with the rest of the world. We used it to communicate with our loved ones, we used it to meet with our teams. Our sons and daughters, brothers and sisters, and perhaps you used it to attend school and book club.

Practically overnight, Zoom became a household word. Everyone and their dog were using it, and that is barely hyperbole: It became at least acceptable, if not de rigueur, to have your pet in your Zoom background while you sheltered, worked, and tried to stay sane.

People still needed to present, so we used Zoom for that, too. We were all bad at it and we were all stuck at home, so we cut everyone all sorts of slack. You were forgiven if you couldn't figure out how to unmute yourself, or if you didn't know where to look when speaking. It was not a party foul if your pitch for Series B funding was interrupted by a doorbell and a pizza delivery. Bad lighting? Poor audio? Camera looking up your nose? All forgiven. Your dog barking? De rigueur.

My own flavor of angst stemmed from the specter, which became a certainty, that we would not be able to hold the Presentation Summit, the annual conference that I have been directing and hosting since 2003. Organizers and patrons alike were chased into our own bubbles to figure out how to stage and attend multi-day learning events from our respective homes.

Urban Transformation
Our family room converted into a broadcast studio, Covid be damned.

Despite my standing as chief organizer, I had no idea what I was doing. I told my presenters that I didn't care about dogs barking or doorbells ringing. I wanted crystal clear audio and I wanted everything live—no pre-records at all.

These are not unique stories—the whole world was trying to figure this out, and just about every hour of every day someone uttered the now-infamous phrase:

"I can't wait for us to beat Covid so that we can return to normal."

Ladies and gentlemen, welcome to our new normal. We have beaten Covid but we still give virtual presentations, and we will probably continue to do so until holographic presenting becomes a real thing. This has very real implications for you, a person who probably owes a chunk of livelihood to communicating effectively in public. This stuff was hard enough before Covid—"Death by PowerPoint" is in everyone's vocabulary. Now add Zoom Fatigue to that and you have a particularly toxic brew.

It's no longer good enough to phone in Zoom meetings (if you'll pardon the mixed metaphor). We who communicate in public do not enjoy the luxury of waving our hand and offering a dismissive "oh, it's just Zoom." We must do better. We must set, meet, and then exceed the standards for virtual presentation. Our audiences deserve our very best effort, and this book was born with that aspiration in mind.

This book places in its crosshairs the worldwide masses who now must communicate virtually as part of their jobs or professions. You are expected to be better than the garden-variety webinar leader—maybe you have an idea how to do that and maybe you don't.

And what credentials me for this privilege of preaching at you across 25 chapters? As mentioned earlier, I've been giving virtual presentations since 2009, but that's not it. I've been operating as a presentations consultant since the turn of the millennium, but that's not it, either.

Hosting the aforementioned Presentation Summit for over two decades has certainly helped broaden my perspective on impactful storytelling, inspiring presentation design, effective use of PowerPoint, and successful delivery. But that's not it, either.

I've been on camera dozens of times in my years as a tennis journalist, as a technology reporter, and as a guest on many shows. I understand the ephemeral quality of warming to the camera. That's not it, either.

And I've been writing books on technology since technology looked nothing like what it does today. Maybe that helps, but mostly that just confirms how old I am.

No, I suffered through the same pandemic that you did. I was thrust into the same position as you of having to learn a bunch of new tech in order to practice my craft. I was as clueless as you were at all of this. Like you, I had to figure all this out in real time, with no manuals, no live support, no pressing F1 for help.

More than anything else, that is what has prepared me to take on a project of this scope.

Across these 275 pages, I won't preach at you and I won't ask you to remember a litany of unfamiliar phrases. I won't expect you to take notes and I won't give you homework assignments for the next time you present. And you do not need to read this book from start to finish—you can browse it and flip through it, stopping at any passage that sounds interesting.

To address the inherent disconnect of reading about a dynamic discipline in a static medium, we want you to have your phones handy, so you can take advantage of the many QR codes that are distributed throughout. They take you directly to short videos that demonstrate or amplify the topic at hand. For the PDF version, those QR codes are clickable hyperlinks.

You will also find several references to files that you can download. Those files are all located at www.crushyournext.pro/files/, so just add the filename to that address to access each one.

I divide the book into five parts, the first four with a call to get something and the last one a call to be something:

- Get Visual
- Get Personal
- Get Physical
- Get Technical
- Be Intentional

That last one might end up being the underlying theme for the whole book. Within those five parts, the chapters are uneven—some of them a few pages and others a few dozen—and that reflects the coverage of topics, where biases are obvious, not hidden. And not just mine: When any one of my technology editors holds a contrary point of view, I do more than just take it into consideration; I invite them to share it with you. Disagreement is good, don't you agree?

Similarly, I neither expect nor hope that you will accept all of my assertions; in fact, if you do, your experience might be a bit diminished. Virtual presenting is still too mysterious and there are too many legitimate and disparate points of view about its effective use for us to expect that we can have consensus on all points. And besides, the greatest reward of all might be in the debate in which we regularly indulge across the Chat screens at the Summit and a host of other online experiences that we hold across the year.

If I have done my job with this book, it holds equal appeal across lines of experience and aptitude. While the sweet spot is those who owe their livelihoods to strong virtual communication, it's not like these concepts are lost on those who Zoom as part of an avocation. And a conservative estimate places the percentage at about 65% of the material in this book that applies to in-person presenting. We still have to do that, too.

I plead guilty to using Zoom as a generic. Most of us use it; most of us use it at the exclusion of all else. But a measurable chunk of our online population also uses Teams, Adobe Connect, and still Webex. Most of the principles in the following chapters are platform agnostic and I simply use Zoom as the common denominator. I try to specify when that is *not* the case and if I blow it anywhere, please hold my feet to that fire and point it out to me.

So let's get started. Just about every point of view that I will share, each stratagem or tactic offered, all of the philosophy espoused can be traced back to three personal truths that I have developed in my more-than-a-few decades of communicating in public and my experience before a camera:

1. A good presentation is made up of what you say, what you show, and what you give to your audience.

2. The greatest quality a presenter can have is authenticity. Your virtual audience members want to know who you really are.

3. Being passionate about your topic will make up for a multitude of presentation sins.

If you would like to explore how these truths play out in the virtual environment, this is the right read for you.

Part One
Get Visual

This book makes the same assumption as just about every work that I have authored since the 1990s: that you are not in possession of a graphic arts degree from any institution of learning. My path to virtual presenting has weaved through electronic publishing, digital graphics, and traditional presentation, and at every stop, I have encountered people without formal backgrounds in the arts being asked to design things, often on a daily basis.

Many of these fine people whom I have met do not really even know what the word *design* means. When they hear that word, they think about making things look pretty, but I'm sorry, if all you have are pretty slides, you don't have much.

So this first part of the book discusses what it actually means to design an effective virtual presentation. If you are one of the lucky few with a background in graphic design, these first few chapters might serve to remind you how fortunate you are!

Designing for Distraction

There was a time when w thought that school-age children had the lowest attention span among our species. That was before we observed humans attending Zoom calls; now we know better. (And to think that during Covid it was the school-age children that had to sit on Zoom all day...so glad our own daughters had graduated by then.)

I have colleagues who believe that 100% attention 100% of the time is an attainable goal. I literally told them that they are on crack—this quote appeared in a 2014 *Forbes* feature story on the emerging trend of webinars:

"If you think you will ever get 100% attention when leading a webinar, you are on crack."

And it has only gotten worse since Covid. Indeed, you might not find an audience for a presentation more distracted than those who attend your virtual ones. It is practically guaranteed that they have their email window open next to their Zoom window, and perhaps a spreadsheet on a second monitor. And, of course, their phone is nearby, dutifully on silent, but nonetheless delivering texts and Instagram notifications.

Do you tilt at this windmill?

So what's a poor webinar leader to do? Do you fight it or do you embrace it? Do you try for the holy grail of complete attention on the part of your audience members or do you conclude that life is too short and you have bigger fish to fry? I want you to do both!

Fight the good fight

By all means, try as best you can to get and keep people's attention. Be undaunted in the face of inevitable distractions. All of the time-tested strategies make up noble pursuits:

- Ask your audience lots of questions.

- Insist that people answer them.

- Conduct polls, either through your streaming service's polling function or by a literal show of hands while in gallery view.

- Have frequent convos with your host or moderator, because the more audience members hear another voice, the higher the likelihood they might pay attention.

You want people thinking, wondering, asking, answering, agreeing, disagreeing. Any engagement is good engagement. Anything you can do to vary the energy level and the vibe, you should do it!

Give up, it's hopeless

At the same time that you are fighting the good fight, you should concede to the insurmountable force. You should acknowledge that most in your audience are doing two things at once, many have places they would rather be, and for some, the only reason they are attending at all is because they know they can be working on something else at the same time.

Concede these points, not begrudgingly or resentfully, but graciously. Show them that you understand their reality and that you are grateful for getting even a piece of them. In fact, go a step further by accommodating their reality: Design your message so it can hold up to divided attention.

In journalism school, students learn about the "inverted pyramid," an approach to reporting in which you lead with the most important information first, before trailing off to less important details. Virtual presentation designers should follow this form. For each topic of a presentation, ask yourself these two questions:

- What is the most important thing to tell about this topic?
- If I only had 30 seconds to tell this story, what would I say?

In the example below, I am leading a conversation about the electric car industry and how far it's come in the last decade. The first few points are salient to all—better range, crazy acceleration, more charging stations. Then I trail off into the weeds with subtopics that are for the EV nerds in the group.

I have even been known to say to my audience, "I know that you might be doing other things, so I will let you know when we change topics." And when I do change topics, I do it prominently: My voice picks up in energy and maybe I wipe the screen with a reversed-out color. In other words, I zealously try to get your undivided attention for a few fleeting moments, and during that time, I hit you with the most important thought of this new topic.

I hope to create a covenant with you: I promise never to shame you for multitasking and you promise to pay attention when I tell you that we are covering important stuff. Audiences appreciate this type of negotiation.

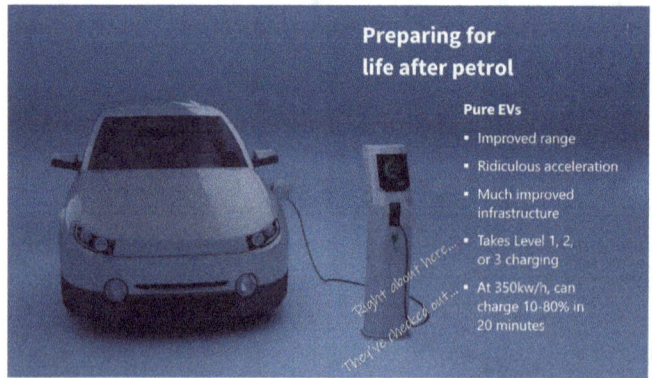 

Your covenant with distracted audiences
This slide about electric vehicles is designed for multitasking audiences. It gives them the most important ideas first, and then assumes that some will turn their attention elsewhere during the minutiae. Scan this QR code to see a video of this strategy in action.

Chp 1 Designing for Distraction

The phenomenon of motion

You could make a strong case that the most powerful tool in PowerPoint's arsenal is the Animation engine. Heaven knows we have all seen the tool used to obnoxious effect, causing us to shake our heads and roll our eyes. That is pretty powerful, all right, just not in the ways that we might want it to be.

Driving this phenomenon is my Universal Axiom No. 1 across all of PowerPoint:

If something moves on screen, your audience members have no choice but to look at it.

This is a response that occurs at a subconscious level. We are like moths drawn to a light; we cannot help ourselves. In response to a skeptic at a seminar many years ago, I prepared the following experiment:

1. I stood off to the side of the room, about 20 feet from the screen and began to talk about this topic.

2. I was careful not to take my eyes off of the audience and equally mindful to speak strongly enough so that their eyes would be on me.

3. In mid-sentence, I sent a rocket ship flying across the screen.

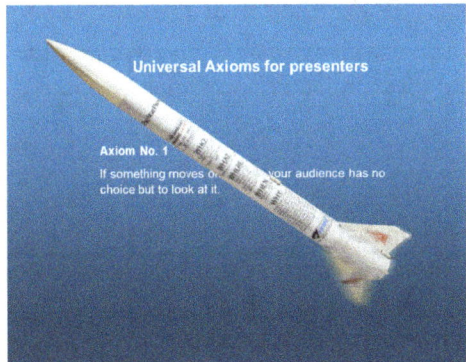

Everyone looked.

"Hey, I'm over here," I said playfully, as the audience returned their gaze to me. Two seconds later, a bright yellow ball flashed momentarily.

Everyone looked. And laughed—they'd been had. I now do this at every workshop I give on this subject, and I can even do it on virtual!

"You can't help it!"
Even on virtual, animation can command your attention, whether you want it to or not. Watch the video and see for yourself.

So please repeat after me these holy vows of animation:

- I will use animation wisely and appropriately.
- I vow not to offend the sensibilities of my audience.
- I promise not to use an animation technique simply because I just discovered it.
- I swear never to make stuff move on screen just because I like to watch my audience members' heads bob up and down.

In the virtual world, these vows have to be balanced against the need to manage the loss of attention that your audience members exhibit.

Change is good

While I rarely advocate for change for its own sake, a dynamic webinar environment is a healthy environment. If a slide sits idle for more than about 60 seconds, people's minds are going to wander, and some might even suspect that their own video has gone wonky.

We seek a tasteful and relevant rotation of visuals—there should be meaning behind the change. If you can find three or four photos that are relevant to the topic, consider bringing them in sequentially, every 30 seconds or so. While that might not be the advice I would offer you when you are in the room, it would be well-suited when in the Zoom.

I am not suggesting that you import them as postage stamps and run them down the edge of the page; Postage Stamp Syndrome is a hallmark of

Chp 1 **Designing for Distraction**   **7**

Death by PowerPoint and a harbinger of Zoom Fatigue. I always urge clients to go big with pics: Anchor them to at least three sides of the slide, and if you can, send it across the entire slide.

If you find three relevant photos, consider a rotating fade of them as the backdrop for your words, as with these slides discussing the criteria for calling team meetings.

Good for 90 seconds of talk time
Place these three slides into a rotation of 30 seconds each to create good visual variety. Same text for all three, just different location and different backdrop.

In this example, the text shifts to accommodate the open space of each picture. This stands in stark contrast to the boring "Content and Caption" layout that floats a photo on one half of the slide and the text on the other half. You can do way better, starting with making photos as big as you can. If you have a nicely honed narrative of just a few words, it will be relatively easy to find space in the photo itself.

To facilitate that, I am a big fan of semi-transparent shapes, as they enable you to blend simple text messages with relevant imagery. If you were to do nothing else than that with your slide design, you would stand apart from 99% of the people using PowerPoint today. The slides left and right apply a gradient fill pattern to a rectangle behind the text—the part under the text is fully opaque, providing contrast to the lettering, while the other side of the rectangle fades away into the photo. You can see how these semi-transparent shapes are utilized by downloading semi-transparent-shapes.pptx from www.crushyournext.pro/files/.

 We will take a deeper dive into the use of integrating photos with your text in Chapter 3.

Change is bad

This needs to be balanced with a larger issue that transcends virtual presenting: gratuitous animation. Too many well-intentioned PowerPoint users go on auto-pilot and apply animation to the text on a slide without regard for whether that improves the experiences of their audience members. In many cases, it does not.

A few years ago, we conducted an informal focus group about this, using this simple slide as an example:

Does this slide need to be animated? Should you animate it? What would happen if you did? What would happen if you didn't?

I believe that you provide no benefit when you animate simple text slides, and in fact, you could be providing a disservice. We learned this almost by accident with that survey at the conference. We showed conference patrons a basic slide like this one, with each bullet set to fade in on the click of a mouse or remote clicker. Our question to them was straightforward: What do you think of this? A majority of respondents believed that the animation added nothing to the audience experience and one out of seven were actually put off by it. "Why are you eliminating all context for me?" asked one.

True indeed: When you introduce elements onto a slide one by one, the audience is not able to see the forest for the trees; you rob them of context, and I have observed that virtual audiences crave context even more than in-person audiences (see the next chapter for more on that topic).

When the data is dense, smart sequencing with Animation is appreciated; when the data is sparse, it is not. Don't fall for the tired old warning that audience members might read ahead and not fully absorb your message. If you can't keep them on point, that's on you—don't blame your slides for that. For properly crafted slides (i.e. ones with simple text messages), it should not matter one bit if your audience wants to read ahead. People respond to simple text differently than they do to long passages. Finely honed and distilled text does not need to be comprehended; it is taken in more like a graphic.

For this reason, I no longer recommend to clients the sequencing of standard bullet slides. You do everyone a service by just getting them out there all at once and speaking to them. You provide them with full context, and what's more, you don't have to worry about forgetting how many bullet points remain and inadvertently advancing past the last one and onto the next slide.

Keeping text slides fresh

So how can we balance these two competing forces? How can you create good visual variety for your distracted audience without taking away their context? This revision of the exercise slide offers a simple solution that anyone reading this book can implement.

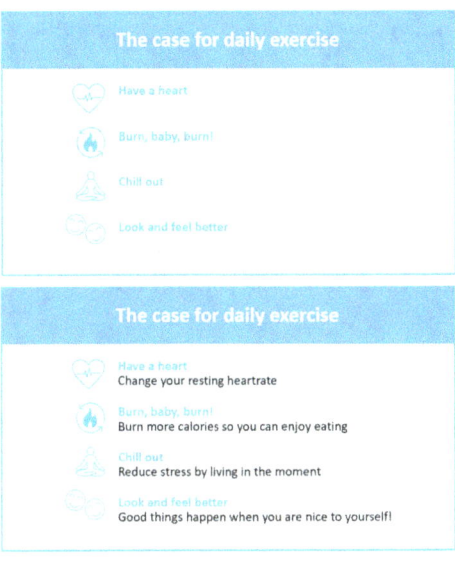

The four lines of text set in bold all appear on the slide together, along with their icons (from the Noun Project). This guarantees context for your audience members: They know this narrative contains four thoughts and they have a pretty good idea what those four thoughts are.

Then the rest of the text can be animated to come up on clicks, one per thought, until the entire slide is built, as shown here. This way, you bring some visual change to the slide but still provide all the context that your audience wants.

A professional designer could have created a much more attractive example of this for you. For that matter, I too could have come up with a more visually engaging slide, but I chose not to. I wanted to show how easily a simple change can elevate the look and feel of a slide. I want you to look at this slide and say, "Hey, I can do this."

◆

What you seek is relevant motion and impactful visual change. Nothing gratuitous—no bullets flying in from the bottom of your slide. You must always ask yourself: "How might I sequence this slide so that I can tell the story better?" Keeping that question top of mind will help you ward off Death by PowerPoint and Zoom Fatigue.

Now do that with your own mug

The logical extension of managing smart change to your visuals is how you control your own video likeness, and this will be the first of many times that I will refer you to Part 5, Be Intentional. Zoom does not make this easy, as its screen share function wants to stuff you into the corner and keep you there, and toggling on and off the Enable Video button becomes tedious.

This is unfortunate because controlling your video likeness should be a fundamental right for virtual presenters, and instead, it is just a foregone conclusion that you will become a postage stamp on your screen. As a result, few virtual presenters think about if, when, and how to show themselves, and yet that is one of the most significant aspects of good virtual storytelling, arguably more important than controlling slide visuals.

This is why we need to look beyond the basic controls of Zoom, Teams, Connect, and the others. Part 4 addresses the *how*; for now, I want you thinking about the *when*:

When should I be on screen and when should I not be?

Maybe I can tell this story better if I were just a voice over my slide.

What if I waited until this next passage to appear on camera?

If you are always on camera, then your appearance becomes a bit cheapened. But if you pick and choose the times to appear, you give your audience important clues about when to pay extra attention. "This is important enough that I want you to see my lips moving."

My whole caper with Axiom No. 1 (you cannot ignore movement of elements on screen) was based on this premise that if I am on screen, I need to be paid attention to more. You tell me which you would heed more between these two images.

The Triad of Good Presentation Design

This is likely to be the shortest chapter in the book and that is intentional, because it is also quite possibly the most salient chapter and I don't want its message to get lost in the weeds.

There are many ways to identify and describe the qualities of a good presentation. Performing a Google search on "good presentation design" unearths an incredible variety of ideas and thoughts. I could probably write an entire book just on those search returns and if I turned my AI agent loose on that assignment, it would have 100 pages written quicker than I could tie my shoelaces.

Preferring not to commit plagiarism, this chapter offers up my perspective on what makes a good presentation.

Three things

A good presentation is made up of these three components, listed here in the order that they typically occur: what you say, what you show, and what you give.

1. What you say to your audience, whether you are standing before them in person or seated before them on Zoom.

2. What you show them, typically through PowerPoint slides.

3. And what you give them, in the form of a printed or PDF handout.

Ideally, these three things would each be given the attention it deserves. Ideally, presenters should aim to make each of these as strong as possible. They would be distinct. Unique. You would reserve independent brain cycles on each of them.

But no. All too often, that doesn't happen. All too often, this is what happens:

- A well-intentioned content creator places way too much text on a slide.
- That compels the speaker to read every word of it.
- Someone then prints the deck and distributes it as a handout.

In other words, instead of these three core elements—say, show, and give—being distinct and unique, they have all become the same thing. And that strikes me as yet another common example of Death by PowerPoint.

The mantra here is to separate: Separate these three critical components of the presentation experience. Think about each one as a task of its own, and strive to make each one as good as you can.

These three core tenets provide the foundation for practically everything you will read in the chapters ahead. They stand as bedrock principles of effective presentation design.

What you **say**. What you **show**. What you **give**.

Chp 2 The Triad of Good Presentation Design 13

And one why

In addition to these three tenets, there is a question that I would like to have hover over every other topic in this book:

Why am I speaking to these people on this day in this way?

I tried to find a place in the text for this question. I could surely discuss it in the context of presentation design. Then I concluded that it is part of the delivery experience. No, actually, it is more personal than that—it is what makes you authentic. Wait, the "in this way" aspect is all about controlling the virtual environment.

You can see what was happening to me. I kept cycling through the four main themes of this book while it became increasingly clear that this question belongs everywhere! So as we just get started, it is my hope that I can bring focus to this question in all four parts and across just about every topic therein.

The Three-Word Challenge

What if a law were passed prohibiting bullet points from exceeding three words in length? Could you abide by it? Perhaps not, but humor me on this one, because it stands as one of the best exercises you can undertake, whether you are the presenter, the content creator, or both.

This chapter represents my stock in trade, as I have been advocating for this technique for nearly 20 years. If you have attended one of my webinars, chances are excellent you have heard me discuss this challenge. It is no less relevant in virtual. In fact, you could make a strong case that it is *more* important for virtual presenters to place their slides on a text diet.

This chapter also represents a lesson in futility: You will see shortly that the exercise that you and I will undergo together is doomed to failure. But from this failure can emerge extraordinary successes. From this failure, you might unlock the secret to better presentation design.

Chp 3 The Three-Word Challenge

Too much text

My friend and colleague Dave Paradi (ThinkOutsideTheSlide.com) conducts a bi-annual poll, in which he asks a simple question: What annoys you the most about PowerPoint? Across a decade of data, there are three responses that have clearly outpaced all others:

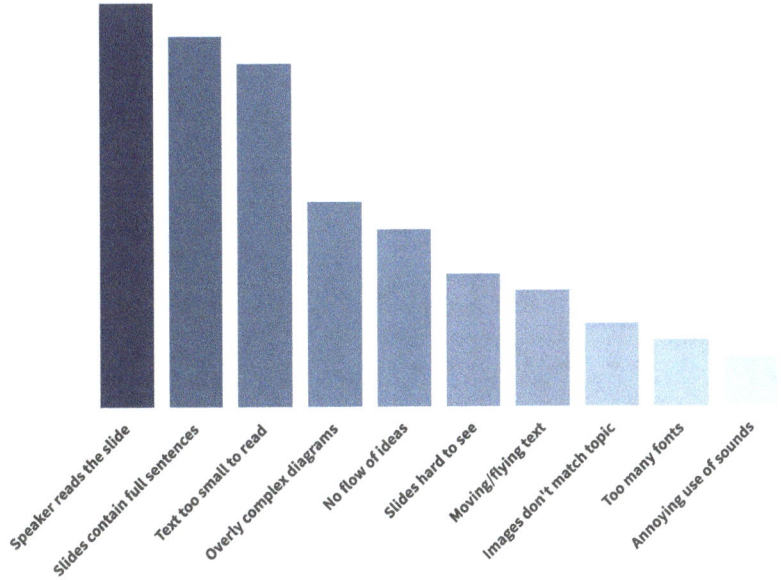

To summarize, people don't like when speakers read verbatim slides that contain complete sentences of tiny text.

Whew, talk about a tale of woe. And what do these three traits have in common? They are all symptomatic of slides that are overladen with text. In my virtual travels, where I am able to interact with presentation builders from all six of the inhabited continents, I see it all the time. Despite research that clearly shows that audience members hate when we do it, we continue to do it. We place too much text on our slides, resulting in reduced appreciation for the message, in turn causing confusion and resentment.

Breakfast gets a makeover

MOM Brands has been one of the most prominent makers of breakfast cereal for decades. Getting its name from the legendary Malt-O-Meal hot cereal, Post Foods bought MOM in 2015 for $1.15B. Everyone eats breakfast and competition is white hot for a stake in this business. MOM competes earnestly in that marketplace and brought me in for slide review a few years ago. Big or small, it seems that all companies must fight the urge to run off at the mouth with slide content. Here was one such example:

Opportunities and Initiatives

- BetterOats
  - Launching three Steel Cut Oat items in April 2015. Kroger expects our participation in Dunnhumby shelf review to identify hot cereal assortment and aggressive support of 3 coupon programs to reward loyal consumers
- Boxes
  - Spooners bags will be presented in June. Spooners bags fill the box voids of sustainability and health initiatives
- Naturals
  - Kroger Natural Foods team wants to be our #1 NF retailer. Kroger is looking for opportunities to partner and be firs to market. Naturally Nora and Natural Bag meets Kroger sustainability initiatives.
- Tube Oats & Hot Wheat
  - Opportunity with tube oats to develop a gusseted bag to have improved pack out and lower case packs.
- General
  - 1ˢᵗ to Market – New items & technologies
  - Promotional Partnership – Creative promotional opportunities, Buy 5 Get $5 Off
  - Dunnhumby – Kroger asked us to continue support of loyalty coupon mailings and becoming shop client. We are partnering with them on both initiatives.

Drowning in text
In wanting to find partners in the competitive breakfast food industry, MOM Brands got a bit lost in its story. Can you spot the typo? It's hard with all that flotsam.

While on site with the team that produced this deck, we were all treated to a rousing example of Universal Axiom No. 2:

If you display complete sentences on screen, it is practically impossible to avoid reading it word for word.

I asked one of the team members to stand up and pretend to be the presenter, speaking to the first bullet point.

He almost became paralyzed. It was tremendously challenging for him to make even the slightest change in the sentence construction and the experience rendered him a mere drone. This is why the fire danger is so high in creating slides with fully-formed thoughts. Let's go inside the head

Chp 3 The Three-Word Challenge

of a typical audience member when you become a drone in front of a slide with this much text on it:

Wow, is he really going to recite all of that to me…I can read it faster than he can say it…I'm already done…why didn't he just email it to me…what am I even doing here…I think I'll just text my friends.

That's pretty much how things go when audiences are subjected to slides like this one. So I want to challenge you. As the name of this chapter foretells, I call it my Three-Word Challenge, and it has acted as my mantra for nearly 20 years:

Can you reduce every one of your
bullet points to three words or fewer?

That might be very difficult for you to do; in fact, it might be an impossible task to accomplish. But you have to try nonetheless, as I'm going to now with that infamous MOM slide:

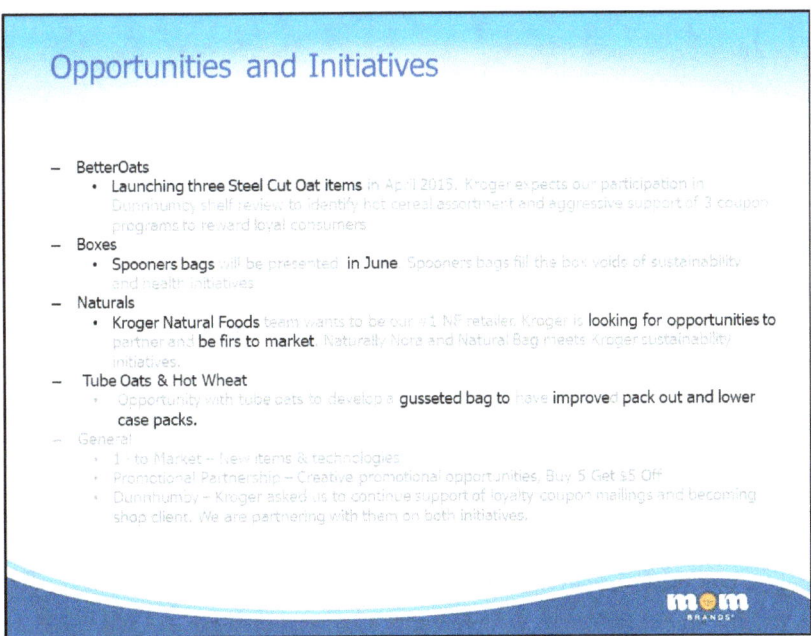

Removing the flotsam
The grayed-out words represent the ones deemed to be unnecessary for the slide. Spot the typo yet? When scrutinizing the text to this degree, it's easier ("firs to market…").

You'll note that I failed just about every time. Except for the final bullet, where I suggested total removal, not once did I actually get to three words. But I assure you that the reward is in the attempt, because look where the slide is now:

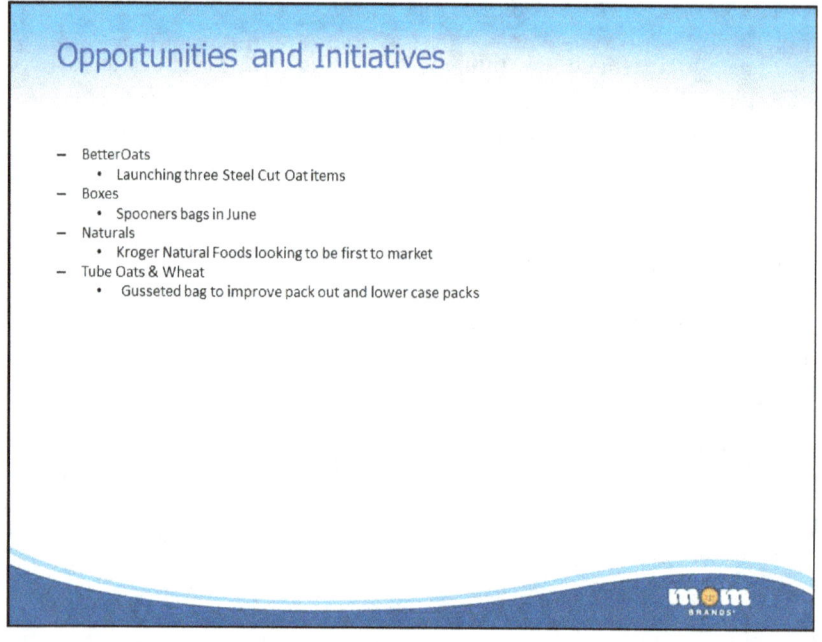

Were I to go no further at all, this slide would be a better experience for everyone attending the webinar. Of course, now we can go further, and perhaps that's the whole point. To those people who declare themselves to be bad graphic designers, who really knows what your instincts might be with respect to slide design, as most slides afford you no opportunity to find out. The finest designer in the world would not have been able to save the original slide, with all that text present.

But now, perhaps for the first time, you have an opportunity to think like a slide designer, and it might become apparent that you shouldn't have bullets with only one item and that this list would be better as subheads with trailing lines of text:

Chp 3 The Three-Word Challenge

Opportunities and Initiatives

Better Oats
Launching three Steel Cut Oat items

Boxes
Spooners bags in June

Naturals
Kroger Natural Foods looking to be first to market

Oats & Wheat
Gusseted bag to improve pack out and lower case packs

Much better
It would be perfectly appropriate to declare this slide done (with typo found and fixed). But could you do better still?

But let's keep going. Now that you can think like a slide designer, I would want you to have the following thought process: Can I find a photo that is evocative of the breakfast experience, and if so, can I size it up to fill the entire slide? I'm pleased to report that no degree in the arts is required for such endeavors. Head to your favorite stock photo house, or use PowerPoint's built-in image search, and have at it. It was crazy how many candidates I found in about 90 seconds of browsing:

These photos all share a particular quality and I wonder if you might be able to guess it before reading further. They all have areas of the image that could be obscured by text without losing impact—white space, as it's commonly known.

And because we have honed and distilled our text, it can fit into that white space. Here are the steps to finish this slide:

1. Choose one photo, discard the rest, and size it up to fit the slide, cropping the photo if necessary. Make sure to start with a photo that is at least 800x600 in size to ensure that it still looks sharp when sized up to fill the slide.

2. Place the branding along the bottom. I rarely think this is necessary but my clients usually do and I don't consider that fight worth waging. However, I did dig in my heels about a straight bar replacing the wavy one. It's cleaner, more professional looking, and less susceptible to having its space violated by the elements of a busy slide. As you can see, there is lots of open space on the left.

White space to the rescue
This becomes the backdrop for our content, with a healthy swath of space on the left side of the photo.

3. Now place the text in that space and set it to be white. You might be alarmed by the result, which is obviously not yet ready for prime time. A slide with unreadable text is the worst form of Death by PowerPoint.

Halfway through...ouch
Placing the text over top this photo would be a fail, but we're not done yet...

Chp 3 The Three-Word Challenge   21

It is now time for one of my favorite PowerPoint tricks, mentioned in Chapter 1: the semi-transparent shape. I find these simple objects—they're usually just rectangles—to be fantastic for solving problems and creating contrast and readability. They can make you look way more talented than you might be. (No surprise that I use them all the time.)

4. Create a rectangle that spans the entire vertical length of the slide and about two-thirds of the width. This rectangle should have a specific gradient fill pattern running from 100% opaque black on the left side to 100% transparent black on the right side.

The opaque part of the rectangle provides great contrast and then the transparent part of it allows it to simply fade away. When you blend simple text with large, relevant photos, you create slides that distinguish you from just about everyone else using PowerPoint.

Now we're talking
Plenty of contrast and readability and a nice, clean slide. Watch a demo of this technique from the QR code.

But as good as this looked, I wasn't satisfied. I really wanted to see some humans in the photo, so I kept looking, and found this gem:

What a perfect breakfast photo! The white space is on the other side, but that is no issue at all. I performed the same gradient fill maneuver, but in reverse, noodled on the title a bit, and found nirvana:

Voilà
Download mom-brands.pptx from www.crushyournext.pro/files/ to watch this sequence and to study how these slides were built. Watch a demo of this technique from the QR code.

♦

The before and after for this slide is dramatic, as will be the high regard that your audiences will hold you in when they see it.

The rewards of three words

Several important things take place when you make an earnest attempt to hone and distill your slide text. And as the previous exercise shows, you don't have to actually succeed at the Three-Word Challenge—that's practically impossible.

Your slides are friendlier

With just that one task, you create slides that are much easier on the eyes of your audience. Eye fatigue is the silent killer of presentations. When you ask your audience to sit in front of their monitor for 30 or 60 minutes, their eyes are going to be the first to check out. The more words each slide contains, the quicker the onset of visual fatigue. Fewer words, less fatigue. Your bullets might not be as descriptive, but that's a good thing: It's *your* job to do the describing.

Your pace improves

Something almost magical happens when you reduce the number of words on a slide. Everything seems snappier, audience members become more receptive, and you most likely project more energy. The entire experience feels more lively and upbeat.

You create intrigue

In three words, you cannot fully explain your points. But that's not bad; it's good. In fact, it's terrific! Unburdened from all that describing, you will become a better writer of bullets. You will begin to write with verve and color. All of this will help you reach audience members emotionally. And that, dear reader, is the holy grail of presenting.

You learn your material better

Of the many bad things associated with dumping complete sentences onto slides, perhaps the worst is how lazy it makes everyone, from designer to creator to presenter. Excess verbiage sends a subtle but powerful message that you don't need to prepare as much, because everything you want to say is already there. It is almost scary how many rounds of review and for how many months that typo in the original slide went undetected.

Parsing the words increases your burden as a presenter, but once again, this is a noble burden. Adhering to the three-word rule forces you to learn your content at a level you otherwise might not have reached.

As for all of that text that was eliminated from the slide? The next chapter suggests a better home for it.

◆

Of the many quotes mis-attributed to Mark Twain, here is one of my favorites:

"If you want me to speak for an hour, I am ready today. If you want me to speak for 10 minutes, it will take me two weeks to prepare."

The Three-Word Challenge is a microcosm of the wonderful dynamic that Twain was said to have articulated. In order to get down to three words, you really need to study the text. You need to truly understand what you intend to communicate and you need to pick three words that best represent each idea. Getting down to three words requires that you practically get intimate with your text.

In the case of bullets, less is so much more. Taking the Three-Word Challenge is one of the best devices to get you to less. It took four passes and over 45 minutes to hone the MOM text. Mark Twain would have been proud.

Copilot vs. ChatGPT vs. human: The battle of the bullets

If ever there were a task that can and should be delegated to a non-humanoid, it would be the cleaning up of dreadful bullet slides. So let's ask and answer the question: Can this task of shortening bullets be given over to AI? And if so, which service does the better job?

The patient

Here are four bullet points from an actual slide, exploring if and when a department should hold meetings:

- If topics can wait until a recurring session/meeting, refining call, then we should discuss adding the topic to a regularly scheduled meeting

Chp 3 The Three-Word Challenge

- If we need a very specific group of people to address a topic/theme and we think the topic/theme won't benefit the entire team and/or will take a lot of time to discuss (30-60 minutes) then we carve out a separate meeting

- Be specific in title of meeting (what is the topic and goal of the meeting, what area of work is this meeting supporting, include details in the meeting invite, etc.)

- Don't end the meeting without agreeing to the next steps: Was there a resolution? Action items? Who is responsible for communicating the decision? Who is responsible for the action items and when will they be complete? How will we communicate the result of the action items?

By any measure, these are dreadful. Complete sentences, parenthetical thoughts, numerous filler words—everything we associate with Death by PowerPoint. Writing this before actually knowing the results, I would be certain that all three agents—human, Copilot, and ChatGPT—could improve upon this trainwreck. Let's dive in...

The human: nuance is the secret sauce

I went first so as to not be influenced by anything that the AI engines might have done, and my conclusion is that these bullets did not need to have a question-and-answer rhythm. All they really needed to do was pose the key questions that made up the set of criteria. The presenter should be the one to provide the answer: Yes, we should call a meeting; or no, we should not. So here is my rendition of the bullets:

- Can the topics wait?
- Need specific people?
- Agree on next steps?
- Identify action items?

I eliminated the third bullet entirely and turned the fourth bullet into two specific questions. I did this because I am a human, capable of thinking in nuance. Writing this before knowing for sure, I suspect that both AI bots will tackle each bullet and just try to simplify them. Let's find out...

Microsoft Copilot: an easy experience

To turn Copilot loose on these awful bullets, I needed only click the little icon that persistently (and often annoyingly) appears next to selected text placeholders. That presents several choices, including Condense:

- If a topic can wait for a regular meeting, consider adding it to the agenda of that session.

- For discussions requiring specific attendees that may not benefit the entire team and could take 30-60 minutes, schedule a separate meeting.

- Clearly define the meeting title, outlining the topic, goals, and relevant work area, and include details in the invite.

- Conclude the meeting by confirming next steps: Were resolutions reached? What are the action items? Who will communicate decisions and complete the tasks, and when will they be done? How will the outcomes be shared?

Copilot did simplify these slides, but not by much. And curiously, it chose to punctuate each bullet with periods, which might be justified given how verbose they are. Copilot is cumulative, however, and I could ask it to keep condensing. After four more passes, the bullets looked like this:

- Include postponable topics in the regular meeting agenda.

- For discussions needing a specific group, arrange a separate meeting.

- Clearly state the meeting title, topic, objective, and details in the invitation.

- End the meeting by summarizing next steps: decisions made, action items, responsible individuals, completion timelines, and how outcomes will be communicated.

These are noticeably better now. Not good enough, but better. And while I had to ask Copilot to condense five times to get to this result, each pass was easy to perform.

ChatGPT: less convenient but worth it

Using ChatGPT required that I cut the text out of PowerPoint and paste it into one of its prompts. Here is what I said to it:

Please condense these bullets as much as you can. Use your judgment to ferret out the meaning and condense this prose however you see fit. The topic is identifying criteria for whether to call a department meeting.

Then I pasted the text word for word. Here is what it produced:

- If the topic can wait, add it to a recurring meeting
- Create a separate meeting for focused, time-intensive discussions
- Make the meeting title clear—include topic, goal, and context
- Don't end without decisions, ownership, and next steps

I was impressed—I felt as if ChatGPT used real judgment in determining the salient points. I told it to use its judgment but I was just being polite. I also said "please"—I tend to do that with mine, I don't know why. I also have named my agent. Then I asked it to return to the text and hone it a bit more. It delivered:

- Use recurring meetings for routine topics
- Schedule special meetings for deep dives or niche groups
- Title meetings clearly with purpose and scope
- End with decisions, ownership, and next steps

I then copied this text and pasted it back into PowerPoint. That extra effort was worth it, as this is now a vastly improved slide.

Verdict: I win

Forgive the lack of modesty, but I would choose my judgment over that of any AI engine any day of the week. And we should all take delight in that: No machine can produce the nuanced thinking that we humans can, to which we should all say *hallelujah!* That is why AI is a fantastic research tool but not as good of a finishing tool. That is why Sky (that's my ChatGPT's name) has offered many ideas for this book but has not written a single word of it.

Sky did much better than Copilot, even giving Copilot five cracks at the task. But both services improved the text, and that is encouraging. Fixing bad bullets is a joyless chore, and if we can alleviate some of the pain by getting a robot to help us, more power to us.

Avoiding Handout Hell

The height of my training season is Q2 and Q3 when I meet personally with hundreds of PowerPoint users and connect virtually with thousands. Nearly unanimously, the following two statements hold true:

- The biggest issue that presentation designers and content creators face is placing too much text on a slide.
- The primary reason that people do this is because they are asking their slides to function both as the visual for the presentation and as the leave-behind or handout.

The frequency with which this strategy fails is breathtaking. In fact, for the sake of round numbers, let's just call it 100%. Yes, this will fail every time you attempt it. And you, in turn, will become an epic failure for attempting it.

That would be bad, so keep reading…

What you give

Recall back to Chapter 2 and our discussion of the three key qualities of a presentation: what you say, what you show, and what you give. Your ideal scenario is to make each of those three experiences as effective and as impactful as possible for your audience members. You want your words to resonate, your visuals to complement your story, and your handout to provide valuable detail.

As noted previously, however, too often they all become the same thing: You place all those words on a slide, you then feel compelled to read them aloud, your audiences receive printouts of slides that recite this same story, and your presentation is deemed something less than a success.

Let's make this really simple for you: *Don't do this anymore!* Do not design slides as if they are handouts. Do not print your slides and call them handouts. Do not write speeches and project them because you think they will make good handouts. Do not do these things.

Separation anxiety

The three slides on the following page show a typical collection from my client files, these from the giant insurance provider Prudential Financial. Prudential's outside sales people have beefy narratives to share about the value of the company's insurance packages, and indeed, these folks did many things right with their pitches to prospective customers. In particular, they:

1. Identified their key message.

2. Knew how to strengthen their argument with compelling facts and anecdotes.

3. Found lots of supporting facts.

4. Created a leave-behind that told their story.

They did all those things right and they did just one thing wrong, but that one wrong thing torpedoed their entire effort. You already know the punchline here: They tried to do all of these things on their slides.

The three slides at right are packed with information, not because Prudential's creative team thought that was the best way to create slides, but because busy slides seemed like the best compromise for handling the needs of their live audiences with the needs of providing a printed takeaway.

Part One: Get Visual

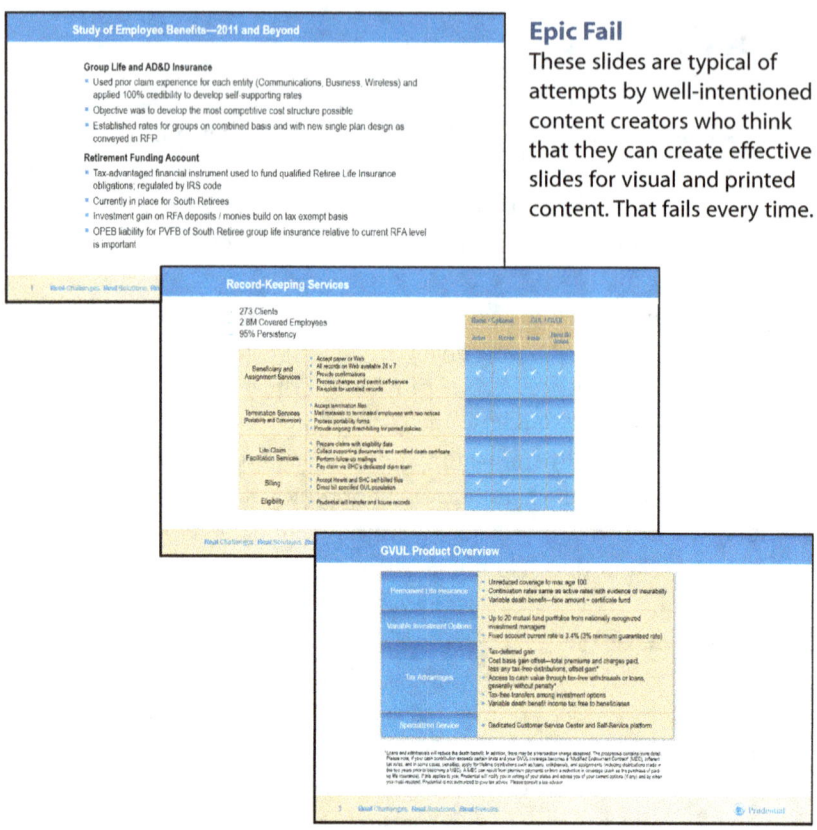

Epic Fail
These slides are typical of attempts by well-intentioned content creators who think that they can create effective slides for visual and printed content. That fails every time.

Based on everything we have talked about in the preceding 30 pages, you can imagine what kind of reception they got. This is right about the time that they called me in for a consultation.

The twain shall never meet

In nearly two decades spent as a presentation consultant, I have not once seen a slide deck that successfully functions as both compelling visual content and informative written material. Not once.

There is just no getting around it: If you create slides for your presentation that follow the ideas laid forth in this book—or the ones authored by Garr Reynolds, Nancy Duarte, Cliff Atkinson, and many others—those slides will necessarily fail as a printed leave behind. And if you create slides that contain fleshed-out thoughts for audience members to review afterward, you create instant Death by PowerPoint when you project them.

Chp 4 Avoiding Handout Hell

These two purposes are hopelessly disparate—the twain shall never meet. And yet you are likely one of tens of thousands who attempt it on a regular basis. Maybe every day.

I'm both mindful of and sympathetic to the demands that are placed on presentation designers and creators in today's workforce. Nonetheless, I am compelled to tell you that you must create two documents in order to do this right. I understand the specter of what I'm saying here, as I know all about 11th hour crises, crazed bosses, ridiculous deadlines, and the like. But that doesn't change my advice; in fact, it just makes me more strident: If you work long hours on presentation content, it becomes even more important that you be doing something that you like and are good at. But nobody likes creating double-duty slides, nobody is any good at it, it's impossible to do right, and audiences usually loathe them.

Rx for the handout blues

I want to assuage your pain somewhat by showing you a technique within PowerPoint that can at least enable you to create both types of content within one PowerPoint file. The following procedure is brought to you by Microsoft's persistent failure to provide an intelligent handout engine within the software, requiring those of us in the trenches to invent workarounds. What follows is my preferred one.

Introducing the Notes Master

The chances are pretty good that you know about PowerPoint's Slide Master, where you control the global look and feel of your slide deck. The other assumption I will make here is that you know about the Notes page, where you can jot down any ideas or thoughts as you create your content.

Odds are pretty good that you know about those two parts of the software, yet odds are equally good that you have never had occasion to visit the Notes Master, where you can control the global look and feel of your deck's Notes pages. Most people just accept the default of a slide thumbnail that consumes the top half of the page and a text box that resides on the lower half.

In fact, you can design the Notes Master as robustly as you can any slide, and therein lies the secret sauce to this solution: I want you to use the Notes pages to create dedicated handouts for your presentations.

The Notes Master has been in the software since forever, but very few people have had occasion to use it. Here is the result of 10 minutes spent with it. You are creating a custom design just for printed handouts.

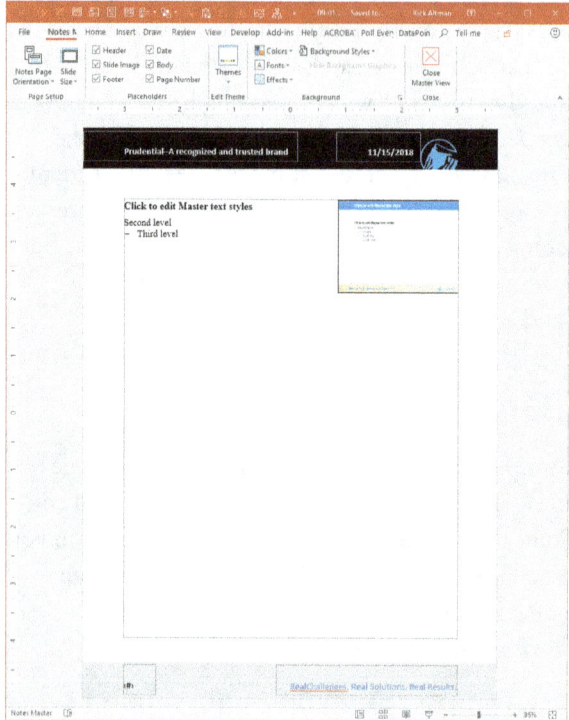

A new paradigm
By redesigning the Notes Master, you can create a custom format for your handouts.

Download handouts.pptx and switch to the Notes Master to see this for yourself.

Watch an extended demonstration of this strategy being implemented:

Nearly anything you can place on a slide, you can also place on the Notes Master. (The only things not available are animation and hyperlinks, as the medium is static.) Here are several things worth pointing out about the elements on this redesigned Notes Master, going clockwise from the top:

- The header is a simple rectangle placed behind white text.

- The Prudential logo is a transparent PNG file, allowing it to sit atop the black header.

- The slide thumbnail is much smaller than the default size that spans nearly the entire width of the page. For that matter, you get to decide whether you want it at all. It's often helpful for a printed handout to connect back with content during a live presentation, but that's your call.

- There is a page number at bottom-left. I am rarely in favor of placing numbers on a slide, but page numbers for a printed piece are different.

- And finally, note the amount of real estate given to text and also the simple (and small-sized) format for it. Just three levels of formatting, all under 12pt.

In just about every way, this is going to function better as a template for handouts than the slide ever could. All of the elements are more appropriately sized (who among us needs 18- and 24-point text on a handout??) and there is plenty of room for the volumes of text that you can now accommodate. Just the fact that Notes pages can be printed portrait is a point in its favor, as most people prefer to hold printouts in their hands that are taller than they are wide.

Moving day

Now that we have a place to put all of that excess text, let's take out the trash-, um, that is, let's find a better home for it. All three of the slides shown back on Page 30 are good candidates for this exchange, and it can be as simple as a copy and paste maneuver to migrate the text from the slide to the Notes page.

Compare the finished results on the next page with the original slides on Page 30. In creating both slides and handouts, you produce a presentation package that speaks well of your sensibilities. You tell your audience that you get it, that you understand the way they would like to receive information. You realize they don't want to drown in text when they are trying to listen to you. You appreciate that they want access to the details so they can refer to them later.

This helps create bonds of trust between you and your audience members that run deeper than what you can muster by simply sitting in front of a camera, speaking, and shoving text in front of their eyes. You're different from most presenters and they recognize that.

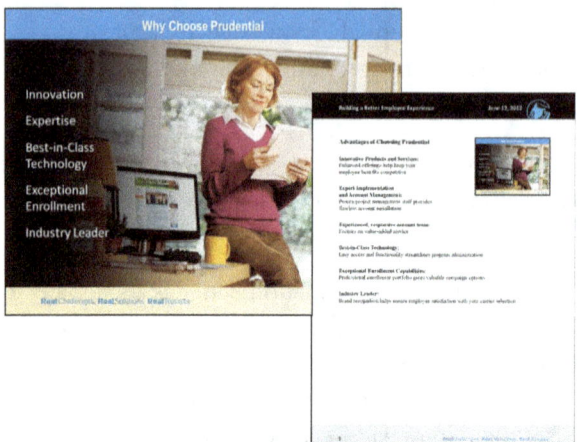

A better handout
By redesigning the Notes Master, you can create a custom format for your handouts.

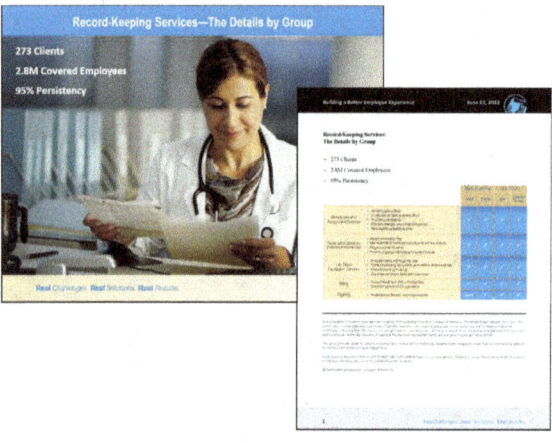

And better slides
With all of that text placed on the Notes page, you are free to design your slides in ways that you could never consider before.

A whole new routine for you

As soon as you separate the tasks of making slides and handouts, you deliver yourself from the impossible assignment of double-duty slides. Further, you give yourself an opportunity to think like an effective presentation designer. Here is what you can ask of yourself or of your team:

- What elements do I need to create the best possible visual to complement our story?

- What are the two or three key points for this slide?

- Now how much detail and research can we gather that our audience would appreciate reading afterward.

You will become so much better at both of these tasks and your work will become more rewarding. You will no longer be frustrated by the pressures to place more and more text on your slides, and you will no longer frustrate those who want you to place even more when you feel like you're already using too much. Your handouts can now accommodate all of it.

Thanks to this process, you will become a better storyteller and more effective virtual presenter, and it bears repeating, you will distinguish yourself from 99% of the people giving business presentations today.

It's almost scary how close to a panacea this is. I don't use the word "literally" lightly: If PowerPoint users stopped the practice of creating double-duty slides, it would literally eliminate at least 75% of all incidents of Death by PowerPoint. Overnight.

So I put it to you: Do you want to make the world a better place? If you create slides that you then produce as handouts, *stop doing that!* 💻

It happened on Zoom

During a recent workshop, a frustrated woman named KellyAnn shared with us the impossibility of her following the advice to separate visual content from printed content. "We are bound by corporate rules that nobody understands, and they dictate to us that we must tell our audience our whole story and then show them our whole story and then send them our deck, with the whole story."

"Would it be good enough," I asked back, "if the 'whole story' is available to them on a click, but otherwise not visible?"

"I don't know—nobody has ever tried that."

I recommended that KellyAnn indeed try that, and we collaborated on a system whereby audience members receiving this deck remotely could choose if and when t o view all of that detail. It uses a semi-advanced technique within PowerPoint, a bit beyond the scope of this chapter. But those who are curious about it can watch a detailed video of the makeover and the use of that technique here:

Better Breadcrumbs

Perhaps I am over-dramatizing the disorienting effect that the virtual environment has on human beings. Maybe we *always* crave context and want to see the roadmap of our journeys. Maybe it is not just when we are on Zoom that we ask "where the hell am I, where am I going, and where have I come from?"

Maybe, but maybe not. I think that we really do tend to lose our way when we stare at those little Brady Bunch squares or when we have to endure someone's shared screen that seems to have no connection with anything that we actually care about in life.

So this chapter provides a quality we humans value: the breadcrumbs of our life. I also just want to geek out with you, because I think the *how* is just as interesting as the *why.*

The challenge

Feeding off of the first chapter, your virtual audience is likely to encounter more distractions than your in-person ones. They are more likely to try to do two things at once, and it is almost guaranteed that at some point in your presentation, they will say to themselves, "okay, now where were we?"

I want for my audiences to never have to say that.

That is an unrealistic goal, I know, but I don't mind failing if the reward is in the attempt, and in this case it clearly is. So here is the challenge that I put to myself, and by extension, to you:

"How can I make it as easy as possible for my audience members to always know what we are talking about now, what we have already covered, and what we are yet to cover?"

Answering that question is challenging. Trying and failing is noble, because remember, the reward is in the attempt. Any steps you take to create those breadcrumbs are better than taking no steps at all.

The background

This entire topic was inspired by ESPN's SportsCenter and its quest to tease you into watching just a bit more. There's good stuff coming up soon. *Just stay with us through the commercial break.*

As you can see in the snapshot of the ESPN studio, the topic at hand is the Denver Broncos and their 6-0 record against the Kansas City Chiefs. Next comes a look at what makes the Broncos so good, then the daily In Case You Missed It segment. You know which is the current topic because it is bright while the others are dim.

I happen to think that ESPN does it backward—scrolling up the list instead of down—and they don't particularly care what topics they have already covered, they just want you to stick around for the ones upcoming. Nonetheless, the "what's next" strategy is sound and worth your emulating for your virtual presentations, where your audience members are as likely to get up and wander off as readily as ESPN viewers.

The dilemma

All fine and well—how do you do it in PowerPoint? How do you create slides that easily show you the current topic amid past and future topics? How do you devise global formats that support that? How do you create a layout that highlights one topic, dims the others, and then highlights a different topic on the next slide?

Native PowerPoint does not have any provision for creating a layout with dynamic content. You can create a layout with one highlighted topic, and conceivably you could then create layouts with the other topics highlighted, but that defeats the purpose of a global formatting device. If you are going to create separate layouts for each topic, you might as well just create slides for that.

Therein lies the dilemma: You want a global formatting solution that changes with each slide. The whole idea of a layout is to lock down a design, not to accommodate constantly changing appearances.

If you concede that some part of this formatting must take place on the slide, how can you maximize what role the layout plays and minimize what content must be on the slide? That's our quest.

The solutions

On the following page you will see a snapshot of me speaking on the value of creating distance from your camera. It is the fifth topic in an hour-long webinar on virtual presenting—sort of a microcosm of this book. That topic, No Talking Heads!, is highlighted on the vertical list running down the right side of the screen. It is bright white while the rest

Chp 5 Better Breadcrumbs

of the topics are dim. Soon, I will speak about gesturing, and at that point, I will want that topic to turn bright and this one to go dim.

I show about 20 slides during this hour, and like any self-respecting PowerPoint user, I have turned to its templating system to streamline the formatting. I have created about a half-dozen layouts for various purposes, including the main character of this little drama: the 10 topics, all running down the right side of the layout.

You are here
This slide design reflects my belief that virtual audiences need more orientation. They appreciate a roadmap that shows them from where we have come and where we are going.

On the following page are two distinct approaches that could be taken to address the formatting challenge. One has all of the text dimmed on the layout, while the other has all of the text set bright. And as I have already conceded, I can't do it all at the global level; some of the formatting has to be done locally. Absent some clever VBA programming, the layout is not capable of dynamic brightening and dimming of the topics. The display of the current topic must be done on the slide.

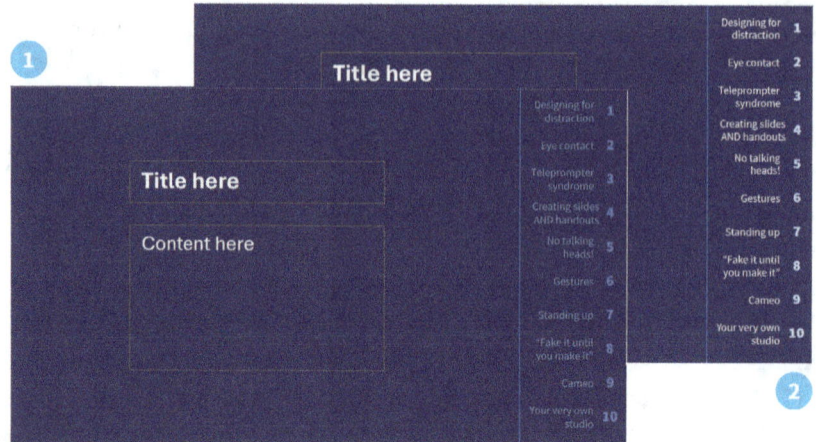

Not-quite-global layouts
Either of these layouts could help create these slides, but they can't do all the work. You will need to create your breadcrumbs on the slide.

In order to use either of these layouts for the slide above, you have three choices:

1. Using Layout 1, place a copy of bright text on the slide, directly atop the dim text, to show the active topic.

2. Using Layout 2, place semi-transparent rectangles over all the non-active topics to make them appear dim.

3. Using Layout 2, place an arrow or some other type of marker next to the active topic.

I'm not wild about any of these, but I would choose Option 1 over 2 or 3. Granted, No. 1 requires that I duplicate the exact location of the bright text atop the dim text. But I would prefer that over having to use multiple dim rectangles to place atop non-active topics, or using a marker or some sort, which could potentially encroach upon my content.

The super-geeky strategy

Ultimately, though, I choose Door No. 4, which requires the least amount of slide work. It has its own drawback, which I share with you on the following pages, but it is the most flexible approach, and employs a

Chp 5 Better Breadcrumbs

little-known PowerPoint technique. Here are the official steps for my official super-geeky strategy:

1. Create the perfect background: Design and create the 10 topics. Do this on a slide, not on a layout. Spend as much time as you need to in order to get them as close to perfect as possible. Slide background color, typeface of topics, size, color, spacing, everything.

2. Export the slide: The easiest method is to use PowerPoint's Save As command and change the format from PPTX to PNG.

3. Use that PNG as the layout background: Now head into Slide Master view and go to (or create) the layout you want to use for your breadcrumbs. From Format Background, choose Picture or Texture Fill, click Insert to find that PNG file you saved. It should fill your entire slide and look no different than if you had created all of those elements on the layout one by one. In fact, there is no point in showing you a screen image, as it would be identical to the one on the previous page.

4. Finish the layout: Place any other elements you might want on this layout: header, footer, logo, text placeholders, etc.

5. Dim the text: Draw a rectangle over all 10 topics and set its fill color to be the same as the background color (use the eyedropper if you do not have the color value handy, and then dial up about a 25% transparency.

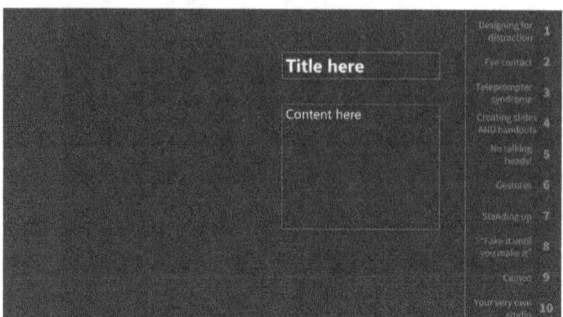

Okay, so why are we doing all of this? If this image-as-background trick looks the same as just building shapes and text boxes on the slide, why bother with all this nonsense? You would be wise to wonder that, and it is all so that we can set up the crucial sixth maneuver.

6. Create the active topic: Here is the coup de grâce. Leave Slide Master view and return to the slide. Create a rectangle and size it to cover one of the topics. From the Format Shape task pane, set the Fill pattern to be Slide Background. In other words, take whatever is in the background at this exact location and show it through this rectangle.

Light shining through

That is the secret sauce here, as it enables you to show the bright white text through the rectangle. The transparent rectangle that you drew on the layout is *not* part of the background; that is why all of the text shows up dim on the slide…except for where you place the magic rectangle. That rectangle effectively drills through the dim rectangle and pulls out the bright text.

Let's say that you wanted to highlight the fourth topic, Creating slides AND handouts. Draw a rectangle around the text; it will first appear with the default fill color for shapes:

Chp 5 Better Breadcrumbs

As soon as you change the fill from the solid color to the slide background, you will see the magic happen:

Changing topics

With this technique, when you want to change topics on a subsequent slide, all you do is copy this rectangle to that slide and then nudge it down to the next topic. The previous topic will become dim and the now-current one will become bright. No retyping, no resizing, none of that.

The one big caveat to this otherwise amazing hack is if you decide to redesign the layout. Then you will have to revise the slide you created, save it out, return to the layout, and re-insert the new image as its background.

To prepare for the possibility that you might need to redesign the layout (Murphy's Law would identify it as a certainty), keep a hidden slide stashed away in the deck with the current design of the layout.

Review

Let's summarize what we did here:

- Used an image as the background for a layout
- Covered up the image with a semi-transparent dark shape, so it will appear dim on the slide
- Created a shape on the slide with fill pattern set to Background
- That makes whatever is under it show up bright 🖥

You can inspect, take apart, and reverse engineer this technique by downloading image-as-background.pptx from www.crushyournext.pro/files. Further, you can watch a video of this process by using this QR code.

Fun with Fonts

It used to be so easy. We chose between Arial and Helvetica when creating slides or designing websites and Times New Roman for anything printed. We were proud to know the difference between serif and sans-serif and we all knew to turn our noses up at Comic Sans.

Life was so simple then.

Today, the world of presentation has a few extra wrinkles, and the world of virtual presentation a few extra still. This chapter will not foist upon you a bunch of terms or definitions. It will not try to teach you the difference between Type 1, TrueType, and OpenType. And it will not provide a tutorial on buying and installing typefaces. You can learn all of that from five minutes with your AI agent.

But keep reading if you seek usable guidelines and rules of thumb for choosing the right type for your virtual presentations.

The hierarchy of type

I probably don't need to teach you this, either, but I want to, just so you can say that you know something that most people do not. Most people have no idea as to the difference between a typeface and a font. Let's make sure that you do...

Type family

This is actually the top of the food chain—the singular name that describes a set of typefaces. A type family shares common design characteristics across each face that makes up the family.

Clarendon is a type family. In fact, it was the first one to be patented, back in 1845.

Clarendon

It is characterized by thick lettering, particularly curly serifs, and tall lower-case letters.

Typeface

A typeface is a variant of a type family. So Clarendon Normal, Clarendon Italic, Clarendon Black, and Clarendon Condensed are all typefaces. Same with these four traditional variants:

Clarendon
Clarendon italic
Clarendon bold
Clarendon bold-italic

Font

Finally, a font is very specific: It is a particular typeface set in a particular size. 12pt Clarendon italic is a font.

12pt *Clarendon italic*

◆

It is merely a point of amusement, not alarm, that so many people get this wrong. People have been using *font* when they mean *typeface* and *typeface* instead of *type family* for decades. Nonetheless, the sun still rises every morning. Meanwhile, here is a collection of tips and advice about managing and choosing type for the virtual environment. In many cases, it is designing for distraction, all over again.

Size is everything

Typefaces were born in the print world, where readers and typophiles could appreciate the elegance of thin serifs and the beauty of statuesque ascenders. As type evolved into the presentation space, designers could be confident that their audiences would be viewing their work at a predictable distance and size. Whether in a smaller classroom with a 10-foot screen or in a grand ballroom with a 30-foot screen—either way, your 36pt titles would be prominent and your 18pt. text perfectly readable.

No such luck in the virtual world, where audience members might be watching on a 72-inch screen or they might be in the kitchen preparing dinner while projecting you from a tablet across the room. Or in the car following you on an iPhone.

So here is the first litmus test: If someone is watching on a laptop from across the kitchen table, will they be able to follow you? If you make sure that the important part of your message can be heard, you will pass this test. But if your message relies heavily on a visual component, you might fail.

And therein lies the conundrum of setting type for virtual. On the one hand, your 12pt sentences might be perfectly readable to an audience member sitting behind his 27-inch monitor displaying a large Zoom window. On the other hand, your 28pt titles might be deficient if they are portrayed through a four-inch thumbnail floating next to your talking head.

Meanwhile, if someone is trying to follow along with your webinar in a bustling office, they might have the sound down and be relying on your visuals. Sigh...

So what are your rules of thumb? That's a tricky question, because as soon as you answer it, I could just as quickly unearth a scenario that defies it. Perhaps it comes down to this question: Might a significant percentage of your audience be watching you from a mobile device?

If the answer is yes, that could have a profound impact on how you design your slides. Simply put, forget about any bulleted text, paragraphs, or charts; consider creating slides that are exclusively imagery and titles larger than 28pt. In this situation, your voice must carry the day—what you say will become much more important than what you show.

Lose the squiggles

If you are reading the printed version of this book, you are looking at one of the most classic typefaces of all time: Garamond Roman. It is a serif typeface, marked by the little squiggles that grace most of the characters.

The serifs help guide the eye from one character to another. They enhance readability on the printed page, where there is sufficient resolution to portray them.

Furthermore, serif typefaces are typically of irregular widths. Look at the e of serif: Note how thick it is lower-left, compared to the thin horizontal stroke. The variance in width is one of the qualities that distinguishes the typeface; it is considered a feature.

Not so with displayed type, like on websites, PDF files, and presentations, where the lower resolution of the display makes serifs problematic. On a computer screen, at 72 lines per inch, the serifs and the thin strokes have been shown to actually *hinder* readability. This issue is why most presentation designers choose sans-serif typefaces—ones without the squiggles (*sans* is the French word for *without*).

The tiny curls and decorative strokes of serif fonts might be charming in novels, but onscreen, especially at small sizes, they blur, bleed, and fatigue the eye.

You are looking here at Source Sans Pro, one of my preferred sans-serif typefaces. Notice how all of the strokes have the same width. I regularly match up a serif face with a sans-serif face for print projects, as I have done for this book. But with presentations, I will limit my use of serif faces to the occasional display of a single word set at a very large size:

There are no resolution or readability issues with this word, set in the well-known serif face of Bodoni. In fact, I think the serifs help to call attention to the emphatic nature of the answer. No exclamation mark needed.

But this is very much the exception to the rule. Sans-serif faces are clean, geometric, and won't become fuzzy if your virtual platform is hit with a latency storm. If you use them 100% of the time, that is one fewer time that you might annoy your audience.

This isn't about personal taste—it's about your audience's tired eyes after the sixth Zoom of the day.

How compatible do you need to be?

My use of Source Sans Pro for most of my presentations, is based on a simple premise: it only has to look right on my screen. If it appears the way

I want it to on my computer, then I know that it will display correctly for my audiences, who are watching a projection of my computer's screen.

If I ever do send a deck to others, I run the risk that it might not display the same on their screens, unless they happen to have the typeface installed. If they don't, their operating system will substitute a generic sans-serif face in its place, like Arial or Helvetica. If the missing face was ornate and distinctive (i.e. did not look anything like Arial or Helvetica), that would be a problem. In the case of Source Sans Pro, a face with a generic stroke weight and letter width—the risk is small.

But what if that is an issue for you? What if you are actively distributing the PowerPoint file to others for them to view on their own screens? What if you need to make sure that your slides appear on other displays exactly as you designed them on your own? In that case, you would be wise to limit your typeface choice to one that is universally available. Of the few dozen that qualify, my choice is Segoe UI.

This is the **Segoe UI** typeface

It is clean, upbeat, and lives on all computers that run PowerPoint. It is also just a bit more distinctive than the common, plain, and just a bit boring Arial or Calibri.

The other factor here is Microsoft's collection of cloud fonts, which install on the fly and are available to all Microsoft 365 (aka Office 365) users. We're talking over 700 typefaces, free to use. I like this for my own use, but I do not trust the system for distributed decks. I have seen too many instances of MS365 faces not installing reliably to trust it with careful presentation work. So I'm still a bit bearish on this feature.

Chp 6 Fun with Fonts

 The topic of typeface management needs its own book, not just one section of one chapter. I refer you to my colleague and friend Julie Terberg, a favorite presenter at the Presentation Summit. Julie's online guide is a treasure trove of advice, education, and inspiration for presentation designers. You can download the fully formatted PDF file from julie-on-type.pptx at ww.crushyournext.pro/files/, or you can view it from here:

The enigma of emphasis

The first thing to be said about emphasizing your thoughts is this: If it is truly important, make sure to say it! If you want your audience to know it matters, the most powerful thing you can do is say it out loud.

If we ended the discussion there, I'd be satisfied that you received my best advice on the subject. But you bought a book, not a meme, so we will not end the discussion there. Here are some additional thoughts on the often-perplexing subject of emphasis.

Typography is the supporting actor

I get it, there are some really enticing typefaces in the wild. And they're tempting. But novelty faces usually just slow people down and cause them to have to work harder. Your audience should be absorbing your message, not decoding your design choices.

Pick one face for titles, one for body text, and stop there. Align them, size them sensibly, and declare yourself done. Your fonts don't need to entertain. That's your job.

If you make everything bold...

Emphasis is a matter of degree and proportion. If you have made everything bold, you have made nothing bold. You can only have bold if you also have "unbold."

This basic principle was lost on this well-intentioned content creator when he intended to clarify the definition of a new patient, according to the American Medical Association.

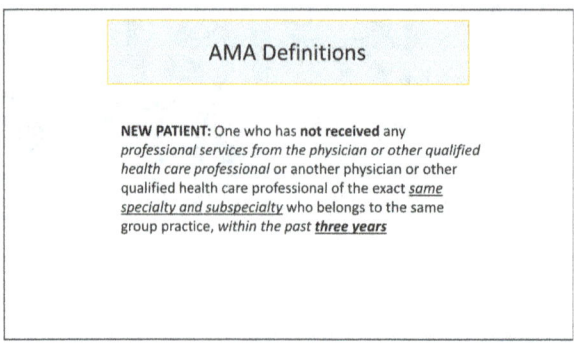

Count the ways
This one slide has type set bold, italic, underlined, and combinations of all three. As discussed in Chapter 3, busy slides have to try harder to get your attention. This is the unfortunate result.

The following makeover reflects the philosophy that for emphasis to have impact, it must not have too much competition. You will also see one of my preferred methods of emphasis: bold and a color that is actually softer than the type around it.

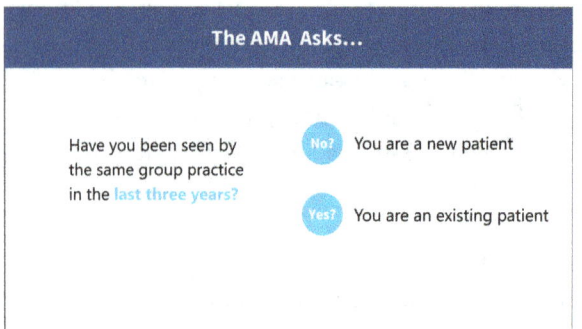

Less equals more
This simplified slide makes it obvious what you are to focus on.

Lose the italic and the underline

For the sake of your virtual audience members, do not consider italic as a tool of emphasis. On all but the largest monitors, italic characters might just fade into oblivion. And underlining is worse, as it tells your audience that not only do you not understand the concept of emphasis, you're old enough to remember when we all used typewriters.

From visual to personal

Part One has been all about the ways in which you can bring more focus to your content, improve the visual component of your presentation, and increase the likelihood that your audience pays attention to the right things at the right times.

Now we transition. Part Two is all about *you*. What can you do to increase connection? What can you do with your eyes and your hands and your body? With your whole person? With other people?

The strategies might diverge, but the goal is the same: I want you to find your most genuine self. I want you to be 100% beholden to the idea of becoming 100% vulnerable. Your audience wants that, too, because that's when great things happen.

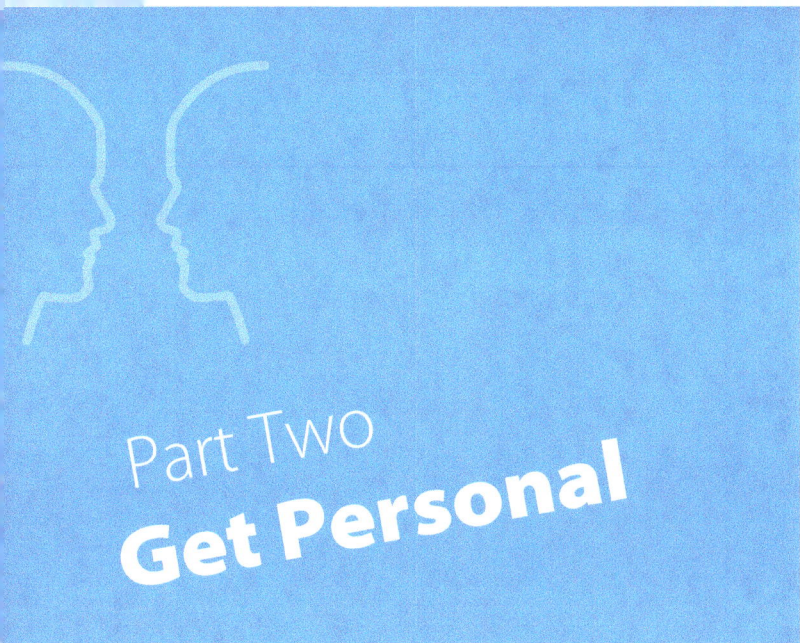

Part Two
Get Personal

Getting personal doesn't necessarily mean sharing intimate stories or baring your soul, although those are pretty good aspirations for any presenter. In the virtual world, it often starts with something simpler: inviting people to participate. Because when someone types a comment in Chat, clicks a poll response, or gives a thumbs-up reaction, that's not just interaction—it's a micro-act of vulnerability. They're putting themselves out there, even just a little, and that creates a thread of connection. And let's be honest, sometimes, a thread is all you can hope for when you attempt virtual connections.

That is the essence of this part of the book. Can you find small, meaningful ways to connect with people who are physically distant? Can you become, and in turn make your audience become, emotionally available?

The moment your audience starts to feel like part of the experience—rather than passive observers—is when your presentation stops being a broadcast and starts becoming a conversation. Every time you engage your audience on purpose, you're giving them permission to care. That's the personal part.

Flex Your Engagement Muscle

When you speak to a virtual audience, you're not just sharing information—you're building a relationship. When audience members see that you care what they think, they feel seen. And when they feel seen, they lean in. Suddenly, you're not just a voice on their screen. You're a presence in their space. And once that bond is formed, they're far more likely to stay engaged, stay curious, and stay with you.

You don't need to reinvent the wheel to create engagement; the wheel is built into your platform. Zoom, Teams, Webex, Connect, Google Meet—they all offer a buffet of tools that can bring your audience closer: chat boxes, reaction emojis, polling, breakout rooms, whiteboards, annotation tools. These aren't just gimmicks, they're connection points. And when used intentionally, they can transform a presentation into a conversation.

The more interactive you make your environment, the more invested your audience will be in it. And you don't have to limit yourself to what's built-in. You can also bring in outside tools—QR codes that link to a quick survey, web apps for voting or brainstorming, even collaborative docs. The goal isn't just to show off your tech savvy—it's to create a space where people feel like they are participants, not just attendees.

That's why it's critical to get them involved early. If you wait too long to bring them in, they may already be gone—mentally, emotionally, or literally. (Please see every word we have written so far about distracted audiences.) So don't save your best questions for the Q&A at the end. Sprinkle them in from the start, and watch the energy shift.

Passive brains wander while active brains remember

Cognitive neuroscience has shown again and again: When your brain is doing something, it's also encoding. When you involve your audience—ask them a question, prompt them to reflect, or better yet, get them to click something—you're activating more regions of their brain. That boosts attention, improves memory, and creates stronger neural connections.

Compare that to passive listening. When people are just absorbing, especially in a virtual setting where distractions abound, their attention can fade within minutes. The brain goes into low gear. You might still be talking, but their processing power has been rerouted—to their inbox, their phone, their evening pickleball, their cat.

It doesn't take much to flip the switch. A one-word chat response, a visual puzzle, a micro-poll—they all trigger what psychologists call "desirable difficulty." That's when your brain has to make a small effort to respond or decide, and as a result, it retains more.

So, when you engage your audience, you're not just keeping them entertained. You're helping them remember what you said.

"Questions and comments, please"

Of the low-hanging fruit in this chapter, the lowest might be your simple declaration that audience members do not have to have a question in order to engage. In my workshops, where we discuss the nuance of presentation strategies, I don't want audience members to just ask me, I want them to challenge me. I tell them the same thing I told you back on Page 8: There is plenty of gray area to these topics, and if you agree with everything I say, your experience won't be as robust.

This is all implied in the very simple call for questions *and* comments. I suggest that you make that part of your regular routine. Every time you call for questions, invite the audience to do more. Some of my best exchanges have come from audience observations, not just inquiries.

It happened on Zoom

Rick: Questions or comments?

Kathryn [on Chat]: I see that you removed the logo from the bottom of each slide.

Rick: That reflects my general belief that branding every slide is overkill. Do you see it differently?

Kathryn: I do.

Rick: Please unmute and we can discuss.

Kathryn [Speaking]: It doesn't actually matter what I think about this. Our corporate guidelines require it. When you suggest otherwise, it's kind of like torture.

Rick: I take your point, and I don't want to torture anyone. But I don't mind a bit of pain around obviously sore subjects. Your bosses probably want to be able to print the slides, right?

Kathryn: Probably.

Rick: And you already know what I think of that practice.

Kathryn: I just don't think you are being realistic in saying we can change corporate culture that easily.

Rick: How did John Lennon sing it, "You might say I'm a dreamer…"

Kathryn: (Laughing) I do think you are being a bit of a dreamer.

Rick: (Laughing back) And you would be right! I dream of the day in which we all present better. It won't happen overnight, and maybe it won't happen at your organization. But you know how it might? If people like you choose to champion the cause. If people like you, with strong instincts and sensibilities, take up the good fight. Take small victories when you can get them. Show those up the food chain what a truly excellent presentation looks and feels like. That will move the needle, I promise you.

Kathryn: Yeah, you're dreaming. But I appreciate hearing it and it beats conceding that we can't do anything about it.

Rick: Dream on!

Chat: the "oatmeal of virtual interaction"

This is a quote from an AI service when asked to offer thoughts about using the standard Chat service offered by all streaming services. Oatmeal. "Unflashy," it went on to say, "unremarkable, but dependable, and surprisingly powerful when used properly."

In a world of fancy platforms and shiny features, Chat remains the simplest and most universal way to bring your audience into the conversation. No learning curve, no QR codes, no plug-ins—just a blinking cursor and an invitation to respond.

But *simple* doesn't mean *thoughtless*. The way you use Chat can either spark rich interaction or fizzle into awkward silence. Here's how to make it work for you.

Be specific

Asking your audience "what are your thoughts about this?" is so general it invites nonaction. Worse, when you ask such a vague question, you either have to wait for responses, risking awkward silence, or just ignore your own question, giving the impression that you never really cared what their thoughts were.

Here are some quick-take questions that are easy for audience members to answer via Chat:

- Share one word to describe your reaction to [the current topic].
- What do you think is the biggest investment mistake people make?
- Be honest, what app are you multitasking us with right now?
- Who is joining from overseas? Chat the country.

You score points for being more intentional in your use of your service's Chat module. If you just ask "Any questions?" and stare at the screen, you risk awkward silence. Instead, ask for interaction, guide the conversation, offer direction, give context, provide a timer.

- "If you have questions about this, I'm watching the Chat."
- "Those last two steps were intricate; hit the Chat if you want me to repeat that part."

- "Here's a question I want you to ponder. Take 30 seconds and tell me which phase you would choose if we could only implement one of them."

In this last example, a few seconds of silence will be fine; it will be expected. But you should be ready with a relevant thought if it goes on for too long.

Refer to it often

People will not be as inclined to engage via Chat if they think no one's reading. So make the effort to show that you are paying attention:

- "Wow, the Chat is blowing up after that story."
- "I see that many of you wish we would explore [topic] a bit more."
- "Michael, your point in the Chat about a 30-day trial is well taken, and if you want to elaborate, raise your hand and we'll bring you on set with us."
- "A lot of you have mentioned 'clarity' as a top challenge. Let's dig into that…"

These simple interactions signal to your audience that what they say matters to you.

What if the Chat upstages you?

What a pleasant problem to have if the Chat blows up and becomes a distraction. Chat is not the backup band; it's the rhythm section. But what if people start using it so extensively, it threatens to become lead guitar?

I am not comfortable telling people to cool it with their chatting; in fact, that is the last thing I would ever want to do. But I acknowledge that if people are running off on tangents and littering the Chat with semi-related thoughts, it could become distracting to other audience members and challenging for you, or for whomever is monitoring it for you.

In this case, the ounce of prevention is the best cure:

- "Feel free to use the Chat throughout—reactions, questions, hot takes are welcome. Just try to keep it on-topic so it doesn't become too chaotic for the rest of us."

Chp 7 Flex Your Engagement Muscle

- "Chat is our coffee house corner—energetic but purposeful. Let's keep the thread connected to where we're going."

If you are not able to preempt a runaway Chat, then…well, I don't really know. Speaking selfishly, as the webinar leader, it doesn't directly affect me, as I am not watching the Chat that closely (see the next chapter). I asked my AI agent what to say, and it suggested:

- "Looks like we've got a party going in the Chat—love the energy. Let's bring that vibe back to [topic]."

- "Great convo happening over there… I'm going to bring us back for a minute so we don't lose the thread."

Mmm, I don't know, I don't see myself saying something like that. Your mileage might vary—my wife Becky said she thought these two responses were great. I thought I would enlist my technology editors to offer their advice on how to rein in an over-active Chat.

John Rahmlow: One possible response would be something along the lines of "It looks like we have a lot of interest in [topic]. I don't have content prepared on that for today, however I'd be glad to set up a session on that in the near future. I do have some great info on [today's topic] and I'd like your comments on that as we continue forward."

Christiane Pusch: I am in a virtual choir, and during rehearsal, Chat is usually closed (important to minimize distractions). So whoever leads the rehearsal declares that "the Chat will now be closed," during which time we can only chat to the moderator, not to one another. Then, when the chat is opened again, the questions and comments come streaming in and usually stay on topic. This helps a lot.

More ways to use Chat

Staying with a module that every member of every audience knows, here are some easy wins that you can score in the Engagement-via-Chat department:

Prediction prompts

When you ask a question, you invite audience members to tell you what they already know. But when you pose a prediction prompt, you challenge them to take a guess, make a prediction, fashion a creative solution. Here are three examples:

Before I reveal the top reason audiences tune out, what do you think it is?

Before I tell you what happened, what would you have done?

We tested three headlines—guess which one performed best?

This engages a different mental process and will be inherently more interesting than just asking for the answer to a question.

Misconception bait

Present a commonly misunderstood fact and ask them to guess what's wrong with it. Every industry has its accepted axioms and challenging them is instantly interesting.

If you didn't sign a contract, it's not legally binding, right? Sounds logical...what's the catch?
This question can launch you into a conversation about oral contracts, implied agreements, and enforceability beyond signatures.

Paying off your mortgage early is always the smartest move, they say. Seems responsible...but why might this be the wrong strategy?
This can lead to a useful discussion about opportunity cost, interest rates, liquidity, and personal goals.

I'm sure you have heard the advice to drink eight glasses of water a day. It's everywhere, but what's inaccurate about it?
This debunks oversimplified health mantras and invites a nuanced look at hydration needs, activity level, and diet.

Using misconception bait is ideal for opening a session, resetting stale thinking, or waking up a sleepy room with a delicious "Wait, what?" Anytime you can debunk or correct a common misunderstanding, you will score engagement points.

Mini role-play

Mini role-play is a valuable tactic with a simple premise: *What would you do if...?* It invites emotional imagination, not just intellect.

Pretend you're your boss and I just proposed a novel idea in a meeting. What's the first question you'd ask—or the first red flag you'd raise?
This sparks empathy for decision-makers and encourages sharper preparation and messaging.

Imagine you're a healthcare provider delivering a diagnosis to a patient. What would they want to know first? What's the most reassuring thing you could say?
Builds compassionate communication skills and reduces jargon.

You're a skeptical investor reviewing a pitch. What's missing? What would make you trust the numbers?
Forces a presenter to anticipate objections and shore up credibility.

Role-playing breaks people out of their own heads and challenges them to see the situation through someone else's eyes. That's instant engagement.

What-would-you-do dilemmas

This one could be an engagement gold mine. Dilemmas hit on values, instincts, and experience. They engage the heart and the head, and because there's no single right answer, they encourage vulnerability and lively back-and-forth discussion.

"You've got a high performer who's toxic to the team culture. Do you coach them, move them, or let them go?"
Sparks discussion on values, short-term performance vs. long-term health.

Your best client asks you to "creatively interpret" a regulation that's legally gray. Do you comply, stall, or walk away?
Invites ethical reflection and shows how values shape real decisions.

A student submits work that's clearly AI-generated. Do you call them out, let it slide, or make them do it over?
Timely, thorny, and highly relatable.

You're in the middle of a talk and someone in the Chat challenges your data. Do you address it now, deflect, or take it offline?
A real-time tension moment—perfect for getting people to think on their feet. This happens to me all the time; I acknowledge it in the moment and promise to address it as soon as I finish my thought. And I make a note of it on a big yellow pad that I keep nearby, because there are few things worse than promising to circle back and then forgetting to do so.

You learn your company supports a political cause you personally oppose. Do you stay silent, speak up, or leave?
Big-picture values prompt, great for exploring boundaries and integrity.

These are terrific as mid-session prompts or as icebreakers, because they encourage people to show up as themselves but you do not put anyone on the spot. People who answer only in their heads, not in the Chat, are still engaged.

Tiny confessions

This is one of the fastest ways to humanize a group and generate laughs, nods, and "me too" moments. When the prompt feels safe but slightly revealing, people can't resist chiming in.

What's something you pretend to understand at work—but actually don't?

What's your go-to fake excuse for skipping a meeting?

How often do you click Join Meeting with 10 seconds to spare, just so you can say you attended?

Have you ever worn pajama bottoms during a client call?

These are easy wins, and again, people who choose not to answer out loud are still answering.

Reverse advice

This one is a delicious twist that invites cynicism, sarcasm, or a little rant—but all in the service of truth.

What career advice should be retired forever?
Watch them light up with: "Fake it 'til you make it," "Stay in your lane," or "Never say no."

What's a leadership tip you received that totally backfired?
Opens the door for nuance, humility, and learning the hard way.

What's the worst fitness or nutrition tip you actually believed?
Cue stories about juice cleanses, no-carb torture, or motivational posters from hell.

What's a piece of marketing advice that sounds smart but isn't?
Things like "Always go viral," or "Post constantly, even if you have nothing to say."

Reverse advice encourages storytelling, not just opinions. It triggers shared eye-rolls and cathartic laughter and it helps surface what not to do without your having to come off as preachy. In my experience, you will get the best responses if these are done when you have established rapport, not as first-thing-in-the-morning icebreakers.

Meaningless diversions

Not all of your engagement schemes have to be on-topic. Here is a short list of other ways to change up the energy and vibe, anytime you think that either might be waning.

Live sentiment check-ins
On a scale from 😀 to 😱, where are you right now?

Two truths and a lie
Share three statements and have them guess which is false?

Build a metaphor
Crowdsource a metaphor for a complex concept you're about to explain. ("If giving a virtual presentation were like driving a car, what kind of car would it be and why?")

Raise your hand if...
This can be anything at all.

One-word waterfall
Ask for a one-word answer to a question. Then say "Type it into Chat but don't hit Enter until I say GO." Then: "3…2…1…GO!" Everyone's responses appear at once, creating a high-energy reveal.

Soundtrack drop
Play five seconds of a song and ask: "If your mood today had a theme song, what would it be?"

Emoji madness
Ask your audience to respond to a question using only emojis.

The miracle of the makeover

Before-and-after comparisons are engagement gold because they tap into some of the brain's favorite things: contrast, story, and transformation. It is not a coincidence that you have seen over a dozen of them in Part One alone. It is no surprise that the most popular seminars at the Presentation Summit follow the before-and-after form. And it is not front-page news that Hollywood produces so many rags-to-riches stories.

Here's why they work so well in a virtual presentation setting.

The brain loves contrast

The human brain is wired to detect change. When you present a "before" and an "after," you're activating the audience's pattern recognition system. It's not just two images or two slides—it's a story arc in two beats.

- Bad slide ⟹ Better slide
- Flat delivery ⟹ Animated delivery
- Dull opening ⟹ Revised attention-grabbing hook

That visual and conceptual gap commands attention, usually more powerfully than simply explaining what to do.

Everyone roots for progress

Transformation stories are irresistible. Whether it's a weight loss ad, a home renovation show, or a reworked slide layout, the improvement is the hook. People engage because they want to:

- See how something got better
- Judge whether it really did
- Learn how to replicate the improvement

Before-and-after scenarios give your audience a reason to care about the process that got you from A to B.

Makeovers activate deeper thinking

When you show the "before," people naturally start problem-solving:

- What's wrong with this?

- What's missing?
- What is here that shouldn't be?
- How would I fix it?

Then, when you show the "after," they get feedback—confirmation, surprise, or a new insight. That back-and-forth interaction builds cognitive tension and resolution, which leads to better retention.

Makeovers invite discussion

Transformation is a strong visual cue, especially in a screen-based environment. You can easily turn before-and-after versions into participatory moments:

- "Before I show you my version, what would you change about this?"
- "Which version communicates more clearly—and why?"
- "What do you like or dislike about each?"

The satisfaction of resolution

The moment you show a "before" slide, your audience members start scanning for what's wrong or what could be better, whether they do this out loud or in their own heads. Then, when you reveal the "after," their brains get the satisfaction of resolution. Instant cognitive payoff.

♦

With before-and-after examples, you are not just telling them the difference. You're involving them in the analysis. Before-and-after is a story with a visual payoff. It invites your audience to play along.

That's high-level engagement.

Beyond Chat

We continue our laundry list of engagement techniques with ideas and services that involve a bit more than just typing into a chat module. Some involve plug-ins, some need nothing more than pencil and paper, some require that audience members get up out of their chairs.

These techniques are all more discretionary than any request you make of audience members to use Chat, so you should expect a lower level of participation. No shaming allowed!

Here's hoping that a few of them are worthy of a raised eyebrow, while at the same time, some might merit an eye roll.

Go grab something

An underrated gem, this one is in equal proportion playful, physical, and personal. It's so simple: You ask people to go get an object from their home or office. It could relate to the topic at hand or could just be reflective of their mood. It signals to anyone who wants to participate that hey, you're not just watching this, you are a part of it. It works on several levels:

It creates movement: People have to stand up, shift, and engage physically. That boosts energy and attention.

It invites creativity: Everyone interprets the prompt differently, which brings surprise and delight.

It's low-risk vulnerability: The objects people choose often reveal something real, but they can share as much or as little as they want.

It's universal: Everyone's got stuff around them. No tech skills needed.

This activity is better with a time limit that is a bit tighter than optimum ("You have 30 seconds...GO!"). Be ready to showcase a few folks, and to that end, if you can have one or two "plants" in the audience (people comfortable sharing whom you know will bring back something cool), so much the better.

And if you strike gold with a particularly good selection of personal artifacts, instruct everyone to hold up their objects so you can snap a killer screenshot of them all.

Here are some possible prompts you could use:

Find something that represents your current mood.

Show us something on your desk you actually use every day.

Show me the weirdest thing you can reach in 10 seconds.

Grab an item that would confuse a time traveler from 1950.

What object would you use to represent our team's vibe?

The selfie assessment

Ask your audience to snap a selfie holding up a handwritten answer to a question you pose. That question should elicit a one-word response, so something like:

Who inspires you? Write their name.

What's your secret weapon for staying focused?

Draw your current emotional state as a face. No words allowed.

What is a ridiculous job title you might give yourself today?

At its simplest, these would be shared in Gallery view and you could stage and snap a pic of everyone holding up their answers. If you are more ambitious, you can have audience members upload their selfies to one of several aggregators—such as Padlet, Mural, or Slido, to name just a few—and then create a QR code to facilitate.

This activity helps humanize the audience, as cameras come on, faces appear, and names become people. And it activates different brain centers than passive listening. Writing by hand + photographing + sharing = deeper processing and commitment.

Give someone the floor

If you were speaking before an in-person audience, you would take for granted that you could see and hear every person who wanted to communicate with you. It's useful to remember that you can do that when leading virtually, as well—you just need to invite people to unmute and/or enable their camera.

Hearing a real voice breaks the often tedious rhythm of screen reading and passive watching. It changes the social dynamic and adds emotional weight to the experience.

It might also be outside the comfort zone of some members of your audience, so you only want to invite people to be seen or heard, never insist, and maybe not even encourage. Let it be their choice entirely. I like the way that my producer (and Foreword author) John Chen does it:

"Feel free to unmute."

Simple and nonthreatening. We usually employ this when someone has asked a question that merits an exchange, and it is part of a procession:

1. Someone asks a good question and my answer involves a follow-up query to that person.

2. "Feel free to unmute," says John, and the person responds to me verbally.

3. "This is a good convo," I might say—can I see you? Are you comfortable joining me on set?"

4. If yes, John adds the person to the Spotlight, and we finish the conversation by speaking and listening.

As I have always said, any opportunity for the audience to hear a different voice or see a different face is a positive addition to the experience.

Charades...sort of

So first off, classic Charades is an easy win, as you can ask your audience to pantomime something silly on camera ("show me your reaction if your WiFi died right now.").

But the real secret sauce is to play Reverse Charades. If the traditional game is played with one person giving clues and everyone trying to guess, imagine the Zoom chaos that ensues in Reverse: Just one person is trying to guess and everyone else is giving the clues! Here is what it looks like:

Better polling

While I enjoy taking polls, the polling functions in most of the streaming platforms are awful. I would rather just use Zoom's Chat than have to wrestle with that half-baked polling module that comes up as an independent dialog box and requires that audience members close it on their own.

I much prefer to integrate my polls into my slides, which I have been doing for over a decade with Poll Everywhere (www.polleverywhere.com) and more recently with StreamAlive (www.streamalive.com). These PowerPoint add-ins let you create a poll as a live object on your slide. As your audience members participate, the slide updates in real time. This is orders of magnitude more capable, more accommodating—and let's just say it out loud—more impressive than using native polling.

Customers of the plug-in can also create polls online, allowing them to be accessed by anyone (including enthusiastic readers of fine non-fiction). If you would like to participate in a simple poll that I have running now, here you go:

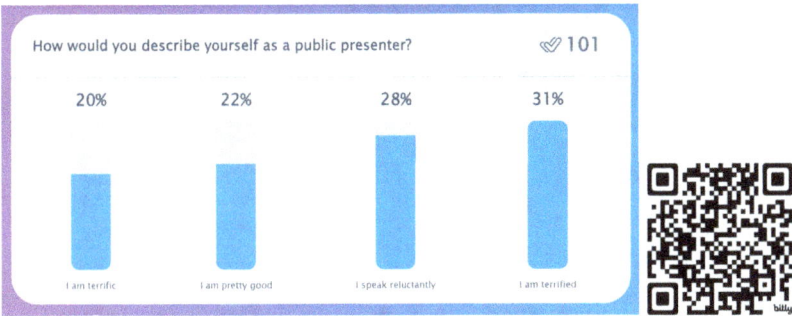

Partnering...or not

Much of the advice in this chapter is influenced by the main thrust of the next chapter, so keep reading for a more thorough exploration of how you can best serve your virtual audience. And let's play spoiler for just a few paragraphs: How easily could you execute any of the initiatives in this chapter if you were on your own? If you were the host, the presenter, and the one working the Chat?

Not well at all, and you shouldn't even try.

An effective virtual presenter always has a helper. *Always.* It doesn't have to be a professional moderator/producer/engineer; it can be a buddy. But trying to create an engaging virtual experience all by yourself is a bad idea on many levels.

Now keep reading... 💻

Everything in Moderation

Let me paint two scenarios for you. In the first, as you prepare to lead a webinar, it is just you and your webcam in that lonely room. Until you click "Join Meeting," and now it is just you and a grid of faces. Or maybe just a sea of turned-off cameras. You have a carefully crafted opener, but all of your prep work, rehearsals, and run-throughs burn to the ground when the specter hits that you must host, present, facilitate, manage, and monitor about a dozen variables. In what universe is this a good idea?

Or there's this scenario. You log in and are greeted with some nice music and a friendly "good morning." This same friendly voice has been bantering with the audience and now introduces you at the top of the hour. When questions flood the Chat, this voice feeds them to you. If something goes sideways with your slides or your screen share freezes, the voice steadies the ship. This voice tells you that you are not alone, you've got backup, you've got a friend.

This chapter is all about why you really want Scenario No. 2 and how to maximize the high potential of working with a partner.

What's in a name?

Moderator, engineer, producer, host, MC, or even the more colloquial moniker of sidekick. They all point to the same essential nature of a person whose job it is to help you with the live experience. An accomplished moderator is one of the most underappreciated assets in a virtual presenter's toolkit. They don't just make your life easier, they make you look better. And if you're thoughtful about how you work with them, they can elevate the entire experience for your audience, too.

This chapter is your playbook for doing exactly that. We'll break down the benefits of working with a moderator, explore how to choose one, and offer practical techniques to make the partnership sing. When it comes to delivering a compelling virtual presentation, everything is better with moderation.

And we are not necessarily talking about a professional, as not all virtual presenters are fortunate enough to be able to hire one. We might be talking about your co-worker or your BFF.

The tangible benefits of a moderator

At its simplest, good moderators monitor the Chat so you don't have to. They read the room for you. They handle what you don't need to, so you can focus on what you're meant to do. And while there are plenty of subtle benefits of having a teammate when you present, let's start with the obvious ones. Good moderators are:

Personal traffic cops, keeping sessions on track, managing Q&A, filtering chat noise, and identifying the audience contributions that will add to everyone's experiences.

Bridge builders, smoothing transitions between segments, and sensing when you might need a reset in tone or energy.

Safety nets in case your tech fails, although we are all at the mercy of the tech gods.

Conversation starters, who are able to stage discussions that feel organic.

Audiences tend to be more attentive when they hear multiple voices. When the moderator makes an appearance, that changes the energy level, usually in a positive way. Good presenter/moderator partnerships understand this dynamic and look for opportunities to leverage it.

A case study in repartee

I am fortunate to have one of the pioneers in virtual engagement as moderator for many of my webinars. In addition to being a Zoom expert and an AV savant, John Chen is a major-league extrovert. He leverages all three of these qualities as he navigates our virtual ship through the virtual harbor. Here is a snippet of the two of us working together:

John knows that I don't mind being interrupted. In fact, I like it—anything to change up the energy level and the vibe, right? And he does so here in a personal and self-deprecating way: by admitting that he does not create handouts for his own presentations as much as he should. This gives us an opportunity for a bit of banter and I rarely pass up the chance to show an audience how two friends might poke fun at one another.

This is virtual presentation gold. Unscripted, unplanned, completely in the moment, and just what audience members might need if their energy levels are dropping a bit.

John Chen multitasks so I don't have to, and that's a winning combination. In this clip, he alternates between Gallery view and Zoom's Spotlight feature to show each of us and both of us. All the while, he is listening to me, responding to me, and monitoring the Chat.

In addition to all of that, John insists that I send him all of my decks and visuals so that in a worst-case scenario—that I become unavailable to lead the presentation—he could step in and *literally take over for me.*

The intangibles

Then there are the less obvious benefits, which successful partnerships develop over time. These might be even more important than the qualities we have already recognized. Good moderators...

Humanize the experience: They assure you that you are not alone in the void, that there is a voice and a presence to keep you company.

Ease stage fright: They tell you they are there to catch you if you stumble.

Add gravitas or levity: Depending on tone, a moderator can amplify the emotional palette of the session.

Create warmth: Audiences can sense good rapport between presenter and moderator, promoting and modeling connection and engagement.

Make you more relatable: A good moderator gives audiences permission to warm to you. *Well, if the moderator likes this guy, maybe I should too.*

Defining roles

The decisions you make here likely rest with the next topic, choosing a moderator. In any event, it is vital that presenter and moderator spend quality time determining who does what, when, and how.

Whose "house" are you in?

Perhaps the most profound influencer of tone is found in this metaphorical question. As the presenter, are you also the host? Is everyone coming to your house? Or are you the featured guest? Is your moderator also the host and everyone is in his or her house?

I'm a guest in someone else's home: I am a regular presenter for the Training Magazine Network, a robust organization that holds near-daily webinars on a variety of topics. For these webinars, I am clearly the guest, entering the home of the host. That virtual home is Adobe Connect, a full-featured platform with a modular look and feel. Each one of those modules is in use, with sponsor shoutouts, a Q&A panel, a download link, various other pods, and a main viewing window for my screen:

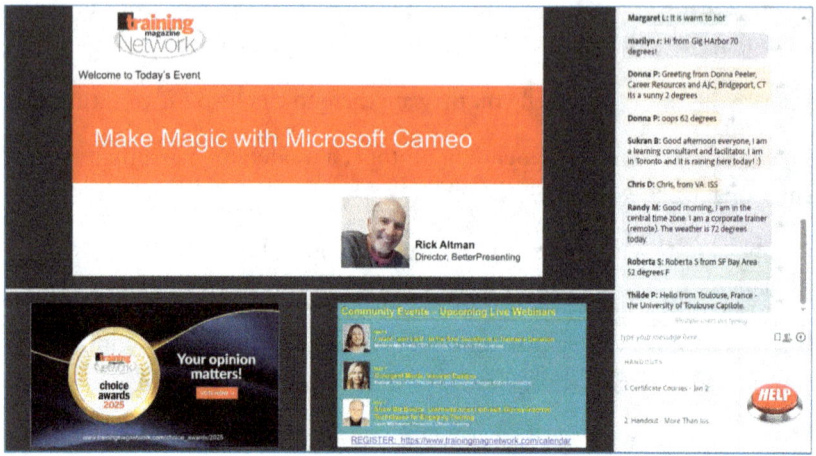

Lots of rooms in this house
For this webinar series, it is clear that Training Magazine Network is the host, I am the guest, and there are lots of places for the other guests to visit.

In situations like this, I know my place: I wait to be introduced. My video camera is not on, I keep my microphone muted, and while I could be active on Chat, I choose not to be. There is housekeeping to be done, sponsors to thank, and nothing would be gained from my calling attention to myself before being introduced. It's not my house.

I'm a guest in my own house: In workshops and conferences that I hold with John Chen or another professional, I am technically the host. It *is* my house, but John opens the door when the guests ring the doorbell. John warms up the crowd and does all of the introductions, but everyone knows they are my guests. I will chat people up and banter audibly. I might keep my video off if I need to prep visuals or go over my notes one last time, but I'm not hiding.

I'm the host and it's my house: In workshops or webinars where I don't have a professional moderator, I need to be more present and more proactive. I do all of the greetings, ice breaking, and warmups—the "connection before content." And whomever I rope into monitoring the Chat for me, I make sure to introduce and thank profusely. That is all I will ask of my friend-turned-moderator—I will take care of everything else.

Know before you go

None of this whose-house-is-it stuff is intuitive or obvious, so don't assume, don't guess, and certainly don't wing it. Talk it all through with your moderator, confer on handoffs, and decide what you will *not* do as earnestly as what you will do. A five-minute pre-show check-in can spare you what will feel like an eternity of confusion later.

The roles outlined across the previous pages are loose and malleable, but above all, they will not define themselves. Make sure you are both on the same page as for who does what:

- Who welcomes the audience?

- Who introduces the speaker?

- Who watches the Chat?

- Who handles the tech?

A professional moderator could literally do all four of these. Your buddy who agrees to help should only try to do one. The key, of course, is to be on the same page.

Who's on set?

Another question that should not be taken for granted is who shows themselves, when, and how? While someone acting as MC will most likely choose to be on camera, you might be doing your nervous buddy a favor by telling them that it is perfectly fine to monitor the Chat without turning on their camera.

The notion of being "on set" became a point of challenge and triumph for me at the 2024 Presentation Summit, when, for the virtual event, we replaced two of our traditional keynote addresses with Q&A style interviews of featured guests. I created much extra work for myself in leading interviews. Although it would have been much easier to let someone just speak for 30 minutes, I refer you back to my strident belief in the value of audiences seeing and hearing from multiple people.

My focus had to be entirely on the guest's responses to my questions, so I could determine the right time to follow up or to change topics. I had to sense a lull in the conversation right before it was about to take place, and above all, look for opportunities when we could really dig into a topic.

This all left me with zero bandwidth for anything else—most notably, I had no idea what other people were asking in the Chat or even *if* people were asking questions. This became problematic during our debut of these interviews, as audience members felt ignored. John needed to get my attention but he did not want to interrupt me or our guest. Private chatting me or even texting me could not penetrate my tunnel vision.

So we stumbled upon the perfect plan: John remains off set and when he wants to share a question from the audience, he adds himself to the spotlight. I can't miss that! Here is a short snippet of what that looks like:

In this clip, John appears right as I am asking a question, so I mentally queue him up to speak as soon as Jordyn, my guest, finishes her answer. John appears on set to pose the question and then, at his discretion, exits again. In this case, as the question needs elaboration, John returns to the set and brings with him the person who asked the question (Marshall Makstein, one of our technology editors).

This is hard work for both John and me, but eminently worth it as it translates to high engagement.

◆

These questions about role, responsibility, and function make up your final layer of prep: not just content readiness, but role readiness. When each person knows what lane they are in, it makes the entire experience feel polished, intentional, and human.

Strategic choices

Here are a variety of thoughts on the general subject of using moderators for your virtual presentations.

Think talk show, not TED Talk

With the last example fresh in mind, I want you to feel as if you are not just speaking, but co-hosting an experience. Virtual presentations can and should be more than solo acts; they should be shared experiences taking place in a shared space. When you bring in a moderator, you create the potential for creating a dynamic more akin to a talk show than a monologue. Think conversation over keynote. Banter over broadcast.

That means leaving space for interplay. It's less about delivering a perfectly polished script and more about creating a rhythm that feels alive and responsive. When you embrace co-hosting energy, the audience feels like they're in the room with you — not just watching from a distance. The result is a more human experience, a better connection, and a presentation that feels less like a lecture and more like a living moment.

Empower, don't micromanage

Give your moderator a lane and then let them drive! Good moderators bring their own instincts, presence, and experience to the job. They know how to read the room, when to jump in, when to hold back, and how to smooth transitions without being prompted.

Hovering over their every move or scripting every word undermines the natural chemistry that you hope emerges when you trust a moderator to settle into the job. That's when the magic happens — when the audience sees not just coordination, but collaboration.

Think morning drive, not morning briefing

One of the more nagging questions of any virtual presentation is what to do with the ten minutes before the official start time. The easy way out is to create a lobby or waiting room and just have your audience members hang out there, and as unimaginative as that is, it beats having them hang out in their Brady Bunch squares and silently ponder the meaning of life.

Meanwhile, not everyone has the luxury of hiring a skilled moderator who can function as an MC and greet everyone in a proper way. If you can, that is the best way to handle the pre-webinar experience.

If hiring a skilled moderator isn't in the budget, it's perfectly acceptable to ask a friend or colleague to help. I suggest the two of you pretend to be morning drive-time DJs like what you hear on radio. As people enter the room, they hear the two of you exchanging banter. And while you won't be as polished as professional radio DJs, you will exude warmth and authenticity. Here are a few tips to get you started:

- During a brief but important collab beforehand, map out five general conversation topics. Try to keep them loosely connected to the webinar topic and order them from most general to most specific. You now have your pre-show roadmap.

- Look for consensus. Within your five topics, identify a few times where you think you can really lean in to some good repartee. "Doesn't it steam you when you see _____," you might say. "Yes, that drives me crazy!"

- Stage a friendly debate. Similarly, find a topic or two where you don't agree and map out a back-and-forth in which you each get to offer your opinion.

- The formal host should sprinkle in a few welcoming remarks, along the lines of "Good morning, everyone, we'll start in a few minutes...we're just hanging out here as we all get settled in...feel free to tell us in the Chat about your favorite vacation destination."

- Use Zoom's Spotlight for the two of you, mute all audio, and disable all cameras. Make it clear to all that this is a conversation between two people and you do not expect anyone to join in. While this might feel exclusionary, it is actually comforting to the audience to assure them that they do not have to be "on" first thing in the morning.

- One minute before the official opening, you might then switch to Gallery view to signal that you're about to begin. To reiterate, a professional moderator might do this exactly in reverse: Start in Gallery view and lead a friendly roundtable and then switch to Single Speaker view right before beginning. While a pro could pull that off, you and your buddy are better off flipping this order.

The magic of good banter is that it doesn't need to be professionally produced or performed. A shared chuckle, a quick observation, a pointed question or two—they all can serve to break the ice and draw the audience into your world.

Choose chemistry over credentials

It's tempting to seek out someone with a long resume or a big reputation to serve as your moderator. But on a virtual stage, rapport is more important than polish. This means two things:

- If your BFF knows their way around a Chat panel, choose that person over a pro you don't know.

- And if you are fortunate enough to be able to hire a pro, interview candidates live and look for the potential for good chemistry.

Chemistry can't be taught, but it can be felt instantly. When you find it, don't let it go just because someone else has a glossier LinkedIn profile. I observed a wonderful example of this at our conference a few years ago. We practiced what we preached and asked friends and colleagues to act as moderators for our virtual seminars. We had engineers doing all of the heavy lifting, but we asked professional colleagues to handle the Chat and Q&A duties.

This paid off handsomely, as all seminar leaders had a friend to keep them company, and audience members were treated to some nice moments. Perhaps none sweeter than this one between seminar leader Bethany Auck and her moderator John Rahmlow. John is one of this book's technology editors, and while he knows his way around a Zoom window, more important, he is a beloved member of the presentation community.

Simple moments like this one pay huge dividends during virtual experiences. They remind audiences that we human beings strive for more than just learning things. It pays homage to the wonderful quote from Maya Angelou: "I might forget what you said or what you did, but I will never forget how you made me feel."

Hiring a moderator

While a relatively new field, there are ample avenues for finding capable moderators for your next virtual event. Here is a brief list:

National Speakers Association: Many NSA members are skilled at virtual moderation and the organization maintains a Virtual Presenters eChapter. www.nsaspeaker.org

eSpeakers: A platform where you can search for moderators by keyword, specialty, or format. www.espeakers.com

Presentation Guild: A close but eclectic group of presentation professionals (full disclosure, I am a founding member) that maintains a robust Slack channel and a job board. www.presentationguild.org

Train your own: This stands as the most likely path as no advanced degree is needed to become an excellent moderator. You want to see general comfort and aptitude with Zoom or the platform of choice, and more important, that simpatico that could lead to magic virtual moments.

The Eyes Have it

It's one of the more delicious paradoxes of virtual presenting: The best way to make someone feel seen…is to stare into a tiny glass dot. Not at their face, not at their smile, not at their reaction to anything profound you might have said—but at a lifeless and soulless camera lens. In the virtual space, that lens represents the face of your audience. It's your eye contact. It's your intimacy. It's the difference between your feeling like a real person in the room and a mere talking head in a box.

But let's be clear here, this isn't about staring. No one wants to feel pinned down by a robotic gaze. You're not filming a hostage video, and you're not delivering an address from the Oval Office. You're having a conversation—one that benefits from rhythm, from warmth, and from the natural ebb and flow of eye movement. This chapter is about learning to make the lens feel like a friend. Learning to treat eye contact, not as a performance, but as a presence. When you get that right, the difference is striking. People lean in. They feel you and they trust you.

If you feel awkward in front of the camera or if you struggle to connect virtually, this chapter will provide techniques, perspectives, and encouragement for your quest to make eye contact feel more natural and human.

Warming to the camera

Looking into a camera lens and pretending it's a person might be one of the most unnatural things you'll ever be asked to do. It doesn't blink, nod, or smile back. It just sits there—cold, glassy, unresponsive. And yet, if you want your audience to feel connected to you, you must learn to treat the camera as your friend. And that's hard.

That's the bad news; the good news is that it is just a skill. It is neither a personality trait nor a unique gift that you had to have been born with. It is a skill that you can practice and master.

The first step is recognizing that it probably won't feel natural at first; you are unlikely to love the lens immediately. Your relationship with it will evolve. It might start out akin to an awkward acquaintance, with whom you do not want to make eye contact. Your eyes will probably dart all over the place at first. Gradually, the relationship will change to one you would have with an indifferent coworker: You are still not sure what you think of it, but it's not worth that level of angst.

And if you stick with it, the camera lens can start to feel like a trusted companion, where you can relax with it, settle in, and become grounded. This helps you reach people, not just present to them.

The value of exaggeration

I learned all of this the hard way, with a series of uncomfortable practice sessions in which I couldn't even smile at first. I couldn't escape the feeling that I was some sort of newscaster and I would adopt the most solemn facial expression ever. Everything was serious, heavy, and decidedly unfun. I couldn't wait for Covid to be over so I could never speak into a camera lens again.

When I reached the point where I could actually muster a smile, it too seemed forced and unnatural. I would watch early 2020 videos of myself with equal feelings of despair and horror. Where was my natural self? I felt no part of my personality projecting through. I also got tongue-tied often and lost my place in the narrative. In reaction to that, I overwrote my notes and succumbed to Universal Axiom No. 2 (see page 16 about reading word for word when confronted with lots of words).

Finally, I had an epiphany: I would mug for the camera. I would get awkwardly close to the lens and exaggerate my every move. I felt like an idiot, and as you can see here, I looked like one, too. I often busted out laughing over the sheer hyperbole of my expressions. But ironically, this exercise in discomfort helped me become comfortable. It helped me feel more natural with my gestures.

In this short clip, I didn't pay attention to my lighting, my backdrop, or even what I was speaking about. I just tried to be overly expressive. This works. Don't let anyone see you, and whatever you do, don't share video of it in a how-to book. But it works.

Natural eye contact

The exaggeration exercise helps you find the line where you are overdoing it so that you can back off ever so slightly. You want to be right on that line; you want to *almost* be overdoing it. Learn what it feels like to open your eyes just a bit too wide, to raise your eyebrows slightly too high, to cock your head more than is natural, and to pierce the camera with your eyes a bit too strongly.

These gestures help you get to natural. You will learn that what you initially thought was too much probably isn't. You will become more comfortable looking directly into the camera while you speak. And once you do that, then (and only then) can you begin to riff off of that. Look to the side while you collect a thought, gaze up as you ponder, look down and shake your head in disbelief over something.

This is all virtual gold. But it must start with your ability to deliver a message while looking directly at your audience. If you are not completely comfortable doing that, continue the exaggeration exercise, or whatever one you prefer, until you get there.

That's like your baseline, from which you can then deviate.

A case study in facial gestures

Here are still images of some spontaneous gestures that I made during a recent presentation:

One of these is not like the other
Five of these gestures are acceptable and one is not. Can you find the one?

Nos. 1 and 2 are the baseline, as I am looking directly into the camera while delivering a message. Conversely, 4-6 are all products of natural reactions. I am either pondering (No. 4), searching for the right word (5), or emoting over some notion or event (6). These are all natural, expressive, and effective.

No. 3 is different. I am either looking at my monitor, a nearby script, or some random event near my camera that caught my eye. In any event, this is a fail and should be avoided. At best, I look distracted, and at worst, shifty. This is what nervous presenters look like, whose eyes dart all over the place for no reason at all. As you begin to get comfortable, this will happen less often, but still, you need to be diligent about keeping your eyes on the camera while speaking. Or veering well off as you naturally would for a number of reasons. But avoid the in-between stuff: eyes either on the camera or well off the camera, but not a little bit off the camera.

Like having lunch with a friend

This analogy works well for putting you in the right frame of mind for warming to your camera. If you were dining with people, you would not stare at them the entire time—that would creep them out. You glance away to sip your drink, you check the menu, you might have your head down while listening.

But when you are actively speaking to your dining companions, you are not focusing your eyes on a point two inches to the side of their eyes—you are looking directly at them! And so shall it be with your camera.

Upcoming…

The following chapters cover subjects that are germane to this one and are worth mentioning here.

Notes are not the enemy

It's perfectly okay to glance down at your notes or your outline. Your audience would rather you keep your train of thought than get derailed, and given the choice between hiding your notes and making it obvious to your audience that you have them, I would always want you to pick the latter. Let them know that you are prepared.

The key is to not overwrite your notes and risk Axiom No. 2 rearing its ugly head. See Chapter 11 for a lot more on this subject.

The Brady Bunch bind

Eye contact is particularly challenging when you are in Zoom's Gallery view and it is not so obvious where to look and when. Fortunately, most presenters don't spend much time in the Gallery, but when you do, how do you direct attention? See Chapter 12 for strategies to help you thrive as a member of the Brady Bunch.

A powerful proxy

The irony of good eye contact while on camera is that it can feel like the least human part of virtual presenting, and yet, it's the very thing that makes you appear most human to your audience. That little lens, as unfeeling as it is, becomes a powerful proxy for presence when you learn to treat it like a person.

Keep practicing. Keep exaggerating. Keep checking in with how it feels. Over time, eye contact won't just be something you remember to do—it will be something you rely on. Warming to the camera will become a source of comfort for you. You can relax when you enter the studio because you know you are about to be with your friend. That's when you know you've really arrived.

Please Read to Us...Said No One Ever

There is no faster way to murder a virtual presentation than by reading it to your audience. You might think it sounds polished, but to your audience, it just sounds dead. Scripted delivery makes every word feel like it's been run through a meat grinder of mediocrity.

You're not performing Shakespeare and you're not delivering the State of the Union. Nobody wants to be read to by a grown adult with a webcam. That's what they have audiobooks for. Virtual presenting is already one step removed from real interaction; why on Earth would anyone choose to take a further step away?

If your idea of engagement is droning through a grammatically perfect monologue, let me congratulate you, because you have just become every high school teacher's worst flashback. This short chapter fleshes out why 90% of the time, you should run as fast as you can away from writing out your presentations. And we do talk about the 10%...

Word perfect, soul absent

I understand the temptation to script your words and I have even succumbed to it a few times. You are nervous...the topic is emotional...you are afraid you'll forget what you want to say...you want it to be perfect. I sympathize with all of these situations, but human behavior is pretty clear on this front: Unless you are a trained thespian, writing out your words practically guarantees that you will not be at your most authentic. Here are a few of the reasons why scripting is bad news.

It flattens your voice: Scripting drains your vocal variety, making every sentence land with the same dull thud. No matter how exciting the words may be, reciting them sucks the excitement out of them.

It stiffens your timing: When you're locked to a script, your pacing becomes mechanical. Natural pauses, gestures, or just adjustments in the moment all become endangered species.

It kills natural delivery: You stop speaking like a human and start sounding like a transcript, with all the spontaneity of a tax form.

It's obvious: Audiences can tell when you're reading—your eyes flicker and your tone goes flat.

It's robotic: Scripts strip emotion and nuance, replacing them with perfectly worded, perfectly lifeless sentences.

It turns you from a presenter into a narrator: You stop participating in the moment and start describing it, like someone reading their own slide bullets to you.

And it kills connection: Real connection requires presence, responsiveness, and warmth—three things a script can't deliver without earnest and dedicated rehearsal and preparation.

How we got here

The urge to script often comes from a well-meaning place. Many of us were taught to treat presentations like speeches or even essays—formal, tightly written, grammatically perfect affairs. Scripting also feeds the illusion of control. If you write it out, you can't mess it up, right? And let's not forget the nerves. When you're nervous, a script feels like a safety net.

Research and observation reveal each of these well-intended reactions to be flawed.

Perfectly paralyzed: In your quest to be perfect, you often become paralyzed. The polish you crave gets buried under anxiety, as you try to recall exact phrases instead of expressing actual ideas.

Fear of forgetting becomes self-fulfilling: If you are beholden to a script, the risk of losing your place increases exponentially. Rarely do script readers adequately see the forest for the trees so any little distraction becomes amplified.

The straitjacket of regimen: When you get trapped in structure, it becomes difficult to respond in real time. Confidence doesn't come from memorizing every word—it comes from trusting yourself to show up prepared and present.

Worse on virtual

It has happened before that clients have informed me that they must deliver a speech from prepared words, and when done in person, there are some tricks that can be employed. Insisting on a lectern is a good start so the presenter is not standing out in open space, having to manage multiple sheets of paper. In addition, I make sure that the type is set at least 14pt so that presenters can stand back a bit from the edge of lectern. This changes the geometry so that shifting their gaze between down at the speech and up at the audience is not so pronounced.

These tricks—coupled with lots of practice and the comfort of knowing that in-person audiences are much further away from the presenter—make delivering a scripted speech in person a plausible project.

Not so with virtual, where audiences sit three feet from your eyes, and all of the factors come into play that we discussed in the last chapter on eye contact. You need a teleprompter to get away with it on virtual, and while there are products to help you with that, I would much rather you wean yourself off of—than become more reliant on—those types of gimmicks.

It happened to me

All of these warnings notwithstanding, I had occasion to consider writing out opening remarks in the fall of 2024. The virtual version of the Presentation Summit was held over the national election, and on the morning of our final day, the world awoke to President-elect Donald Trump. Our conference leans a bit left, and I suspected there would be some sad faces in our galleries that morning. Sure enough, that morning was punctuated by puffy cheeks, heavy eyelids, and sad faces.

We are a decidedly apolitical event, but when I saw these sad faces, I knew I needed to say and do something to lighten the mood. I changed into a bright shirt, instructed John Chen to play upbeat music, and I decided to say a few words about the situation. Notwithstanding all of the risks I have written about here, with no time to prepare or rehearse, I typed out a few paragraphs and taped them right next to my camera.

This video represents about the best that I could do without a teleprompter, and to me it is obvious when I am not making proper eye contact—like in the snapshot I chose here, where my gaze is on my script, to the right of the camera.

Am I being overly sensitive? Perhaps so. Did anyone notice? Perhaps not, and in the video snippet, there are times when I connect intimately with the camera. But when there are complete sentences in the vicinity, even an experienced presenter finds it impossible to not look at them.

I have two regrets when I look back on this event. I wish that I could have spoken from the heart during this poignant moment. But I, too, was emotional, and as I often advise my clients, when you feel at risk of losing composure, give yourself a break and write out what you want to say. So that regret is mitigated by the circumstances. The second regret is that I didn't own it. Yes, I wanted to make sure that I didn't step all over my words, so why didn't I just say that? "This is an emotional time for all of us," I could have said, "so please indulge me as I read from prepared remarks."

I wish I had said that.

The other exception

The other time that it is acceptable to script out your words is if you have a passage that you want to nail. The introduction of an important topic, a critical transition from one topic to the next, or a part of the talk that is carefully timed.

If you want to script that out, fine, go ahead, but do these things:

- Prepare a clean slide that provides a strong canvas for your words.
- Practice it diligently so you can read it naturally. Vary your cadence, insert pauses, maybe even throw in an *um* or two.
- And turn your camera off!

Here is an example that I provided for a recent workshop, where I share my angst over buying an electric car during the height of demand. In the video, notice the devices and tricks that I employ to make it sound as natural as possible. I pause and hesitate a few times, I throw in a few exclamations, and I try to create a lot of dynamic range (difference between soft and loud vocal tones).

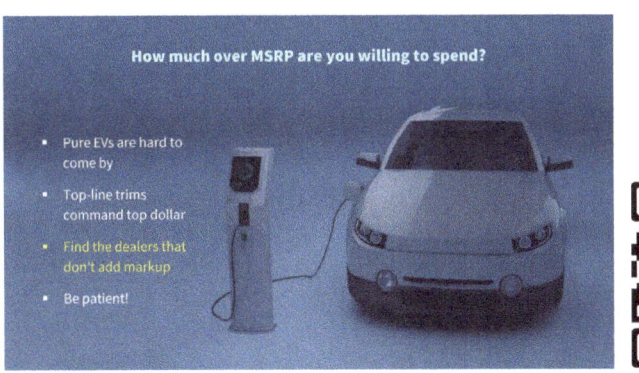

This is no different than an actor learning his lines: You say it enough times that you begin to own it.

Teleprompter syndrome

Virtual presenters can buy a variety of cool toys and impressive tech, all of which promise to make you better, and all of which probably produce exactly the opposite.

Suction cup cameras: These are small webcams that can be adhered to any point on your screen, the idea being that you have your script up in Word and the camera right next to it. But unless you are skilled and practiced at speaking from a teleprompter, your audience will see your eyes darting across their line of sight and will feel the disconnect.

Mini teleprompters: I have had occasion to see three different products that connect directly to your camera and act as small teleprompters. The most impressive is from Elgato, the makers of the popular Stream Deck. Elgato's Prompter drops a veil in front of your camera lens, onto which you can choose to show: your script, PowerPoint's Presenter view, Zoom's active speaker view, or the Chat. This ensures that you can take care of your business and look directly into the camera at the same time.

As impressive as this technology is, it can become like crack cocaine, making you ever-more dependent on it. That is the last thing I want for myself or for any of my clients or readers.

Your mileage might vary. You might love these things. Ultimately, all that matters is giving your audience the impression that you are speaking directly to them. If teleprompters help you get there, all good fortune to you. More often, I find them to be barriers to connection.

The right thing to memorize

As we sum up this short chapter, I want to impress upon you how much more beneficial it is to rehearse your ideas, not your sentences. Memorize the structure of your talk, not your lines.

You want to sound like a person. You want to sound real. No virtual audience member ever said, "Wow, that was a beautifully recited paragraph."

The points made in this chapter go hand in hand with those of the next one: all about creating good notes. So keep reading... 💻

Notes to Self

If the last chapter was all about what *not* to do, this chapter is the yang to that yin, focusing on what you *should* do. No matter how confident you are, how well you know your content, or how off the cuff you want to sound, walking into a virtual presentation with nothing in the way of prep is a gamble. Notes are your scaffolding—they support you without boxing you in.

The difference between scripting and note-taking is the difference between building a cage and setting up a trampoline. One locks you in; the other gives you bounce.

This chapter is about making notes that help you bounce—so you remain present, stay organized, and sound like a real person while doing it. I will make the case that notes are not just acceptable, they are essential. I don't want you to think of them as a crutch, but as a launchpad.

Why notes work

Let's disabuse ourselves of several notions right away: Notes are not a form of cheating, they are not a crutch, not a sign of weakness, not something to sheepishly apologize for. My AI agent wrote that "good notes are the secret weapon of great communicators," but I dispute that also—they should not be a secret! I want my audience to know that I have notes. I want them to know that I have been thinking about how best to service them.

Think in ideas, not sentences

The moment you chase exact phrasing is when you veer away from all that makes a presentation great. Notes help shift your focus from word-for-word recitation to concept-by-concept delivery.

I don't want you to memorize a script; I want you to visualize the narrative arc of your story. That only happens if you stay above the weeds.

Notes provide structure and preserve spontaneity

Good notes are like a trail map: You can take detours, knowing you can find your way back. They anchor main points without imposing rigid phrasing. You can digress, knowing how to return to the trail. Notes allow you to speak naturally with the reassurance that you're never far from home base.

These two ideas—structure and spontaneity—appear to live in tension. Spontaneity implies improvisation and reacting in the moment, while structure suggests planning, order, and constraint. How can you be off-the-cuff while working from notes? Isn't spontaneity supposed to come from scratch?

That's the myth. In truth, they're not opposites at all; they're dance partners. Without some kind of structure, spontaneity easily devolves into rambling or distracting filler. And without any spontaneity, structure can turn wooden and lifeless. It's the interplay between the two that makes a presentation feel polished and real. Real life holds many examples of this:

A jazz musician works from a chord chart. The structure gives shape to the song, allowing the French horn solo to soar.

An improv comic has a scene framework. A loose outline sparks spontaneity without scripting the laughs.

A dancer rehearses choreography, but brings it to life with nuance. Every step is mapped, but expression and artistry make it feel spontaneous.

Great chefs follow a recipe, but taste along the way. They measure key ingredients, but they don't follow blindly. They adjust seasoning, change course, and improvise based on what the dish needs.

A wedding officiant works from an outline, but speaks from the heart. They know the key moments and their order, while leaving room for warmth, humor, and presence.

A teacher has a lesson plan, but reads the room. They might plan activities down to the minute, but if students are confused, curious, or stressing out, will adjust in real time.

Late-night talk show hosts have cue cards, but they follow the guest. There's a rundown of segments, but the magic happens when they go off-script in the moment.

A stage actor memorizes lines, but finds fresh emotion every night. The structure never changes, but each performance is alive with subtle shifts in timing, tone, and connection.

And a great presenter has notes, just enough guidance to stay grounded, with plenty of space to speak like a real person.

So yes, it feels like a contradiction—and that's exactly what makes it worth exploring. Notes can keep you grounded while giving you room to roam. They let you take tangents without getting lost. They keep your content tethered without tying you down. When you embrace both elements, you unlock your best self as a virtual presenter.

One of the most insightful takes I've ever heard on this subject comes from Julie Andrews:

"Some people regard discipline as a chore.
For me, it's a kind of order that sets me free to fly."

That's what good notes do. They give you a framework so you're free to move, to adapt, to sound human. Notes let you take detours without getting lost. They let you fly, knowing the ground is always beneath you.

Notes can calm your nerves

There is real comfort in knowing your thoughts are close at hand. When nerves creep in, your notes act as an anchor. Just a glance can remind you where you are and what's next, confirming you are on track.

That tiny hit of reassurance can steady your voice, slow your breathing, and bring you back to the present. Your audience doesn't sense your tension, they sense your composure. And you have your notes to thank.

Notes provide comfort

Sometimes, the best thing about notes is simply knowing they're there, even if you don't refer to them. Their presence is calming. Like an understudy who never goes on stage, they stand ready just in case.

That quiet backup gives you peace of mind, especially in moments when your mind races or the tech glitches. They are your silent partner, always in the wings, reminding you that you're not alone out there.

Bad notes vs. good notes

Not all notes are created equal. The way you format them can make the difference between helpful cues and a hot mess of distraction. Bad notes make you fumble. Good notes let you glance and glide.

Paragraphs are bad

Long blocks of text make your eyes work too hard. You'll lose your place the second you look away, and in a live presentation, that's all it takes to unravel your momentum. Full sentences invite full-on reading—and we all know where that leads.

Bullets are better

Breaking up your thoughts into clean, scannable chunks (not paragraphs or long sentences) helps you stay on track. Bullets make it easier to find your spot again and reduce the temptation to speak in written prose.

Keywords and prompts are best

This is the gold standard. You don't need full thoughts, you need a phrase to jog your memory, a word to spark the next idea, a reminder of your transition. These notes work with your brain, not against it.

Visuals, colors, and spacing matter

Use line breaks. Use bold or highlight. Even add emojis or icons if they help you scan quickly. When your nerves spike, your ability to process dense text drops. Make your notes glanceable.

Before and after

Here is a Notes page view from a client who got a bit carried away (left), along with a makeover (right). While the six bullets for the six life skills are clearly delineated, there are way too many complete sentences in the original, all but guaranteeing that the presenter would not be able to glance at this nor avoid reading it word for word.

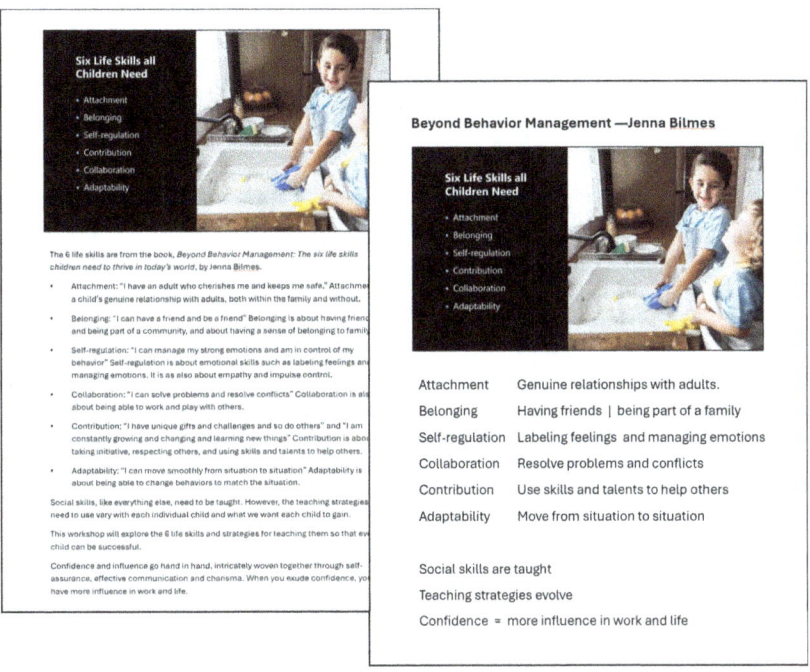

The critical assumption is that the presenter can speak to the six life skills with very little help. Same with the three conclusions at the bottom. The only thing I don't leave to memory is the title and author from whom this work is derived, and I moved that to the most prominent location on the page. Forgive the bluntness: If the presenter can't tell this story without a script, they should not be before an audience.

Formats that serve

Now it is time to ask where they should live: at what location and on what type of medium. You need a form that's easy to access, easy to read, and above all, will not compete for your attention or focus. Here are some of the most common formats, along with the pros, cons, and little tricks.

Presenter View

If you're using PowerPoint or Keynote, Presenter View is worth considering, as it is built into both programs. It gives you a slide preview, your speaker notes, a running clock, and several other tools, all of which live behind the scenes, away from audience view.

Many tools...maybe too many tools. Here I am in mid-presentation, with Presenter View on my top monitor. Within that top monitor, the large top-left image is the current slide, the smaller top-right image is the next

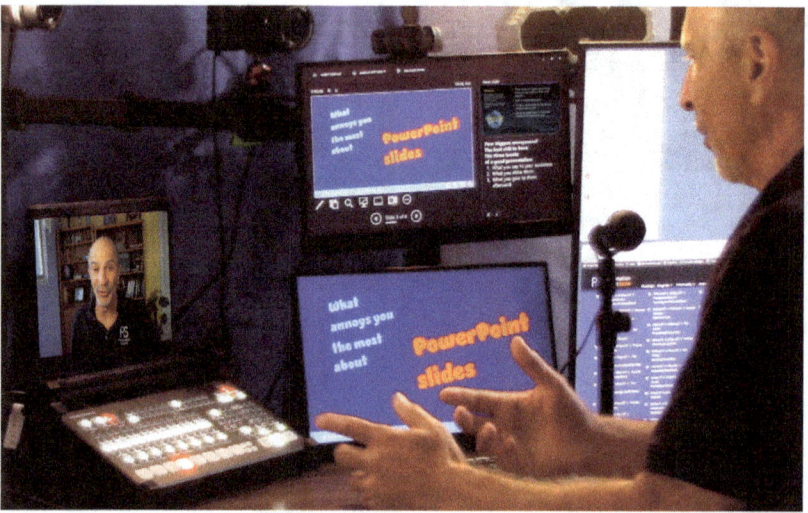

slide, and my notes are lower right. With so much busyness, I need to ensure that my notes are terse.

That's a good thing, to be sure, and if you tend to create slides with one thought per slide, seeing just one slide worth of notes works great. With my tutorials or makeovers, one theme will stretch across many slides and it becomes tedious for me to parse out my notes across so many slides. I prefer that my notes not be so strictly aligned with my slides, so I do not use Presenter View often.

Printouts

Never underestimate the power of paper. A printed sheet on your desk is simple, reliable, and uncrashable. You don't have to worry about window placement, battery levels, or software updates. Just make sure your notes are formatted for quick scanning: large font, bullet points, wide spacing, key words bolded or highlighted. It should feel like a roadmap, not a novel.

One downside: Your gaze will drop to your desk, so practice how you then return to the camera. A smooth lift of the eyes is all it takes to stay connected. I don't mind my audience knowing that I have notes on my desk; again, I want them to know. So I don't mind being seen looking at them.

Paper next to the camera

This classic technique involves your notes and a bit of scotch tape. The closer to the camera the better, and taping your notes literally to the lens is the best. That way, you never have to look away at all to see your notes.

This works fine as long as you are at least five feet from the lens. Then it will not matter if you look at the camera or at your notes. That's good, because with your notes so close to the lens, you will look at them often, whether you need to or not. You will likely alternate between the two rapidly.

But if you are in tight to your webcam, this rapid switch between lens and notes will make you look nervous at best. And if you focus just on your notes, they will turn you into the person who's reading from a script. Better to just have index cards on your desk.

 See Chapters 9 and 18 for further discussion about eye contact and your relationship to your camera.

Mobile phones

While a tablet is a plausible option to display your notes, I have yet to see anyone pull off the natural use of notes from a mobile phone. A curse seems to come to people who try. Their words become mechanical, their muscles tighten, and they strain to read the screen. Even young people with sharp eyesight are not used to how far away the phone needs to be in order to be out of camera view.

And let's not even talk about having to scroll the damn thing.

I root hard for someone to show us the way, given how convenient mobile phones are. But I'm still waiting and I expect to be waiting when I am old and frail.

Practicing the glance

Rehearsing with notes is different than rehearsing a speech. You are not trying to memorize lines—you are training your eyes to find the right word at the right time, and then return to your audience. You are not trying to do it quickly; that makes you look nervous and will call attention to the very act you are trying to do discretely. You are trying to do it naturally.

This kind of rehearsal is all about rhythm: You're learning how to glance down without breaking connection. You're practicing your transitions and smoothing out the moments that tend to trip you up. Rehearsal isn't for polishing the words, it's for polishing you.

With this video, I call attention to something that I think/hope that you would never have noticed on your own. In this short snippet, I look down at my notes three times. Each time is in the middle of a sentence, the objective being to note the next topic before I finish with the current one.

Were my notes closer to the camera, the move would not have appeared as natural—it might have appeared to you as nervous, jittery, and maybe shifty. But a longer glance down is much more natural, and as I said earlier, I do it while I am in mid-sentence.

The goal is flow, not perfection (that's a microcosm of this entire book). You don't need to recite anything flawlessly. You need to get comfortable finding your footing in real time.

So don't just write the notes. Don't just print them and tape them somewhere. Speak with them, tell stories with them, become one with them. That is the day that you stop delivering presentations and start inhabiting them.

How low-tech can you get?

I am a proponent of having notes nearby anytime I am live, but those notes take different forms depending upon the circumstance. This breaks

Chp 11 Notes to Self

down into two distinct categories, both decidedly low-tech: index cards and legal pads.

The convenience of index cards

If I am in full view, I work off of index cards. This is often the case with extended interviews, whether in person or virtual. I might be seated on a stool, with my lap in full view. Each index card is a question I want to ask, and I don't mind at all if the camera captures this.

This was the case in 2020, when Guy Kawasaki joined us on set to share his perspective on good presentation content.

I remembered the keynote address he gave at our 2015 conference in which he said "You can steal from me all you want. All of my videos are available on YouTube, if you want to use them, go right ahead. That's just good marketing."

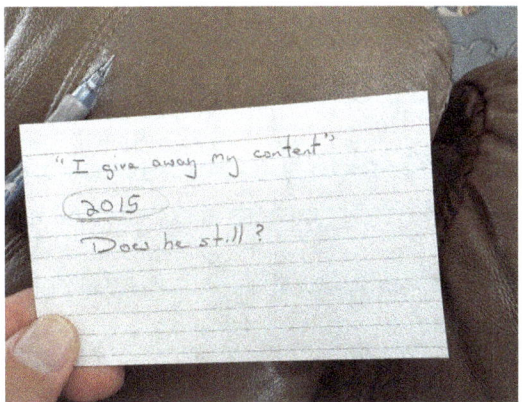

Low-tech notes
When it comes to on-set notes, the simpler the better.

I wanted to know if, five years later, he felt the same way, and this simple index card on the next page was all I needed.

A few things to note here, pun intended:

- I handwrite my notes. I want them to be as tactile as possible.
- I use pencil, so I can erase stuff and make it bigger if I need to.
- I thought about these things out of order, and while I could have used my eraser, instead I just circled the year to indicate to me that I should start with that.

The incredible comfort of the legal pad

Continuing the low-tech theme, my notes are pieces of paper that feature my bad handwriting. Here's one from the 2024 conference:

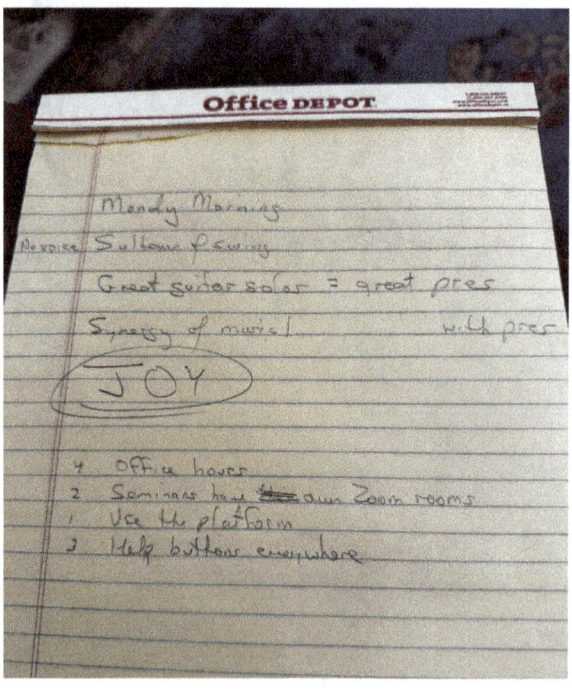

The small left column is for cues to myself. In this case, after being introduced, I went right to a short clip of one of my favorite songs ("Sultans of Swing" from Dire Straits), and that is me telling myself to remain silent.

As you can see, my plan was to make some sort of connection between great music and a great presentation, and during run-throughs, I tended to forget to speak about how each can bring such joy—hence the big circled word.

Finally, I had to take care of some hostly announcements, which I wrote down in the order I thought of them, and then ordered them with simple numbers next to each one.

The amazing dividends of reminders

In a more classical virtual environment, in which I am a talking head, nothing beats a full-size sheet of paper and a mechanical pencil with an eraser head. That is my go-to, and I always bring them onto the set and make reference to reminders that I need to make for myself. I share the video below with you, not to try to show you how brilliant and innovative this strategy is; it is neither of those things. It is about as old-fashioned as an interaction can be ("let me write a reminder for myself...").

First off, it's good to make reminders, because if you're like me, you will forget stuff all the time, especially if you are promising to address it 24 hours later. Moreover, I am constantly reminded by how much audiences appreciate this simple gesture. When they see me with pencil and paper in hand, in the words of one audience member, "I can feel him through the screen. It's like, wow, he's just like me, he writes sh*t down!"

In a world of high-tech virtual wizardry, it is noteworthy when a pad of paper and a pencil can have that kind of impact.

A final note on notes

Notes are your partner, not your prison. Get them right, and they disappear—leaving only you and your audience. The best notes aren't there to be read—they're there to remind you what ideas matter to you, and what type of journey they comprise.

They don't need to be fancy, they don't need to be neat, and they don't need to be invisible. Whether it's a scribbled cue on a legal pad or a perfectly spaced digital cheat sheet, they just need to work for you. Notes are not a sign of weakness—they're a sign that you care. For your message, for your audience, and for your own peace of mind.

The Paradox of the Gallery

You enter a Zoom room and, bam, there they all are. Several dozen faces staring back at you in neat little boxes. It looks like an audience, but does it feel like one? Is it one?

That grid of faces might be alternatingly reassuring, confusing, or downright terrifying. Why have they shown up? What do they want? Are they engaged? Are they bored? Are they doing three other things while waiting for you to cast off a pearl of wisdom or two, after which maybe they will pay you more attention? Such pressure!

Gallery view is the only speaking situation where you are presenter and audience member at the same time. You're watching them. They're watching you. You're watching yourself watching them watching you. Yikes, no wonder it can be so disorienting. Gallery view promises connection, but the strange physics of the grid can mess with your instincts and affect your efforts to deliver your genuine self.

This chapter is about navigating that mess and helping you make intentional choices about how you see your audience and what you show your audience. When used wisely, Gallery view can be a useful tool of engagement. It can and should work for you, not against you.

Gallery view is not your go-to

Gallery view is one of the most recognizable features of virtual meeting platforms. The tiled wall of faces has become a symbol of our remote era—that is why we represented it on our cover! For many, it feels like the natural way to see your audience, and it won't be too long before a group of young professionals joining the workforce will not remember a time before Zoom.

But that doesn't mean it should be your default setting. It shouldn't be.

When you're presenting, Gallery view can do more harm than good. It splits your attention across dozens of micro reactions. This makes it harder to focus on your content, harder for your audience to focus on you, and pressures you to "read the room" in a context where the room isn't reading you back. Instead of delivering a message, you risk delivering a series of second guesses.

Furthermore, Gallery view can become draining to your audience members. They have come to hear what you have to say on a topic that matters to them. They don't want to be "on" all the time. This is one of the root causes of Zoom Fatigue.

Use Gallery view as a strategic choice, not a reflexive habit. Smart moderators will switch to it for a Q&A segment or will do a quick cutaway to it during a monologue, just to change up the energy. This is shrewd use of Gallery view, as the exception, not the rule.

A Gallery by any other name

While we choose to capitalize it, we are using the term Gallery view generically, as all three of the major streaming platforms—Zoom, Teams, and Google Meet—offer it. Zoom and Teams refer to it by this name, while Meet calls it Tiled view. Most of this chapter applies to all three and I will do my best to point out when a particular topic does not.

The illusion of attention

I remember during one of those very first Covid-induced virtual gatherings how fleeting the joy was that I could speak live while sheltering in place. Gallery view felt like a gift: so many faces, so much audience—and they are all listening to me!

I think. I think they are listening to me. Are they listening to me? Hmm, I actually have no clue if they are listening to me. Do they care? Are my words hitting the mark? What if they are not? Did I just see someone yawn? That person is looking down blankly...was it something I said? What if I am bombing and I don't even know it? Yikes, I'd better wrap this up and get out of here!

This freak-out moment was brought to you by...me. I did this to myself, all by myself. It seems as if I am never more tuned into audience reaction than when I don't want to be.

How you *think* your audience is responding shapes how *you* respond to them—this is just human nature. But facial feedback in Gallery view is unreliable at best, and imaginary at worst. What you're seeing is a delayed, pixelated, sometimes distracted slice of reality. Don't make the mistake that I made that first time of basing your performance on it.

Instead, anchor yourself to your message, not their expressions. Stay grounded in what you came to say. Trust that connection comes from clarity and conviction, not from a grid of facial cues that may or may not be real.

You are the only one responsible for your energy. Resist the urge to scan the grid for affirmation that may never come.

Your energy is the thermostat

One of the trickiest dynamics of virtual presenting is the mismatch between what you give and what you get. You bring your energy, your personality, your message—and in return? Crickets. Muted microphones. If you're lucky, a few nodding heads.

Connection is still possible in Gallery view, but it takes more intentionality to make it feel like a shared space. And let's always keep in mind that Gallery view is not your default as a presenter: When you are in your true zone, you are most likely being spotlighted. You switch to Gallery view because you want to spark a conversation, so speak to the group as if you are all together in someone's living room. And as the conversation leader, you are looking for the slightest morsel of consensus. "Sam, you look like you want to jump in here...I see Dana nodding her head...lots of eye rolls from that rant."

These small but very human signals create warmth and you score connection points for encouraging and cultivating them. This is all part of humanizing the grid, a topic that could probably be an entire book unto itself. Suffice it to say that behind every Brady Bunch square is a real person craving connection and acknowledgment just as much as you are. Every small ritual of interaction—every nod, every smile, every chatted emoji—gets you one step closer.

Talk to the glass

Let me share with you one of the most ironic contradictions in all of virtual presenting:

To make someone feel seen, you have to look away from them.

If you and I were engaged in conversation in a physical room, we would do what all humans do: We would look at one another. Not all the time, but most of the time. And because we share the same physical proximity, we would have other ways of showing our connectedness. We might nod, exchange *uh-huhs* or *yeahs*, a light touch of the arm to emphasize a point, or one of a dozen other empathetic gestures that friends typically exchange.

But it would be different for us in a virtual room. Those nice human gestures—the nods, the uh-huhs, the touches? Most of them disappear or get flattened. A nod might go unnoticed, while a smile might lag. A confirming "yeah" might be muted or garbled. And forget about anything remotely resembling actual physical touch.

And eye contact itself is all bass-ackwards on virtual. Yes, we would still look at each other...sort of. You'd probably be watching my face on your screen, and I yours, but the feeling would be hollow.

Instead, what I would need to do is stare into a cold, glassy lens while I speak to you. That is how I would show you that I am really present with you. My instinct would be to read your expression, but my job would be to resist that instinct.

When you speak directly into the camera, your audience sees your eyes—your real-time presence. That's where the connection lives. Not in your glance downward to check their reaction, but in the steady, human focus of your gaze.

That's not intuitive; it's the opposite of intuitive. You show your audience members you are paying attention to them by not looking at them? No wonder this sh*t is so hard...

A blueprint for sanity

The ideal scenario is that you train yourself to always look into the camera during a Gallery conversation. As they speak, you look into the camera. As you speak, you look into the camera.

But that is practically impossible and entirely unrealistic. Not only does it go against all of your instincts, but you miss too much nuance by looking away for the entirety of a conversation.

Instead, here is the strategy that I have hit upon after countless hours of self-reflection and frustration about conversations in Gallery view:

When you are speaking: I, the presenter, look directly at your square. I watch your gestures, I listen to your inflection, I try to pick up on subtleties that are so easy to miss on virtual. My eyes are not on the camera—I am looking at you. If I am able, I arrange the squares so that yours is as close as possible to my camera.

When it is my turn to speak: I look directly into the camera. I might miss the nuance of your reactions to my words, but I accept that risk. The more important sense I create is that I am speaking directly to you.

So when you speak, my eyes are on you. When I speak, my eyes are on the lens.

♦

This strategy is not easy to pull off. It takes a lot of conscious thought and repetition to become second nature. You might feel like you're staring into a void and speaking to nobody. So you just need to drill it into your head: to make them feel seen, you need to look away from them while you speak. So yes, talk to the glass. That's where their eyes are.

Hide Self View, save your soul

Many yoga studios disallow mirrors in their floor design so that their customers can focus inward, not on outward appearance. Most theaters cover or remove mirrors during rehearsals so that cast members can inhabit their characters without having to observe themselves. Same with many places of worship, where mirrors and reflective surfaces are believed to be distractions from introspection.

In all of these cases, the belief is clear: Staring at yourself while presenting is like trying to give a speech while also being your own hair and wardrobe consultant. It divides your focus, amplifies your insecurities, and keeps you half in and half out of the moment.

At first, seeing yourself on screen might feel reassuring—proof that you're centered in the frame and that your lighting is working. And to be sure, you do need to make sure you have taken care of these simple set requirements. But the longer you watch yourself, the more your attention drifts inward. Why am I making that face? Is my collar crooked? Is that how I really look? This is the "mirror effect," and it's a recipe for distraction and loss of focus.

Hiding Self View is one of the most underrated moves in virtual presenting. It doesn't mean you disappear; it means you free yourself to be fully present. You still get to show up for your audience—you just stop showing up for yourself every second of the way. (Research suggests that the mirror effect is a leading cause of Zoom Fatigue.)

Let your delivery matter more than your hair. Talk to the lens, trust the tech, and get out of your own way.

Turning the Gallery into a gallery

Most people think of Gallery view as a static wall of faces—more observational than interactive. But with a little creativity, it can become a shared canvas, a co-created space. A gallery not just of attendees, but of participants. When used sparingly and intentionally, it can become wonderfully inclusive. As we detailed in Chapter 7, "Flex your Engagement Muscle," simple tasks you assign to visible gallery members can pay big dividends. Ask people to show something on camera—a prop, a book, an object—that represents their mood or mindset. Run a quick show-and-tell session. Invite people to hold up answers on paper. Turn the Brady Bunch into a story circle.

None of this has to be formal. Even just asking, "Linda, can you unmute and weigh in on that?" changes the dynamic. The grid shifts from being a wall to being a room with movement, rhythm, and presence.

This is where Gallery view shines—not as a passive screen of nodding heads, but as a living, breathing space for interaction.

Your go-to views

Let's reiterate that for a presenter shaping a narrative, Gallery view should not be the default view. Here are some better places to be.

Spotlighting

Zoom and Teams offer the Spotlight function, whereby the platform locks one or more people in view for everyone. When the host activates Spotlight, everyone's view automatically switches to Speaker view and becomes "locked." That's not a technical term, as far as I know, but you know how when you are in Speaker view, an unmuted person coughs, and that person is suddenly shown? That cannot happen when there is a Spotlight on. Everyone is better able to focus on the presenter when that person gets a Spotlight.

Because the inmates run the asylum on Zoom, audience members could switch back to Gallery view, plowing asunder your best efforts to create the right environment for them. But they would have to do this deliberately—if they do nothing, Spotlight automatically switches to Speaker view.

Google Meet calls it "pinning," and while it produces the same effect, there is no provision for a host to implement it universally. Each audience member engages or disengages it.

Side-by-Side Speaker view

This is a view choice that is available during a screen share, allowing each audience member to choose the relative sizes of the presenter and the presenter's screen. Unlike Spotlight, the host cannot control this; each audience member does. And we have learned that this is not well-known, despite its potential to greatly improve the viewing experience. At the Presentation Summit, we distribute a video tutorial to make sure that each of our patrons is familiar with the feature:

Chp 12 The Paradox of the Gallery

Teams does not have this option, but its Presenter Mode is arguably more powerful, with its ability to overlay the presenter atop shared content, news anchor style.

Google Meet does not offer anything like Side-by-Side Speaker view.

◆

Gallery view is a tool, not a philosophy—its value depends on how and when you use it, and how infrequently you choose to employ it. As a special occasion, consider some of the high-interaction activities that lend themselves well to a gallery.

Up next

Part Two has focused on your face, your eyes, your voice, and your vibe. In the end, the personal side of virtual presenting isn't about being perfect—it's about being present. It's about showing up fully, quirks and all, and making your audience members feel like they're in good company.

In Part Three, Get Physical, we'll explore how to use the rest of yourself. Because presence is only part of the equation. What you do with that presence—how you move, how you sound, how you command the screen—is its own secret sauce. And that's where we're headed next. 💻

Part Three
Get Physical

You have crafted your message, rehearsed your slides, and framed the shot like you were preparing a cameo for Oprah. And then it happens: Your voice goes wobbly, your hands forget what to do with themselves, and you suddenly develop a deeply intimate relationship with your water bottle.

Welcome to the war between mind and body. You could be talking about quarterly profits, early childhood education, or whether pineapple belongs on pizza. If you're human, your body is going to react to the stress of live presenting. Sweat happens.

This part of the book is about the aspects of presentation that don't show up in an outline: managing nerves, controlling your energy, and pretending you're calm until, news flash, you actually are. It takes all of yourself to find your most genuine self. Let's start looking.

Fighting Nerves

I remember the first time I came face-to-face with paralyzing nervousness, and all I was doing was sitting on a couch. It was 1978 and I was just a kid. This was just a few years after I stood up in front of 200 people and chanted in Hebrew for my bar mitzvah. But that was nothing compared to this scene.

It was the ninth inning of Game Two of the World Series between the Dodgers and Yankees. I was sweating vicariously for L.A. rookie Bob Welch, as he faced Reggie Jackson, who had earned the nickname Mr. October for his postseason heroics. As he approached the mound, Welch looked like he was about to come before a firing squad. But he not only faced Mr. October, he struck him out.

I'd never seen anyone so nervous, and I've never been so nervous for someone else. What I didn't consider, however, is whether Jackson was nervous. Years later, he told us. "If I'm not nervous," he said, "then there is something wrong. If I don't feel those butterflies, it means maybe I don't care as much as I should."

I always feel better about my own anxiety when I think of that quote, and so should you. It is neither realistic nor helpful to believe that you can quell your nerves; it would be better to learn to live with them. If the greatest World Series performer of his era was nervous, it's okay for you to be. Here are a few strategies to help you become one with your nervous half.

The lowdown on laughter

This might be the oldest advice on record: Start with a joke. Laughter relaxes you, it makes you feel more comfortable, and it allows you to loosen up. It is the classic icebreaker, so why would that not be good advice?

In fact, it is very bad advice. First off, what if you are not funny? What if nobody laughs? Now you're in a deficit; now you're nervous *and* flustered.

Second, in a virtual setting, you have no idea whether your joke landed or bombed and that is the most uncomfortable feeling for someone who purports to command the environment and the tone of a presentation.

The risk is just too high to start with a joke, and besides, I have a better idea than trying to make your audience laugh:

Make yourself laugh.

I'm very serious about this, pun intended. If the audience laughs at your joke, it might make you feel better. If you laugh, it is virtually guaranteed to make you feel better. And the stakes are much lower.

Laughing uses good muscles, not bad ones (more on this soon), and it's easier to make yourself laugh than it is to make a gallery full of strangers laugh. So all around it's a better strategy to employ.

This talk today on warehouse efficiency, it's funny that I should be the one leading it…[chuckle]…and if you ask my sisters about this, they'll agree…[snicker]…because you've never seen a childhood bedroom messier than mine. How I got to this point where I am expected to act as an authority on this subject is…[laugh]…well, that's just beyond me.

Audience members might laugh along with you or they might not, but it doesn't matter either way. You're not trying to be comically funny, and so this isn't a joke that can bomb. It's funny to you in a reminiscent way and therefore it is appropriate for you to see the humor in it. Here is an opening that I once employed while traveling:

You know that story about "If it's Tuesday, this must be Belgium?" I now know what they mean. This is my fourth city in four days, and yesterday I woke up and literally forgot where I was…I [laugh], I thought I was already here in Austin, about to speak to all of you. I left the hotel and immediately got lost, until I realized that I was still in San Antonio. So…[laugh] to say that it's good to be here takes on a whole new meaning for me.

This anecdote might not have been funny to my audience but anyone can see why it might have been funny to me, so again, it doesn't seem like forced humor. It almost doesn't matter what kind of story you share—make it up if you have to.

How slow can you go?

Why do we speak so quickly? It's not enough to just say we're nervous and that's why we speed up. What is making us speed up?

Much of the time, it's a fear of the unknown: You don't remember what's next or you're not confident about your next transition. You have stopped living in the moment as you fret about what you are to say next.

When you speak quickly, you do more than just make yourself nervous; you make your audience nervous. The quicker you go, the more fidgety you get. You don't give yourself any time to make large gestures, so all of your gestures are small ones involving small body parts. Small, fast, fidgety little gestures. And out comes the dreaded "flashing fig leaf." That's when presenters speak so quickly, the hands can't keep up. They remain cupped in front of their private parts, except for the occasional flip of the wrists.

This metaphor was written for an in-person audience. The virtual equivalent would be the "pixelated pelvic panic," when your hands get locked in a tight little knot just below the camera's view, frantically broadcasting discomfort that none of your audience members will ever be able to unsee, even if they don't actually see it in the first place.

The whole thing spirals, as your fidgety gestures make you speak even quicker, which in turn makes your body try to keep up, and so your gestures become even more halting and spastic, because that's all you have time for. You are constantly trying to catch your breath, and the quicker you speak, the higher your voice gets, and that raises the frequency of the entire room, and through it all, you drive your audience crazy.

But if you slooowww down your speech…

…you'll slow down your entire body…

…and that will calm everyone down.

When the world is traveling a million miles per hour and your heart is beating out of your chest, the one thing you have control over is the speed at which you speak. And when you know what your next thought is, it's uncanny how much easier you can speak about your current thought. Absent of panic or dread, you can practically luxuriate in your words. And then, you can indulge in the holiest of all moments before an audience:

You can pause.

  A long pause.

    Longer.

      Longer still, and look right into the camera.

This is not an awkward pause; it's a commanding pause. You have complete control of the room and everyone knows it. And how have you won the virtual room? Why have you become so confident? Because you know where you're going. You know what you want to say next, so you can live in the moment, without sweat, fear, fig leaves, or pelvic panics.

I can't imagine a better feeling when speaking before an audience—when I know my material so well that I can completely control the pace. I can linger on points, look silently into the camera, take questions, invite debate. Once I have established this level of control, no reasonable pause feels uncomfortable.

Nailing your transitions makes all this possible. In my opinion, practicing transitions between topics is as important as preparing the topics themselves. Maybe more important, actually.

Air under the pits

The symbiosis between the voice, the body, and the nervous system makes for a fascinating study. Unless it's your own body we're talking about, whose byproduct of this relationship is usually profuse perspiration. Then it's not fascinating; it's frustrating. Each one of these parts of the system is responsible for changes in the other:

- If you are nervous, it will show in how you move your body and how you speak.
- Changes to your vocal pattern create a change in body motion, which affects pulse and heart rate.
- Command over your body can create command over your speech and your nerves.

We have discussed the syndrome whereby a nervous speaker accelerates his or her speaking pattern, which in turn causes the entire body to speed up. Whether fidgets are the cause or the byproduct of your nerves, they are not your friend, as they perpetuate the cycle and they affect your audience.

So think big.

Make big gestures, not little ones. Create a reason to raise both hands to or even above your head. Get some air under your armpits!

Working gross motor skills is equivalent to slowing down your vocal pattern. Your body responds more positively to a big action than to a little one. A big gesture can actually help relax you. At a minimum, it takes longer to make a big gesture than a fidget, and that creates a better, slower pace for you. My advice about making yourself laugh has relevance here: Laughing uses your diaphragm, a big muscle.

I've found that raising both arms over my head, can be interpreted many ways and audience members are generally willing to view the gesture in context.

Context: Question from an audience member about a situation that troubles her.
Me: That frustrates me too [gesture]. It's like whatever you do, it comes back to bite you. Try doing this…

Context: We solved a problem or addressed a difficult issue.
Me: [gesture] Thank the heavens, you figured it out!

Context: I ask an intricate question and an audience member answers it correctly, showing that she understands its nuance.
Me: [gesture] (Nothing needs to be said—the gesture serves as a "Eureka!")

I have been offering advice like this for the better part of two decades to presenters who speak in person, and I am not inclined to change the advice just because we are constrained by virtual surroundings. While I will temper the gesture just a bit on virtual—both hands to my head, instead of my arms over my head—even if I didn't, it would still be effective. Even if my hands and arms left the camera frame, audiences would understand the meaning of the gesture.

📢 The one caveat is if you use a virtual background without a green screen. Then your hands might become disembodied. See Chapter 20 for more about virtual backgrounds.

However, if you feel like an idiot performing big gestures, then don't! The gesture has to be a part of you, but it's worth the effort to find one you are comfortable with.

Leveraging your body

The tactics discussed here are specifically to address nerves, and no doubt, the more you move around, the more readily you can combat nervousness. As we transition to the next chapter, the emphasis will shift to how your gestures can help you better connect with your audience.

That said, these two dynamics are closely linked and that is why I want to start that convo here. Controlling energy helps you control your nerves. Controlling your nerves helps you make better use of your energy. And this all flows through the big muscles in your body.

One colleague likes to cup his hand to the side of his head and then move it away, as if he has just had an epiphany and all this amazing stuff is flowing out of his brain. He uses that to great effect in many scenarios.

I know a woman who likes to hold one finger up, but she really goes for it, raising it above her head. She uses it to mean "Listen up," "wait a minute," or "here's the thing."

Another uses her hands very effectively to create relationships in time, distance, or some other set of variables. "Over here, you have the question of cost," she might say with her left palm outstretched all the way out to one side, "and over here is the issue of resources," as she stretches out her right hand. Having created those two spaces, now anytime during that conversation, she can stretch out her left palm and the audience knows she is talking about the cost factors. She has created a terrific spatial and cerebral connection with her audience. And she gets to put air under her pits.

All of these people developed these gestures initially to help them quell nervousness. Then they began to use them more naturally. I encourage you to seek out your own big gestures and use them to engage your audience, to improve your pace and vocal pattern, and to help quiet your nerves. The next chapter offers lots of ideas.

◆

As I look back on this chapter, I have to laugh. It seems as if we are advising you to become a phony:

- Fabricate a story to laugh about.
- Conjure up situations in which you can make long pauses.
- Make up a gesture and fake your way into using it.

But let's face it, speaking in public might always feel like an artificial situation to you, so it makes sense that a few artificial devices can help you with it. Anything that helps get you to a place where you can speak naturally and share ideas freely is a good thing. See Chapter 16 for a related conversation about what it means to "fake it until you make it."

Natural speaking through fabrication—what a concept...

Sit Tall, Stand Strong

How do you know whether you have given a good virtual presentation? There are many markers for this and we have already covered many across the first two parts of this book. I have a much more visceral one than any we have uncovered so far: I know I have done a good job on virtual when, at the end of the presentation, I have a headache and my back hurts.

I don't say that as a martyr or a masochist—I say it because showing up fully on camera takes real effort. Not just mental effort, but physical. I can be sitting in a chair the entire time and still feel like I just ran a 10K.

A good virtual presentation is not a casual affair. It is not a Zoom call in sweatpants. It's not flopping into a chair and talking off the top of your head. It is, in the best possible way, a performance. And that means your body gets involved, whether you want it to or not.

This chapter is about that physical involvement. Not the adrenaline-fueled anxiety of nerves—that got its own chapter—but the intentional, chosen actions you take to deliver your message with strength and presence. We'll look at posture, gesture, movement, and yes, eventually, the possibility that you might want to get out of your chair entirely.

Sit like you mean it

Sitting is the default for most virtual presenters. At its core, this is a computing experience, and most of us practice computing from a chair. But unlike most of our digital activities, this one is practiced in public, and comfort can be a trap. Slouch into your chair, and you might as well slump into your message. Audiences can sense it, even though they can't see all of you.

Good sitting is active, not passive. It's a physical stance that says, "I'm present, I'm alert, I'm driving this thing."

It starts with the feet

It is our prerogative as virtual presenters to choose any footwear we want. That said, the key criterion is that we be able to sit with our feet planted firmly on the ground. Not crossed, not dangling, not propped on a box of printer paper. A stable base sends positive signals all the way up your spine.

I live in flip-flops, especially in the summertime, but they do not suit me when on camera. Without any ankle support, I find myself too often on the balls of my feet, or even up onto my toes. This is better than the opposite, leaning back on my heels, but it places strain on my calves, and just like the stable base, this unstable base sends signals all the way up.

Also flip-flops and sandals can clack around too much. When I once had to apologize on air for the thwack of my Tevas, when the Velcro on my strap got wrapped around the table, I concluded that I needed something softer and quieter. So for me, it's just socks, no shoes. Athletic socks—super-thick Thorlo-branded socks.

Straighten that spine

Think tall and relaxed. Your back should support you without locking up. Your head should float above your shoulders, not jut forward like you're chasing your webcam.

Then check your framing. You want your shoulders square to the camera with the lens at eye level, not staring up your nose or down your forehead. Even if you're only visible from the ribs up, the rest of your body will still impact how you show up on camera. Your slouch changes your voice. Your spine affects your breath. Your position influences your presence. All of it adds up to the nonverbal version of *I'm ready for this* or *I'm not*.

The following diagram shows a variety of typical postures with No. 1 being the gold standard: feet planted on the floor; feet, knees, hips, waist, and shoulders all in alignment; shoulders back; eyes looking straight ahead.

Chp 14 Sit Tall, Stand Strong

Five common postures
No. 1 is perfect, the others are all something less than that. It is impossible to have perfect posture throughout an entire presentation so read on for when and how compromises are acceptable.

All the others have varying degrees of imperfection. In No. 2, our presenter is up on the balls of her feet, creating stress on her calves. In 3, she is hunched over to look at the screen. In 4, she has her legs crossed, causing her to sink down and create stress on her lower back. And 5, she is slouched, bringing down her entire upper torso.

If you can make No. 1 your go-to posture, you're ahead of the game. But can you sustain perfect posture across a 60-minute presentation? How about a two-hour workshop? No, you cannot, but the good news is that you don't have to, and you shouldn't try. Here is the official Rick Altman Posture Recipe for leading webinars and workshops:

1. **When you are speaking into the camera:** Adopt Posture No. 1 above. Be as upright as you can be and speak as forthrightly as possible. Move air from your diaphragm and be expressive. This will be fatiguing if it goes on for more than a few minutes, but it's a good fatigue. It means that you are really working it.

2. **When you are speaking off camera, like when showing slides:** You can relax a bit. You still want your voice to project, so No. 3 would still be verboten, but if you need to cross your legs, relax your lower back, roll your shoulders a bit—all good. Just make sure you are still speaking from your diaphragm.

3. **When you are taking questions:** Do whatever you have to do to be comfortable. Stand up, lean back, curl forward, hand on chin—all good. You have 30 seconds or so while listening to address whatever body part is sore or achy. Take that time so you can be ready to answer the incoming question while in Posture 1.

Anchor your body, amplify your message

Your body is either reinforcing your message or undermining it, and the latter happens sooner on virtual. Audiences are generally willing to give the benefit of the doubt in person, where they can see all of you. If you shift your weight, scratch your nose, cough, sneeze, stutter and stammer, all of that is contextualized. There is a cushion of grace.

But in a virtual setting, that cushion disappears. The frame is tighter and every motion is magnified. Every hesitation is more conspicuous. The audience sees less, so they assume more—that's terribly unfair but it's our reality as virtual presenters. The virtual space strips away the context that normally softens rough edges. If your presence doesn't project clarity and confidence on camera, the audience won't assume it's there off-camera; they'll assume it's missing. If what they do see appears nervous or fidgety, they interpret that as the whole picture. That too is unfair.

In the virtual world, your upper torso is the whole stage. There are no grand entrances, no pacing across the floor, no walking and talking with a lav mic clipped to your jacket. What audience members get is a rectangle—head to midsection if they're lucky, head to sternum if they're not—and you will want to know how to own every inch of that rectangle.

That starts with "anchoring"—creating physical stability in your body so that your energy is focused, not scattered. When your base is grounded, your movement becomes deliberate. When your posture is intentional, your presence becomes magnetic. You trade nervous motion for purpose:

- Feet planted
- Core engaged

- Spine tall
- Shoulders steady
- Hands free to move, not flail

From that foundation, your gestures have space to mean something. A hand lift signals emphasis. A pause in motion draws attention. A simple nod says "I'm listening."

Stillness is power. Movement is punctuation. Anchoring is what makes both possible. This is the physical equivalent of the "unbold" reference that I made on Page 51. In the case of typography, bold is only prominent if you have unbold type around it. Similarly, gestures have more meaning if they come from a base of calm.

Finding your signature moves

There are two ways to approach gestures: Lean into the ones that come naturally, or build up a library that you can draw from intentionally.

The key is purpose: You want to use them purposefully, not mindlessly. Learning to talk with your hands is not the critical skill here if all you do is roll your wrists in circles with each phrase. That falls into the mindless category. Wanting to practice what I preach, I started wondering: What are my signature moves? What are the gestures that I use to punctuate my thoughts and words?

I didn't know.

I knew that I did stuff with my hands and with my expressions, but I couldn't describe them. Then I started to wonder if that is maybe a good thing, because too much awareness of what my body does might create paralysis of analysis. And to be sure, lights/camera/action is *not* the time to be narrating your every physical move. But there is certainly a place for self-critique and reflection—looking at yourself on playback is one of the best ways to discover which gestures are helping you, and which are just filling space. The goal is not to choreograph yourself. It's to become familiar with what your body already tends to do so you can lean into the useful parts and dial back the noise.

What follows is equal parts analysis and roast. I dug through hours of footage looking for signature moves. What I found was a mix of intentional gestures, subconscious expression, and some truly ridiculous freeze frames. Here's the tour...

📢 Freeze-framing your video is nearly guaranteed to make you look like an idiot and certain to creep out those whom you are making watch it. You've been warned...

The neutral position

This is my stock pose, while waiting to be introduced, listening to someone else, or otherwise not speaking. I find the closed-mouth smile easier to maintain than a toothy smile. Hopefully, I am doing all of the things spelled out in Posture No. 1 from a few pages ago.

This thing over here

With this gesture, I am defining space in my frame, in this case by referring to my slides that would be behind me in a conventional in-person setting. Once defined, I can make this same gesture repeatedly to communicate that I am talking about my slides.

The countup

This is your basic counting up from one. Do this when you have four or fewer things to count, because the thumb becomes awkward. And when you do it, make sure to start with your index finger and not your thumb.

Hands touching hands

There are lots of interpretations of joined hands. I have no idea why I am touching fingers in the left image, I think I look stupid doing it, and I have made a note not to in the future. With the other two images, however, I recognize that as a sign of gratitude: I am either grateful for people having connected with me or grateful for the opportunity to present. And given that I find gratitude to be a very powerful emotion, it is no surprise to me that I found many instances of my adopting this pose.

Eureka!

This is one of my favorite moves, as it is expansive and expressive. It can take on many meanings, similar to the discussion on Page 120. I use it to express discovery, surprise, resignation, and exasperation—that's one serious multi-purpose gesture. I've had to practice this one to make sure that my arms stay in the frame, although I'm not sure what bad thing would happen if they strayed.

The clasp

Experts in non-verbal communication interpret this gesture to be a show of solidarity, faith, and mutual support. I hold sacred the bonds of the community that has grown up around the Presentation Summit, so perhaps that explains why I use this one so often. Maybe it has nothing to do with that, I just know that this one makes me feel good.

The world is your oyster

This gesture is said to make you feel powerful, as if you are "holding the world in your hands." It can also project authority and mastery of a subject. I will just say that it is slightly more effective with one's eyes opened rather than closed.

The epiphany

This fun gesture is usually a two-parter, as I begin with both hands on my respective temples and I then release them outward, as if a whole bunch of super-smart brain matter has exploded out of my head. Overuse of this gesture would be problematic, as one should really limit one's epiphanies to one per day.

The oy vey

I'm not one to express angst too often, but when I do, I want to get my money's worth. So I do it up like a thespian in agony. I have been known to actually slap my forehead and audiences have been known to actually hear it.

The eye bugout

What can I say, this one is just ridiculous. But in a 30-minute video clip, I found six instances of my having done this. In context, I guess it works to show surprise, amazement, or shock. I don't advocate you ever trying to overtly use this gesture, but if it comes naturally, it does serve the general point that a bit of overemoting on virtual is not a bad thing. We all have to try just a bit harder to express ourselves. I guess I have succeeded in that.

One caveat to this study in overapplication: If you get a bit overactive with your hands, as I have done in the third image, and they fly toward the camera, some lenses will try to focus on them instead of your face, which would leave you blurry. Plus, anything too close gets distorted, like you're reaching through a funhouse mirror. So, bug out to your heart's content, but keep your hands closer to home.

Talking heads

Finally, there are situations where I am much closer to my camera than my primary setup. As you see in the top part of this image, when I choose to go split screen, I do this with my tighter shot. This shows just my head down to my sternum, so gesturing with my hands is not recommended (the closest I come is the finger point).

Now all I will have is my face, so I really have to go for my facial gestures. You see more eye bugouts, raised eyebrows, and tilted heads.

I should point out that much of this occurs at the subconscious level. I don't choose to keep my hands out of the picture. But when I can't see them, I tend not to use them, and when I don't have access to my hands, my face just sort of takes over.

◆

Generalizing a bit further, none of the examples of me looking foolish is done on the conscious level any longer. They once were; there was indeed a time when I sat in front of a mirror and practiced facial expressions and body gestures. But nearly two decades later, now they are simply my body reacting to the feeling I want to convey about the topic.

After all, nobody would choose to look like an imbecile, but apparently, my body disagrees.

Who says you have to sit down?

Anchoring your gestures, making use of torso space, finding subtle movements that match meaning—all of this assumes you are seated for your webinar. But where is that written? Who says you have to be?

Sitting might be the default, but it's not the only option. And if you're ready to shift your presence from strong to dynamic, standing up might be the better option.

Standing changes everything

It changes your energy, your breath, your posture, your presence. It invites your whole body into the conversation—not just your shoulders and face. That shift in stance can trigger a shift in mindset—from casual to commanding, from reactive to proactive.

Standing gives your gestures room to breathe. When you're upright and untethered, your hands can move more easily. Your posture naturally lengthens. Your voice gets a lift from improved breath support.

More than just losing the chair

I wish that the switch from seated to standing were as simple as the elimination of a chair. It's not. Here is a list of the things you will need to buy, do, and change in order to try it out.

Start with a better camera: Built-in webcams are notoriously bad for standing presenters. Locked into laptop lid height and wide-angle, they are designed for seated users at arm's length. The second you stand, they betray you—angling up your nose, warping your face, and shrinking your body as if you are being seen through the wrong end of a telescope. You need a dedicated webcam or standalone camera, one that you can position exactly where you need it: straight on, at eye level, and centered. You don't need studio-level gear—a $50 external webcam from Amazon would do, as would a mobile phone on a tripod mount.

What matters is flexibility. You want to move the camera to match your posture, not contort your posture to match your webcam.

Get your gear in order: Wireless earbuds or a lapel mic are your friends—no dangling headset cords to box you in and no desktop mic that would make you sound like you are in a warehouse. Make sure your lighting is adjusted for your new height, and that your background is intentional.

Mind your frame: Give yourself enough headroom and chest room. You want your upper torso, shoulders, and expressive hands all visible in the shot; this gives your gestures space to land. But you neither need nor want a head-to-toe shot; that puts you back on the wrong end of the telescope. When I stand, I'm usually still wearing shorts or sweats.

Check in with your content: If you're screen-sharing or using visuals, you may need to adjust your screen position to ensure that you're not constantly looking down or away. If your slides live on a separate monitor, elevate that too. Wherever your eyes go, your presence follows.

While more ambitious, the real money shot to virtual stand-up is if you can bring your visuals onto the set with you, as I am doing here:

This was back in 2020, during the height of Covid, when we were all still figuring this stuff out, but this seminar ended up being one of the best-received of the conference, in large part because we went to such lengths to make it feel un-Zoom-like. Our audience appreciated that effort.

Let's also return to that question of *contextualization* from a few pages ago, when I said "the audience sees less, so they assume more." The opposite is true of a standing virtual presenter: They see more, they assume less, and they have more benefit of the doubt to bestow upon you. This was certainly the case in 2020, when standing up helped me pretend that I was in a room full of people. I was much more animated than when seated and I felt as if my audience could more readily feel the energy flow between us.

Surgical standing

If you want to test-drive this for yourself, you don't need to commit to it for the whole session. You can use it surgically—for your opening remarks, for a passionate story, or to finish with authority. Standing, even for just a few minutes, creates contrast. It signals intention. It raises the stakes (in a good way).

To test the waters, you will need a lapel microphone, but you could get by with the rest of your existing gear. Just take a step or two back from your desk, so your webcam can still serve you. I'm willing to bet that you will become more animated with your gestures as you become more unconfined.

♦

You're always delivering a message with your body, whether you mean to or not. Your audience doesn't just hear your words; they read you. Your posture. Your stillness. Your motion. Your presence. All of it speaks.

So why not make it intentional?

Whether you sit tall in your chair or rise to your feet, ground your gestures with calm authority. Let every physical choice deliver the same message: I'm here. I'm ready. This matters.

Talk Human to Me

When you speak in a virtual space, your voice does far more than carry your words. It carries you. It conveys your energy, your confidence, your intentions, and your mood. It reveals things you might not even realize you are saying.

In the absence of a firm handshake or eye contact across the room, your voice becomes the primary way your audience experiences you. This is a bit counterintuitive and even ironic, because it is your camera that shows what you look like and it is your video likeness that captures most of our attention. This book will probably spend twice as much time discussing video than audio and will dive deeper into how you show yourself than how you sound, and it will advise you to spend more money on cameras than on microphones.

And yet, it is your voice that is the barometer of how you feel. Your voice is your emotional channel and your layer of personality. It becomes your virtual body language.

This chapter is all about knowing what your voice is capable of and learning to trust it enough to let it do the job it was made for: connecting you to other humans. This chapter is not just about sounding "good," however that might be defined. It is about sounding real. And that is a word that needs no further definition.

Why voice matters in virtual

Your voice is more than a delivery mechanism—it's a mirror of your energy and your presence. In a virtual setting, your body language gets compressed. Your gestures shrink to the size of a window. Your posture is mostly hidden. But your voice? It still arrives in full. And often, it does so before your face even appears. It's the first impression and the ongoing presence.

That's why your voice has to do more work online than it ever did in person. It has to compensate for everything the audience can't see: the nuances of your body, the movement of your hands, the lean-in of genuine engagement. It carries outsize importance on virtual, and in my case is precisely why I often end up with headaches and back pain after long sessions in my studio: I speak in more animated fashion on virtual than in person.

Listeners pick up on subtle cues just by how you sound. Your energy level, your spirit, your focus—you might not even be aware of how you feel while your voice is conveying these feelings to your audience. But your audience will know. They will know if you are hesitant, rushed, happy, or bored. They don't need to see your face to know how you feel; they can hear it.

In the virtual world, how you sound is usually how you are judged. Which means your voice doesn't just carry your content. It carries your credibility.

The Sound of you

One of the oddest parts of working on your voice is coming to terms with how it actually sounds to other people and for most of us, that moment is unpleasant. That epiphany came very early in life for me: May 27, 1972, the day of my bar mitzvah. A friend brought a tape recorder into the sanctuary to capture my Torah chanting (he probably sneaked it in,

as it surely violated some observance of the Jewish sabbath), and he played it back for me.

I told him that was the wrong recording; it must have been of the bat mitzvah the previous weekend. That was the voice of a young girl, not of me. It was at least a half-octave higher than what my blossoming baritone was at the time. I wish I had kept that recording for you to hear, because as should be plainly evident by now, 15 chapters into this book, I am not at all above embarrassing myself.

This is a universal reaction. Ask anyone how they felt the first time they heard themselves in a voicemail or on a recorded Zoom call, and you'll get the same cringey reaction: *Do I really sound like that?*

Yes, you do.

Let me throw just a touch of science at you. When you speak, you hear your voice not just through the air, but also through the bones in your skull. It turns out that your bones transfer sound pretty well; in fact, *bone conduction* headphones take advantage of that by transmitting sound waves through your head, leaving your ears open to the environment.

The bones in your skull add resonance and depth to sound; kind of like having your own personal subwoofer in your head. That's the version of your voice that you hear, while everyone else hears only the air version—the thinner, usually less flattering version. Recordings capture the air version, too, so that full and resonant version of your voice is a gift from the gods bestowed only upon you.

And it's more than physics and biology—hearing your own voice also triggers a kind of psychological dissonance. You're being confronted with a version of yourself that you don't control. You can't make others hear the you that you know is inside of you. They hear the you that is outside of you and there is nothing that the inside you can do about that. The outside you is just…you. Unfiltered, undeniable, unavoidable. And that makes many people want to run for their own mute button.

There are three points of advice to be made about this and I share them here in order of increasing importance:

Get lower: Most of the time, one's outside-the-head voice is a higher pitch than the inside-the-head voice, and if you prefer that one, you can practice speaking with a lower register. That's coming up later in this chapter.

Acceptance is everything: You don't need to fall in love with your voice; you just need to get comfortable enough to trust it. You need to come to terms with the fact that it only sounds off to you; everyone else has had a lifetime to accept your outside voice.

Perfection is not the goal: Your job is not to sound perfect. Audiences don't want perfect presenters. Your job is to sound present and real. That's challenging enough without having to also sound perfect.

When you stop fighting your voice, you free it up to do its job—expressing your thoughts, revealing your personality, and letting your audience hear not just your words, but the real you.

Add vocal variety, no cartoons allowed

It's tempting to think that energy in your voice means turning up the volume or speaking with big dramatic swings. But that's not energy, that's theater. And your audience didn't log in for a one-person stage play.

While yes, we advocate for big and bold physical gestures to compensate for the confines of the virtual space, your voice doesn't need to go big and bold indiscriminately. The real secret to vocal presence lies in variety, not volume—more subtle shifts in pitch, tone, and rhythm that help your voice stay fresh and your message stay clear. Just like a good melody needs highs and lows, your voice needs contrast to stay engaging.

That said, there's a fine line between adding variety and going over the top. You don't want to sound like you're narrating a children's audiobook or auditioning for a cartoon—unless, of course, you are doing one of those things. For the rest of us, the goal is to enhance meaning without drawing attention to the method.

Dr. Jackie Gartner-Schmidt is a professor of Speech-Language Pathology at Carlow University in Pittsburgh PA. She has a Ph.D. in Communication Sciences and Disorders, and when she spoke on these topics at the 2021 Presentation Summit, it was a meta experience for all, as she made every effort to practice what she preached.

Chp 15 Talk Human to Me

As she says in the video that you can watch here, "Just by listening to my voice, you have made a perception about who I am. We are really good at listening to the voice for personality attributes. Are you aggressive, are you confident, approachable, trustworthy—just with your voice."

She also made the case for good vocal hygiene, such as proper hydration, avoiding ice water (which could cause vocal cords to contract), and breathing through your nose during pauses from speaking.

Jackie is trained and paid to go deep into this type of research; the rest of us would go a bit loony if we intentionally tried to use our voices to portray ourselves in certain ways. So it's helpful to continually return to the prime directive: Be real. Speak so that your true self comes out. And there are some practical guidelines that you can follow:

Vary your pitch to ask questions, signal transitions, or emphasize curiosity. A gentle rise at the end of a sentence can keep people leaning in. A drop in pitch can signal closure or finality. Pitch is your steering wheel, telling your audience where the conversation is going and inviting them to follow along.

Leverage volume to punch a key point or pull back for intimacy. A slight increase grabs attention and says *this part matters*. A whisper draws people in and says, *listen closely*. Volume isn't just about being loud enough to hear; it's about knowing when to fill the room with your words and when to fill it with the silent echo of them.

Adopt tone to match your emotional intent, be it excitement, empathy, or seriousness. As Jackie said to us back in 2021, if your words say "I'm thrilled," but your tone says "I'm bored," people will believe your tone and then wonder if they can trust your words at all.

When voice and body sync up

We could write an entire book analyzing vocal patterns and how they convey emotion. Instead, I would like to introduce you to Sally Zimney, a presentations coach and good friend. Her website describes her mission as helping people discover "that unique blend of story, style, and substance that makes audiences say 'I've never heard it put quite like that before!'"

At the 2024 Presentation Summit, Sally shared a personal challenge that scared and threatened her. This clip has impact even if you do not know what that challenge is, and if you want to play along, watch the clip first, and then I'll share it with you on the other side.

Sally lives in Minnesota and she has taken to outdoor swimming and cold plunging in the dead of winter. The video that she proceeded to share exposed her total vulnerability and sheer dread at the prospect. She then expertly wove in the parallels with public speaking and how you can find your best self when you face those types of threats and challenges. It was gold.

As you watch and rewatch this short video, I want you to focus on her vocal intonations and her variance of pitch and pace. How she draws you into her saga with her tone and tenor. "Just doooooo it," she admonishes herself as the video concludes.

Then I want you to appreciate how her physical gestures match her vocal tone. None of this is indiscriminate—she is feeling every movement, and in turn, making us feel them right along with her. This is elite-level storytelling as her style, her tone, and her message all come together as one.

"My main objective," Sally told me afterward, "is to get my audience to visualize the story in their own minds, right alongside my telling of it. I want them to experience the story as if they were there with me. Once they *see* it, they will remember it."

"It is not about choreographing your every move—there's nothing like choreography to turn off an audience. It's about telling the truest story I can possibly tell that will bring everyone in with me."

◆

It is worth reiterating throughout this discussion that in the previous chapter, you were encouraged to amplify your physical gestures—bigger hand movements, more open postures. But when it comes to your voice, exaggeration is not the goal, authenticity is. The goal isn't to *perform* your message, it's to deliver it with just enough variety to keep people's ears tuned in and their minds engaged.

Exercises for the masses

Absent Jackie-like understanding or Sally-level skills, how can you begin to exert more control over your vocal patterns? Here are some practical exercises to consider:

One sentence, six meanings

Here is a fun and approachable challenge to help you with varying your vocal patterns. You can do this in your head, but it's more useful if you say it out loud. The following sentence can be recited six different ways:

I didn't say he stole the money.

I didn't say he stole the money. (John said it over there.)

I **didn't** say he stole the money. (Did so. Did not. Did so.)

I didn't **say** he stole the money. (I was just wondering out loud.)

I didn't say **he** stole the money. (I think it was Nancy who did.)

I didn't say he **stole** the money. (Maybe he just borrowed it.)

I didn't say he stole the **money**. (I think he stole your credit cards.)

A participant in a workshop scored extra credit when she managed to place the emphasis on "the"—he didn't steal **the** money, he stole some other money. She actually pulled it off! That's the power of modulation.

The pitch ladder

Read a sentence like you're climbing a staircase—gradually raising your pitch with each word—then read it again coming down. This trains your ear and vocal cords to recognize tonal range without sounding sing-songy. Here are two good ones to try:

RECITE THIS: "We should probably get started"
Climb to create uncertainty: *Do we really want to?* Then descend to make it sound like a concession. *Uggh, let's get this over with.*

RECITE THIS: "So...this is happening"
Climb for nervous anticipation, and try to hit three different notes on "happening." Then descend for comedic resignation. And on descent, it is difficult to keep the "So" at a higher pitch than the "this." Do it slowly.

The pause practice

Record yourself reading a paragraph with no pauses. Then read it again, inserting short pauses after commas and full pauses after periods. Compare the two. This builds rhythm awareness and discourages verbal steamrolling. Try this one:

Thanks for joining us today. We've got a lot to cover, and some of it might challenge the way you think. That's a good thing.

Version 1: No pauses (read like a single breathless paragraph):
"Thanks for joining us today we've got a lot to cover and some of it might challenge the way you think that's a good thing."

Version 2: With intentional pauses:

"Thanks for joining us today. (two beats) We've got a lot to cover, (beat) and some of it might challenge the way you think. (two beats) That's a good thing." (two beats)

Let me point out the two beats after you're done reading. This suggests that whatever you are going to say next, you want to pause before it.

Loud/soft drills

This drill is similar to the emphasis drill about who took the money, but with a subtle difference that is worth your appreciation. Let's look at this sentence:

This is the part I really want you to hear.

If you say it all at normal volume, nothing stands out. It's all neutral, and that is not necessarily bad; many sentences don't merit anything more. Nosay it a few different ways, first with selected words louder:

This is the part I really want you to hear. (emphasizes urgency)

This is the part I **really** want you to hear. (signals passion)

Now say the selected words softer:

This is the part I really want you to hear. (adds intimacy or sincerity)

This is the part I really want you to hear. (signals gravity or emotional pull)

Emotion switch-up

Pick a neutral sentence and try to infuse emotion into it. I'm not going to tell you what words to focus on—just try to let each different emotion be your guide. Here's a good sentence to use:

I didn't expect that.

First, say it flatly, with no emotion. Then try bringing the following emotions to it: surprise, excitement, annoyance, amusement, hurt.

This is a challenging exercise that trained actors employ often. When they do, they usually go through dozens of takes. In a workshop I led on this topic, one woman really nailed the hurt emotion just by adding a pause after the first word:

I…I did not expect that.

It was all done with a whisper, and in the moment, she repeated the "I" and took apart the "didn't" contraction. They both gave tremendous emotional weight to the moment. It is almost scary how tiny intonations like this can make such a difference in the meanings we convey.

Mirror monologue

Finally, stand in front of a mirror and describe your day for 30 seconds. Try changing your pitch, slowing down, pausing, and emphasizing key phrases. This helps tie vocal awareness to facial expression and natural rhythm.

The tone traps

Even the most experienced presenters fall into vocal habits that could become distracting to an audience. Some are physical, some behavioral. Some sneak in unnoticed, others drive a Hummer into the virtual town square. Some don't bother anyone, others drive everyone mad.

This section isn't about shaming you for those habits. It's about surfacing them, getting curious about them, and above all, deciding which ones are worth fixing and which ones are best ignored.

Monotone

This is the most prevalent attention killer. Even with great content, a flat delivery could put audiences into a mental drift that they won't (want to) recover from.

And it's not just boring; it's confusing. Your voice gives cues as to what matters and what doesn't, especially on virtual. If everything sounds the same, how are listeners supposed to know when to lean in? They don't, so they will most likely choose not to lean in at all, and that's when you know you've lost them.

Most people aren't monotone by nature. They become that way when they're nervous, overly scripted, or trying hard to sound like a broadcaster. The irony is that this effort to sound polished often scrubs away everything that makes a voice interesting.

Even highly trained speakers at our conference have fallen into the trap of overpreparing and then appearing stiff and unnatural. We have seen the following in the post-Covid era:

Reading from a script: It is really hard to inject emotion into scripted dialogue. That is why trained actors rehearse dozens of times. Absent said rehearsal, presenters appear stiff, rush through their words, and rob themselves of the opportunity to feel and convey their meaning.

Memorized transitions: Same thing with this microcosm of scripting. If you practice a word-for-word transition, you can own it. If you don't practice, it will more likely own you. In 2022, one of our presenters insisted on creating transition slides with fully-formed sentences. In accordance with Axiom No. 2 (page 16: It is impossible to avoid reading complete sentences when shown on screen), that person read the transition word for word, and any hoped-for emotional impact was lost entirely.

Nerves: One of our more accomplished presenters was speaking virtually for the first time and it got the best of him. He almost literally forgot how to breathe and sounded out of breath through most of the talk. This dramatically affected his emotional range, as most of his focus then became about when to inhale and when to exhale.

The fix is both easy and hard: Record yourself. I know, cringe, but build a bridge. Have a dry run over Zoom with the recording option on. Then swallow hard and listen to it. Most likely, it will be completely obvious to you when you sound natural and real and when you sound stiff and fake. "I really should wait a beat here," you might say to yourself, "and then sound a bit more excited here."

Rehearse with exaggeration, listen to how it sounds, keep tweaking, and then record again.

And keep reminding yourself: The goal is not to sound dramatic, it is to sound *alive*.

Uptalk

That rising pitch at the end of a sentence? The one that makes statements sound like questions? The thing that you might do without even knowing it?

That's uptalk.

And while it might sound casual or approachable in conversation, it can undercut your authority in a virtual presentation. It makes otherwise confident presenters sound uncertain. Even when you know what you're talking about, uptalk could suggest to your audience that you are asking for their confirmation.

The other fail with uptalk is its effect on the rest of the sentence: It tends to flatten all of it. When you are about to ask a question, you typically do not start low and gradually rise; more often, you keep the same tone all the way to the upward inflection. This becomes boring pretty quickly.

Uptalk is especially common among younger speakers, but anyone trying to sound non-threatening or agreeable can slip into the habit. And that is the insidious part of this: It is often born out of good intentions. Non-threatening and agreeable are good qualities…until they are not.

Fixing uptalk involves practicing with intentional downward inflections to the ends of your sentences. As you feel yourself finishing, focus on dropping down a few notes and letting the finish sink for just a moment.

Because the first cousin to uptalk is quicktalk and the former practically compels the latter.

Here is a good sentence to practice with: "The deadline is next Friday." If you finish that sentence with a question mark, you invite someone to say "no, that's too tight." But if you finish it with intentionality, you make it clear that the deadline is not subject to debate.

In her 2021 talk, Jackie offered an excellent example of what uptalk sounds like and how the simplest focus on a sentence's finish can make a world of difference:

You don't need to sound like a news anchor; you just want your tone to match your conviction. Practice reading declarative sentences, like the one above, and landing them, firmly and cleanly.

Vocal fry

You've surely heard it before, perhaps without knowing that it was a thing: that gravelly tone that settles in at the bottom of a person's vocal range. It often creeps in at the end of sentences, where your voice trails off into a low, buzzy whisper. It could interfere with your clarity and diction, but even if it doesn't, audiences infer all sorts of bad things from it: fatigue at best, disinterest and untrustworthiness at worst.

It also comes at a physical cost: true to its name, bottoming out your lower range could fry your vocal cords. Fortunately, it has well-defined solutions:

Breathe: Fry often comes from running out of air.

Project forward: Keep your voice lifted and engaged, especially at the end of your sentences.

Record and review: Listen for creaky fade-outs and practice finishing sentences with energy, not collapse.

I am aware of the potential contradiction here: For uptalk, the advice is to finish with a downward note, while for vocal fry, the advice is to "keep your voice lifted." In either case, I want you to speak through the end of your sentence—not up into the air, and not down into the gravel. Think of it not as going up or down, but outward—projecting your voice forward with energy.

Verbal tics: When your mouth arrives before your brain

I approach this topic with a bit of trepidation. There is no question that presenters who litter their words with a procession of *like, you know, so, I mean, um, uh* risk disconnects with their audiences. That's real.

What is also real is that audiences often don't notice or care and presenters often turn a non-problem into a problem by fixating on it. So this topic is a bit more complicated than face value might suggest.

Jumpstarting the brain

At their most innocuous, verbal tics like *um, uh, so*, and *you know*, are a simple and effective way of getting your brain up to speed. As you are thinking of saying something, your mouth starts up a few seconds prior, and it doesn't yet know what it wants to say. So out comes whatever is on your bingo card of verbal filler.

The one that amuses me the most is *I mean*. That has become everybody's favorite jumpstarter of sentences. The original intent of that expression is to clarify: *I mean to say.* You use it after you share a thought and then you elaborate to make clear what you mean. But in modern parlance, it has become the prefix to a thought, not a suffix, and it has reached the highest echelons of public communication. Anderson Cooper and Kaitlan Collins of CNN and Jen Psaki and Chris Hayes of MSNBC all do it. Here was Collins in a recent interview with a foreign leader: "I mean, isn't it fatiguing to have to issue the same statements day after day?"

She surely doesn't realize she is doing it, and a tiny percentage of her viewing audience notices it, so this falls squarely in the harmless column.

Case studies in verbal flotsam

I'm going to be pretty hard on myself soon, but first, let me put myself in good company. One of the biggest offenders of the uhs and ums is also regarded as one of the greatest communicators of our time: former President Barack Obama. Search YouTube for any interview of him and you will run out of fingers and toes counting his verbal tics.

In his case, his mouth outpaces his brain, not because it goes too fast, but because he takes the time to consider what he wants to say, and he fills the silence with his tics. In a way, his brain goes too slow, and I don't mean that as an insult. Just the opposite, actually, as the ability to slow or even turn off the brain is one of the keys to high performance. But his mouth didn't get the memo, so it slows down by flooding the zone with flotsam.

In this extended clip, he begins with a *well, uh,* and then proceeds to tell a story that is 50% longer than it needs to be. And it's not just a litany of tics; he also indulges multiple asides and rabbit holes. The central message of this clip is this: "I recognize Lyndon Johnson, who was able to overcome his background and say 'I'm going to make this happen.'"

He begins that sentence at 1:40 into the clip and doesn't finish the sentence until the 3:08 mark.

Obama took many rounds of voice lessons, and they surely helped, as he delivered generational addresses before a teleprompter. But without prepared remarks, he struggles to get to the point.

And I struggle, too. My affliction is more traditional: My mouth starts racing mindlessly and until my brain catches up, there is nothing to say. It is almost always a product of fatigue, appearing late in the day, and it is more pronounced on virtual. Watch for yourself...

Chp 15 Talk Human to Me   151

All of these scenes took place in the afternoon; a few of them I remember all too well. They are not all ums and uhs—some of them are almost like stutters, where I just repeat the first word in the sentence several times. And they are particularly maddening because when I dribble like that, editing them out is made that much more difficult. Why must my mouth never stop? Why can't I just be silent instead??

Indeed, when I show more self-control, my pace is much better and I am able to employ confident pauses instead of high-strung verbal twitches. I search for a way to do that even when I have begun to fatigue. In theory, it should be easy: If I am tired, do less, not more. Move more slowly, not more rapidly.

I will be interested in learning whether my technology editors, or my wife and daughter for that matter, will report being aware of my tics, and as I write this, I don't know the answer, as they haven't weighed in yet. I suspect they will tell me that they haven't noticed them in me, and in fairness, the above video is sort of a greatest hits of verbal diarrhea. Because I get through them quite quickly, they are probably not as distracting to my audiences as they are to me. So let's try to categorize: When are verbal tics troubling and when should they be ignored?

Be concerned if...

They are a crutch: Do you feel like you can't speak without them?

They are part of a pattern: Does every one of your sentences begin with *so* or end with *you know?*

They break your rhythm: Do you feel like you get into a groove and then something happens to you?

They make you sound uncertain: Is your credibility in jeopardy by your verbal utterances?

They are distracting: Have they become a barrier between you and your audience? Has your audience started keeping count of your *you knows?* Do they play the drinking game, made famous by Robin Scherbatsky in *How I Met Your Mother?*

If your verbal tics fall into one of these camps, start by recording yourself so you can understand what your audience sees and hears. Try to identify the most prevalent filler word you use and attack just it. Tics are usually a product of too fast, rarely too slow—can you replace it with silence? Can you slow down your cadence?

These are all the things I tell myself on a regular basis, and they do help. I need to always be conscious and aware of my tendency to race and to continually remind myself to slow down.

Let it go if...

It is just once in a while: Occasional filler sounds might just sound natural and conversational.

They do not annoy: Audiences will forgive personal quirks that don't interrupt clarity.

It's just you: Is it part of who you are? If it sounds like you, don't fixate on it.

If you are in this camp, consider yourself lucky and move on. Nothing good comes from too much awareness of something that is not a problem. I'd rather you be blissfully unaware than diligently pondering. Let it go!

♦

Remember, the goal isn't to become a flawless speaker. It's to become a real one. That means being aware of your vocal habits but not at war with them. Which ones need attention and which ones can you live with?

The pitch penalty: a voice bias worth naming

It is time to discuss an uncomfortable dynamic with voice: As a society, we are biased toward deep voices. Especially in leadership settings, we tend to associate low pitch with authority, calm, and control. The higher the voice, the more likely people are to (consciously or not) question its weight.

There is a preponderance of research into this. An Illinois 2018 survey, a 2014 study of all 435 House of Representatives elections, 2020 ScienceDirect research, and numerous other studies have all concluded the same thing: Lower register equals higher authority.

In addition to being inaccurate, this is completely unfair and definitely not gender-neutral. Women and naturally high-pitched speakers often find themselves scrutinized more closely—not for what they're saying, but for how they sound while saying it. Their voices are described as "shrill," "piercing," or "annoying," even when delivering the exact same message as a deeper-voiced counterpart.

If you fall into that category, you are stuck between two bad options: Force a tone that isn't yours, or face judgment for the one that is. But the news is not all bad: You can work with your pitch, and you can do it without compromising your identity. It is entirely your prerogative to protest on principle having to concede to this cultural discrimination, but while you are protesting, hear me out and try the following exercises.

Good vowels and bad vowels

Controlling your vocal register starts with knowing which vowels tend to send you high and which help you go low. In general, the i and e sounds are made from your throat and tend to accentuate higher pitches. In contrast o and u sounds come from your belly. The a is the swing vowel, with the short a belonging in the first grouping and the long a in the second.

Knowing this, it would behoove you to be quicker with throat vowels and longer with belly vowels. To practice this, take the ice cream test:

1. Record yourself saying "I like ice cream."

2. Channel your inner child and say it with an excited voice that emphasizes the i sounds. Say it loud.

3. Now say "I love ice cream."

4. Say "I love chocolate ice cream."

5. Accentuate the love: "I looooove chocolate ice cream."

6. Linger over the word chocolate, also.

7. Finally, just as you were long over the o sounds, be quick with the i sounds.

I staged this exercise with my high-talking daughter Jamie, and here is how it came out.

The first time you watch this video, what should become clear to you is that speaking from your diaphragm brings out your lower registers and the deeper-sounding vowels facilitate that. If you watch the video a second time, notice two things:

1. When Jamie stands up, she can find that lower register more readily. As her posture straightens, it becomes easier to move air from lower in her frame.

2. When she was breathier over those o sounds, it positively influenced the i sounds, also. Compare how the *ice cream* lines

sounded between her first time ("I like ice cream") and the final time ("I loooove chocolate ice cream").

The laughing exercises on Page 117 will also help you find your lower register. You need to move a lot of air to laugh and I want you to tune into that. Shallow breathing creates weak and rushed delivery, while deep, intentional breathing gives your voice strength and consistency. Lean into the laugh and to those o and u sounds—indulge them with full breaths and long landings. The more you can fully shape your vowels from your diaphragm, the more you can explore the deeper parts of your natural register.

> 📣 It is worth noting the opposite: Men with baritone voices often have trouble projecting without becoming boomy. They can focus on their throat vowels to be more piercing.

Let me reiterate that those with higher pitches should not have to do this; it is unfair that society forces this upon you. But as a book author, given the choice of changing societal norms or offering you a tactic to outsmart society, I'm a realist about the power of my particular pen.

And for the rest of us: If you've ever found yourself reacting more favorably to a lower-pitched voice, take a moment and ask yourself if you're responding to the message, or just the tone it came in, and if that is fair of you to do that. Awareness isn't everything, but it's a good place to start.

◆

Your voice is the most personal tool you bring to a virtual presentation. It's shaped by big things like your personality, your history, your life experiences, but also by little things like your breath and your pacing. You can't trade it in for a new one. But you can train it, trust it, and use it more intentionally.

This isn't about sounding slick. It's about sounding human. Not polished to perfection, but present enough to connect on a personal level. Not free of flaws, but full of awareness.

Whether you're adding vocal variety, clearing out filler, or confronting unconscious bias, remember: Your goal is not to mimic someone else's voice—it's to claim your own. And then use it with care and confidence. That's what it means to talk human. That's what makes your voice worth hearing and worth listening to. 💻

Fake it 'Til You Make it

This phrase can rub people the wrong way. It can sound like pretending, like putting on airs, like being inauthentic. But that's a shallow take. What if "faking it" is really about stepping into a version of yourself that hasn't fully arrived yet? What if it's less about deception and more about evolution?

This short chapter ends Part Three by reclaiming the phrase and reframing it as a tool for growth. Confidence doesn't have to come first. Sometimes it follows.

Act first, feel later

You don't have to feel confident before you act confident. In fact, it often works the other way around and an entire body of research supports this. When you sit up straight, breathe fully, make eye contact, and speak with energy, your body starts sending signals to your brain that say, "Hey, we've got this." The way you carry yourself can change the way you feel. It's not just psychology, it's biology. Your brain listens to your body more than you think.

This does not mean you're being phony. It means you're building a new habit. You're rehearsing a version of yourself who can lead the meeting, hold the spotlight, deliver the pitch, teach the class. Sometimes you have to act as if you belong before you believe it fully.

Mimicry, too, gets a bad rap. Imitation is often dismissed as unoriginal. But in real life, mimicry is how we learn. Children mimic adults to learn how to navigate their world. New professionals mimic mentors. This is not stealing—it's scaffolding. When you mirror someone's confidence, tone, or poise, you're borrowing a structure until your own voice can grow into it.

Your intentional self

The key is to remain intentional. You're not hiding your true self behind a performance. You're allowing performance to *stretch* your sense of self. Think of it as a confidence costume—not to disguise who you are, but to give that part of you a chance to take the stage.

Of course, nerves don't just vanish on command. You may still feel your pulse rise, your breath shorten, your thoughts scatter. But those are not indicators of failure; they're signs that you're stretching. That you're doing something that matters. And that's precisely when this technique becomes so valuable. When the ground feels unsteady, posturing into confidence can be the act that steadies you.

Sometimes it takes standing taller to feel more grounded. Speaking louder to feel more heard. Slowing your pace to feel more in control. None of these things is fake. They are strategic growth behaviors, and the more you practice them, the less they feel like performance and the more they feel like you.

One caveat: This technique only works if you're using it to become more of who you really are. If you're faking it just to look good or to score some cheap applause, you are not being intentional, you are being a bullshit artist, and people can smell it a virtual world away. That's not confidence; that's performance art. But if you're using the posture of confidence to grow into it—if you're walking the walk until it becomes real—then you're not faking anything. You're becoming.

So, when you find yourself thinking, "Who am I to do this?" or "I don't belong here," try flipping the script. Step into the behaviors of someone who does belong. Treat confidence like something you can wear, not something you have to earn.

All the world's a stage—and confidence is a costume that fits better the more you wear it.

◆

And once you've stepped into the spotlight—body aligned, voice steady, presence strong—it's time to make sure your gear doesn't trip you on the way out. Confidence might carry you far, but lousy lighting or a glitchy mic can still take you down. So it's time to get technical... 💻

Part Four
Get Technical

You might have brilliant slides, a magnetic presence, and a rock-solid message. All good, but can audience members hear you, can they see you, and can they stop staring at the moonscape that makes up your virtual background? Technology is no longer just the delivery system; in the virtual era, it has become part of the message.

These next five chapters will not try to turn you into a gearhead, but can we please not give your audience the impression that you borrowed your kid's Chromebook five minutes ago? We'll break down the things that matter, the things that don't, and the tech that you might want to invest in.

Good tech doesn't steal the show, it disappears. When everything works, your audience forgets the platform and leans into the moment. That's the goal. Let's get your tech to shut up and make you look great.

The Sound of Trust

In the hierarchy of virtual presentation essentials, nothing ranks higher than sound. You can get away with soft video and you can survive a slide that doesn't advance. You can even forget to turn your camera on—something I seem to do on a daily basis—and audience members will not only forgive it, they will likely find it endearing.

But your spoken words convey most of your story. If your audience cannot hear you well—if your voice cuts out, echoes like a canyon, or sounds like it's coming from a tin can—you undercut your message, you risk disengagement, and you erode trust.

This chapter, and the ones that follow, are not just gear round-ups; there are literally thousands of publications that will do that for you. I *will* share with you the products that I have chosen and why, but our focus will be on how to achieve the kind of audio clarity that evokes authority, credibility, and trust.

Audio is the engine that drives presence.

Can you hear me now?

It is deliciously ironic how much we are about to obsess over cameras, lighting, and backgrounds in the following chapters when your microphone does more to shape your audience's experience than any of those. Audio is the No. 1 determinant of a good virtual experience. Clean, intimate sound makes people feel closer to you, while muffled or echoey sound creates distance, confusion, and fatigue. Here is an exaggerated case study:

Pick your poison
Given the choice between bad video and bad audio, most people would choose to hear you better, even if they can't see you better. Judge for yourself...

Let's remember our roots: It is a relatively recent phenomenon to see the presenter during a webinar. For the first decade, they were audio-only experiences. And before there was television, our ancestors crowded around their vacuum-tube radios. We are wired to listen.

Way back on Page 23, I wrote that "eye fatigue is the silent killer of presentations." I should have included ear fatigue. The quality of your spoken words impacts every aspect of a virtual presentation: clarity of message, emotional weight of story, integrity of the takeaway. Clear and crisp audio contributes to all of these. If they can hear you, they'll stay with you.

The right mic in the right place

Not all microphones are created equal and you can spend as little as $25 or as much as $2,500. But this much you can be confident of: Just about any external microphone will be better than just about any built-in laptop mic. Built-ins pick up too much room noise and not enough of you. Whether you are clipping, wearing, or placing them, external microphones make a world of difference.

USB condenser microphones

A popular choice for virtual presenters, the USB condenser microphone is desk based, plugs directly into your computer, and delivers warm, full-bodied sound. The term "condenser" refers to the process by which sound waves are converted to electrical signals. They are ideal for stationary setups and they give your voice a studio-like presence. They also pick up a fair amount of room noise, so your space needs to be quiet and controlled.

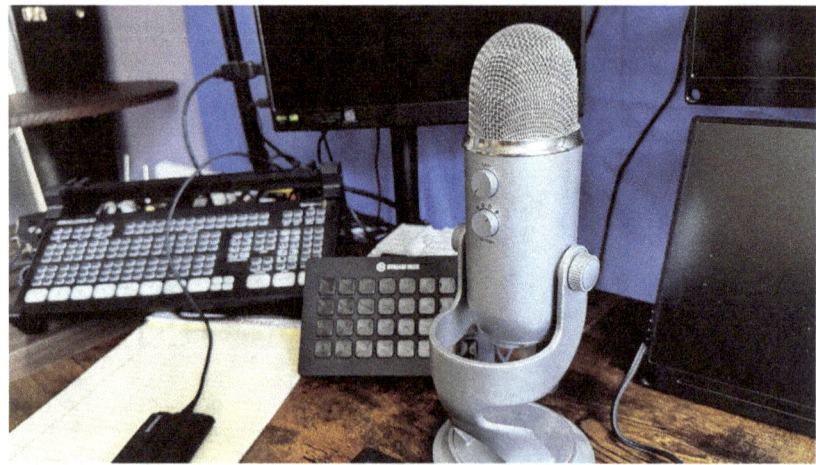

I have had the Blue Yeti condenser microphone for over five years (mine is silver, but oh well). It connects via USB, Windows and iOS both find it automatically, and all streaming platforms recognize it as a source.

While desktop mics do chain you to your desk, sound quality is superior to built-ins and they are super-convenient—always there, always plugged in, always listening. In the fall of 2025, the Blue Yeti sold for $110 on Amazon and was seen for as low as $83 at Walmart.

One last advisory with desktop mics: Placement matters. Too far away, and you sound like you're across the street. Too close, and you risk breath noise and *plosives* (those distracting puffs of air on Ps and Bs). The sweet spot, as shown here, is four fingers away from your mouth, nearly at chin level, and a few degrees off to one side.

Lavalier microphones

These clip-on mics offer freedom of movement and consistent sound, as they travel with you and remain a consistent distance from your mouth. The term "lavalier" is an outdated French word for an ornamental necklace, and you do wear it like a pendant. These are often referred to as *lapel mics,* and that term is indeed more descriptive.

Lavalier mics are great for presenters who don't want to stay in one place. If you take to heart any of the advice about standing up while you present virtually, you will want to pick up one. Our conference purchased a dozen lavs from AKG back in 2008 and we still use them to this day. But for my studio, I now use the Rode Wireless Pro, a beauty of a system that practically fits in the palm of my hand.

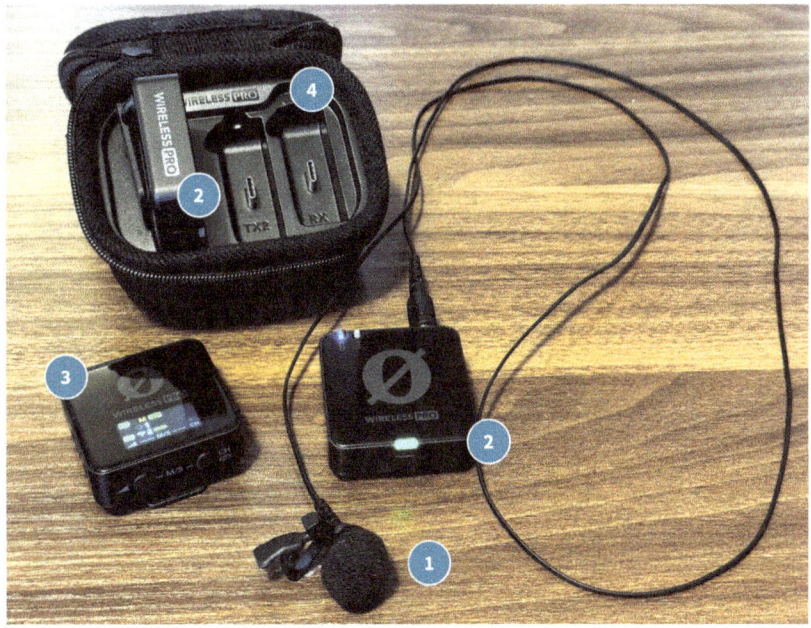

The lapel mic (No. 1) connects to one of two wireless packs (2). The pack fits in a pocket or is clipped to a belt and transmits your voice wirelessly to the receiver (3), which has a standard 3.5mm jack to connect with just about any audio input. (Bigger mixing boards have 1/4-inch inputs, so you might have to pick up a $5 adapter on Amazon.) The transmitters and the receiver all live inside a small case (4) that keeps them charged.

This sub-$300 system is noteworthy for several reasons. First, they are tiny and take up very little space on my desk. Second, there are two transmitters and both can be connected to the receiver at the same time. And third, the transmitters have their own recording chips and can hold as much as 40 hours of voice recording. They even have a built-in mic, which, while not sufficient for studio work, is handy for quick recorded memos.

The sound quality is excellent, the form factor is ideal, and I love not having to constantly monitor the life of a disposable battery.

This setup is analog: Sound waves picked up by the microphone are carried to the transmitting pack, sent to the receiver, and pumped out the output jack...all analog. Also analog is my "AV switcher"—a hardware device that takes several different audio and video inputs and outputs just one.

Without an AV switcher, analog audio is a bit more complicated. I would need to get this analog sound source over to my PC's digital neighborhood. This would involve a converter—a small $50ish device that equalizes the gain, volume, and signal. While it is conceivable that I could go straight from my receiver into my PC's 3.5mm microphone input, the risk is high that audio quality would suffer.

Score another point for the Rode system, as its USB-C ports are digital outputs as well as charging inputs. The receiver is equally facile supplying analog sound to my AV switcher as it is providing digital audio to my PC.

Headworn microphones

This microphone style wraps around one or both ears and positions a small boom mic right near your mouth. It delivers consistently clear audio because the mic stays in the same position, no matter how you move. (Although it's conceivable that mobile presenters could move their heads independently of their shoulders, thus moving the lav off of the mouth.)

I have only worn these a few times, in person when I needed my hands to be free. You know, like when I needed to wield a head of lettuce:

Chp 17 The Sound of Trust

I normally sport a handheld microphone for my opening remarks, but my lettuce caper required me to improvise. This type of microphone felt too stagey and a bit rock-star-meets-fitness-instructor for my tastes, but it accomplished the objective of freeing up my hands. *Seinfeld* buffs will enjoy the clip.

Like with the lav, this one is fitted with a wireless transmitter that you keep on you, and an analog receiver. That means that you will need some sort of converter to use it with a computer.

♦

That was a lot of geek I just threw at you, so let's summarize:

- Desktop microphones are very convenient in that they just sit on your desk and are ready to go.

- Lavalier or lapel microphones are advantageous in that they allow you to move more freely in your virtual space.

- Headworn mics provide even more freedom of movement.

- The sound from lav and head mics is potentially superior, as the microphone is a constant distance from your mouth.

- Moving from analog to digital requires an additional converter or a wireless system with built-in conversion.

> It goes without saying (and yet here I am saying it) that you need to test your audio in the environment in which you will present. Most platforms have preview options, and if you take my advice from Chapter 8, you will always have a human being available for a sound check.

Your room has a voice, too

The sound of your space is part of your sound. Hard floors and bare walls turn your voice into a ping-pong ball, while soft furnishings absorb those harsh audible rebounds. Rugs, curtains, bookshelves—even a few well-placed pillows—can make your room feel less like a warehouse and more like a recording studio. And don't forget the uninvited guests: barking dogs, leaf blowers, the neighbor's grunge band practice. Great mics are no match for bad environments. Here are a few specific recommendations to make your room more audio friendly:

Put down a rug: A single area rug can make a noticeable difference, especially if you're working on hardwood or tile.

Close curtains or hang fabric: Thick drapes or even just a blanket over a window can absorb sound and reduce echo from glass surfaces.

Add soft furniture: A couch, armchair, or even a pile of pillows can help break up and absorb reflective sound.

Fill your bookshelves: A bookshelf full of irregularly shaped items—books, frames, plants—acts as a natural diffuser.

Record with the door closed—and covered: Close the door when presenting, and consider hanging a beach towel if it's thin or hollow-core.

Mute the outside world: It's probably not realistic to expect that you could approach your neighbors and ask them to be quiet from 8:00 to 10:00, but still, silence your phone, unplug ticking clocks, and if you are responsible for answering folks in the Chat, use a quiet keyboard. Oh, and keep pets in another room. Or not...see Page 81 to be reminded of how disarming they can be.

 If your environment makes it impossible to control noise—leaf blowers, HVAC systems, open windows—there are apps available that use AI to filter background sound in real time. They aren't magic, but they can help in a pinch. Our technology editor Christiane recommends Krisp.

The loudspeaker-or-headphone question

Hundreds of thousands of Zoom and Teams users don headphones or earbuds for their virtual presentations because they were told that it eliminates feedback and echo. As the advisory goes, if the sound that comes out of the speakers makes its way into the microphone, it will then cycle through this little loop. And because the speed of sound is not instantaneous, that small delay will become part of the cycle, and any tiny echo will grow into big ugly feedback.

Chp 17 **The Sound of Trust**

Unless it doesn't.

While I am on record across this chapter touting how important good audio quality is, I also loathe wearing headphones or earbuds while presenting virtually, as they make me feel even more detached and removed from my audience. But good audio quality supersedes my sentiment against phones or buds, so I would wear them if I had to.

But I have never had to. I get no feedback whatsoever from my Altec-Lansing Bluetooth studio monitor. It sits behind my microphone and the mic is designed to pick up audio from in front, not behind. So I get to fill my studio with the happy sounds of happy virtual audience members.

Perhaps your studio can be this happy, too. It's worth a try!

> 🔊 There are numerous Zoom settings that could help improve audio quality during Zoom meetings. That conversation begins on Page 215 within Chapter 21.

◆

The right mic, the right space, and a little intentionality is all it takes to sound like you know what you're doing. Let's be clear that you do actually have to know what you're talking about, but that said, when your voice comes through clean and confident, people lean in. You're no longer just talking through a screen—you're being heard. 💻

Get Your Shot Together

Before you say your first word, your audience has already formed an impression. And in virtual settings, much of that impression comes from what your camera shares with the world. Your gear, your framing, and the visual vibe of your shot don't just affect how you look; they affect how you're perceived.

This chapter isn't about acting natural on camera (that was Get Personal), or sitting with intention (that was Get Physical). And even though Part Four is gear-head heaven, it will not be a round-up of products. This is about the frame that holds it all together. A good shot builds trust. A bad one creates distance. And the best part? You don't need to be a cinematographer to get this right.

You just need to get your shot together.

Your laptop camera might be lying to you

Most built-in laptop cameras struggle to handle real-world lighting. They blow out highlights, they drown out shadows, and they make your skin look dull or shiny—or maybe dull *and* shiny, both at once. In short, they make you look worse, not better.

Because they're fixed to your screen, built-in cameras often shoot from below eye level, creating the classic "nostril cam." Nobody looks their best from that angle. And while I will tell you soon the same thing that all camera consultants advise—to get your camera at eye level—I know how hard that advice is to follow when we're talking about your laptop computer. It usually involves a few strategically placed books.

Very few built-in cameras offer the sensors needed to render accurate skin tones or keep the image balanced when light changes. You look either ghostly or muddy, depending on the time of day. In anything but ideal lighting, your image can turn soft, noisy, or choppy.

Worse, built-ins can give you a false sense of adequacy. You open Zoom, see your little face in the corner, and think, "Looks fine." But that preview window is deceptively forgiving: To your audience, watching full screen on a monitor, you look underlit and disconnected.

So yes, your laptop camera is lying. It will be fine for Zoom calls, where you just need to show yourself to others. But it should fall well below the standard you set for leading a virtual presentation.

📣 The pages of the printed book might not adequately show the difference in image quality of the various camera options outlined here. Please see our **camera test at www.crushyournext.pro.**

The upgrade your face deserves

If you have $75 to spend, you can completely change how you come across on screen. A better camera won't make you more qualified, but it will make you easier to see, easier to watch, easier to pay attention to. This isn't about looking glamorous—it's about removing one of the many potential barriers between you and your audience, so your presence comes through without visual distraction.

Get a USB webcam

These are the workhorses of virtual presentation. They're affordable, plug-and-play, and most offer big leaps in image quality over your laptop's lens. You'll get crisper focus, better light sensitivity, and more control over your framing.

If you search "USB webcam" on Amazon, you will be presented with about 10,000 choices, and you cannot go wrong with the Logitech C92x line, ranging between $60 and $100. Here is a side-by-side with it vs. my built-in, and just a reminder, you can inspect these comparison photos at www.crushyournext.pro/files/camera-test.ppsx:

Built-in webcam   **USB webcam**

The printed book might not show the superior tonal quality of the USB webcam, but you can certainly see its better angle and perspective. And while granted, I could have made the effort to raise my laptop to eye level, very few people do. Perhaps that is the key takeaway here: If you have no choice but to use your built-in, do whatever you must in order to raise its camera to the level of your eyes.

Use an old phone

Some presenters use an old iPhone or Android as a webcam, taking advantage of apps like EpocCam, Camo, or DroidCam. For people on a tight budget or those upgrading in phases, it's a viable in-between option, as they all offer clean HDMI and better than decent video quality.

Use a "real" camera

If you are ready to level up further, DSLR or mirrorless cameras (together known as interchangeable lens cameras or ILCs) can turn your feed into something almost cinematic. The depth of field alone can make you look like you're sitting in a professional studio. It is probably unfair of me to lump these two into one, but they share the same virtues of interchangeability of lenses and profound control over the light that they are able to capture.

ILC cameras are a bit more complicated and they certainly cost more than good USB webcams, but for many, they are the only way to go. They will get the lion's share of the ink in this section, starting with how to choose:

Choose a DSLR if you have an old one lying around. That Canon Rebel from 2010 would be perfect to use in your studio.

Go with a mirrorless if you are buying new, as they win out in almost every comparison. They are smaller, easier to mount, optimized for continuous shooting, and more intelligent with face tracking.

Here is what you will need in order to add a high-end ILC to your virtual studio:

1. **Clean HDMI Out.** This quality refers to the ability to project an output signal that eliminates all of the stats shown through the viewfinder (ISO, aperture, magnification, shutter speed, etc.). Most ILCs offer Clean HDMI Out, but make sure before you pull the trigger on an off-brand ILC, because if your audience is constantly being told that you are shooting at F8 with ISO 800, white balance on Auto, 20mm zoom, and exposure compensation at -1.25, this will be an epic fail.

2. **A physical mount.** Even the lightest ILCs are bulkier than USB webcams and cannot just sit atop your monitor. You will need to use a tripod that sits on your desk, or better still, one that attaches to the edge of your desk or to a pole. These are cheap and plentiful, but should not be overlooked.

3. **A capture card.** Just like with the analog microphones we spoke about in the last chapter, ILCs need to convert their picture to digital so you can plug them directly into your PC as USB devices. These cards cost as little as $20.

4. **A "dummy battery."** You will not want to run your ILC from a battery, as the constant video image will drain those poor things the way shooting video drains your iPhone. Instead, pick up a battery-shaped adapter that connects to AC power. Your camera won't know the difference but your patience will.

You can purchase a current Canon, Sony, Fujifilm, or Panasonic ILC in a range of $500 to $800, but let me share with you my bargain of the century: the Sony a5100. Introduced in 2014, this is the entry-level model of Sony's wildly successful Alpha series. Sony had no idea that it was creating the perfect Zoom camera before anyone knew what Zoom was. But this little mirrorless gem offers clean HDMI, reliable face detection autofocus, a flippable screen, and an excellent sensor.

I troll eBay for them, where I will find used bargains like these:

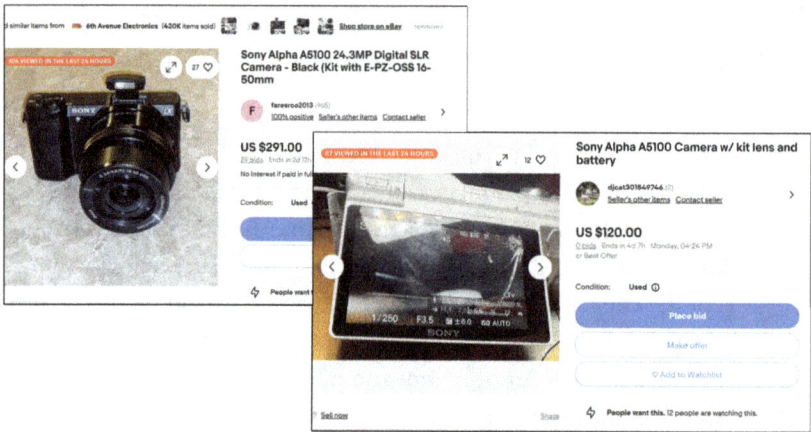

The one on the left has a shutter count of 350,000, and that is why it is $100 cheaper than the typical used price. But here's the thing: In your studio, you might not depress the shutter once across the next five years. All you care about is the quality of the lens and the sensor, and they tend to have half lives like plutonium.

The one on the right has a cracked viewfinder, and while I am not advocating that you gamble on damaged goods as I often do, you will never frame a shot with the viewfinder; you will do that with your confidence monitor or within your streaming platform.

I have three used a5100s in my studio, one of which I bought from a vendor in Thailand for under $200. I have outfitted them with dummy batteries, they pump high-def HDMI directly to my AV switcher, and they have been marvelous, trouble-free performers. Two of them do most of the heavy lifting, one fixed at 18mm and the other at 22mm:

My main shot, at 18mm **Tight shot, at 22mm**

 Compare all four camera types at
www.crushyournext.pro/files/camera-test.ppsx.

Show up in your own shot

Zoom goes to great lengths to allow you to present while seated in front of the Eiffel Tower or from the peaks of Machu Picchu. It also helps you look good even if your lighting is bad. These are good qualities, which we will discuss soon, but more important than your background and your lighting is your *framing*. Shot composition is one of the simplest ways to elevate your virtual presence, and one of the easiest to overlook. When your face is too low, too high, too far, or too close, it could send subtle signals of awkwardness or disconnection. Even if your content is great, a poorly framed shot can quietly undermine your credibility.

The rule of thirds...sort of

One of the true elements of photographic gospel, the rule of thirds creates a grid from two horizontal and two vertical lines. The principle is to cluster main characters on the intersection of those lines and to place horizons along one of the horizontal lines. The rules apply differently to virtual presenters who are looking directly into their cameras, but nonetheless it is worthwhile for you to understand the entire concept, so we will start with still photography.

The photo on the next page follows these two principles perfectly.

The young couple (my daughter and future son-in-law, no less, captured by my other daughrer while hiding in a bush) is placed in the top-right third and the horizon is along the top line. This type of positioning provides context, energy, and vitality to the photo. This is considered quintessential framing for still photography.

These rules also apply for people on camera who are *not* speaking directly to the cameras, as seen in just about every interview you have ever watched on television. Here are stills from a profile of a young crocheting phenom named Jonah and his mother.

Chp 18 Get Your Shot Together 175

Adhering to the rule of thirds allows interview subjects to face into their scenes. Again, this is standard operating procedure for placement of people who are not speaking to the camera, but those who are (like virtual presenters) would not follow all of these guidelines. Let's go deeper:

Lining eyes: Your camera lens should be level with your eyes. That's how we view each other in real life, and that's what creates a sense of natural connection on screen. If your camera is looking up your nose or down at your forehead, your audience feels it, even if they can't articulate why.

Noggin space: The other key quality for virtual presenters is headroom, the space between the top of your head and the top of the frame. If there is too much, you look like you're sinking. Too little, and you're crowding the shot. Just an inch or two keeps you centered.

Partial thirds: When speaking directly to your camera, the rule of thirds applies horizontally but not vertically. In other words, you want your head to be on the top horizontal third line, but you do not want to move laterally to one of the vertical thirds. If you choose to move a tiny bit left or right in order to accentuate your own good side or that of your background, that's okay. But if you moved all the way to one of the vertical thirds, the shot would feel off.

Here is an example of good framing and video composition:

This woman has sufficient headroom, is looking directly into the camera with level eyes, and is positioned very close to the center of her frame. Her background is diffused and flat; the only thing I might quibble with is the color of her shirt, which blends in a bit with the background. I might have advised a darker color for better contrast, but everything else here is spot-on.

Be tight, hang loose

In this chapter, and in several earlier ones, I have written about the relative merits of tight shots, which enable you to create intimacy with your audience, and looser ones, which allow for more upper-body gesturing. In particular, Chapter 14 is replete with examples of both and how they impact gesturing and emoting.

My hope for you is that this is not an either/or situation, and for that I refer you to Chapter 24, for how you can use hardware to accommodate the use of multiple cameras.

Support behind the lens

Eye contact is one of the most powerful tools in any communicator's toolkit and we have discussed it in all five parts, across many chapters. In virtual settings, it becomes a trick of geometry: If you look directly into the camera, you can't see the people you're speaking to. And if you look at your screen—where their faces live—you're no longer looking at them. I devoted a section of Chapter 12 to this paradox: The more you try to see your audience, the less seen you appear.

To address this conundrum, there is a wide range of solutions, strategies, and products at your disposal, and I offer them to you in increasing degrees of tech.

Move your Zoom window!

The simplest solution, and the one that I employ, is to move your streaming platform's window close to your camera. Furthermore, Zoom users can reorder the Brady Bunch squares to place the person speaking right below the camera. Coupled with the strategies on Page 110—where I detail where to look and when—this stands as the simplest, cleanest, and cheapest solution.

But it's not perfect: You are still looking away from the person you are speaking to instead of right at them. And that is potentially bothersome when trying to be present for your audience. To review, what you are hoping to avoid is Brady Bunch syndrome, where you are looking at a person's square while speaking (left), instead of looking into the camera (right).

Stick your camera onto your screen

A new collection of products enables you to bring your webcam down from the top of your monitor and place it anywhere on the screen, including over the face of the person you are speaking with.

These range from very slick little suction cups to fully hinged solutions that hang your camera down from the top of the monitor's edge. Some are dedicated cameras and others are more generic mounts that will work with nearly all webcams. They range in price from $25 to $250.

The most evolved are from Plexicam, an outfit that focuses on accessories for virtual presenters. Plexicam's products include mounts that hang down from the top of a monitor as well as suction cups that can be placed anywhere on the screen.

On the next page are four uses for screen-mounted cameras, ranging from simple to sophisticated, and clever to misguided.

1. Hang a cam: The most popular way to place a webcam on the screen is to hang it from the top of the monitor and slide it up and down to the desired vertical position. These cost between $75 and $100.

2. Suction action: This webcam is literally suctioned to the screen, along with two lights and a microphone. It's effectively an entire studio on one 32-inch display Each cup costs about $50. Coffee cup is extra.

3. Eyes on the slide: If you want to maintain eye contact with your audience while being displayed next to your slides, you can place your camera literally right within your slide.

4. Read and stare: You can also place your webcam right on top of your script and use it like a teleprompter. Please don't—this usually fails epically, turning you into a lifeless zombie. See the last section of this chapter for my little diatribe against teleprompters.

Monitor your confidence

In the ballroom of an in-person event, a confidence monitor is a screen placed at the foot of the stage that enables speakers to see their slides, a timer, their notes, and anything else that helps them stay grounded in the moment and present for their audience. A confidence monitor is not just about displaying information; it provides assurance—hence its name.

Virtually, these same principles apply, as does the goal of maintaining awareness and orientation without breaking connection. But monitors are cheap and space around you is like gold, so it pays to go big when thinking about how to set up shop.

Chp 18 Get Your Shot Together

At a minimum, you want to see what your audience is seeing, and typically the streaming platform can do that for you. Additionally, you might want to have PowerPoint's Presenter View visible, so you can see the current slide, the next slide, your notes, and current and elapsed time.

If you have more than one camera in operation, you will want a monitor to confirm for you which view is being sent to your audience, and before you know it, you are ordering up two or three extra monitors. That might help you and it might make you drown.

Below is a repeat from Chapter 11, where you can see many displays in front of me. Here is a tour:

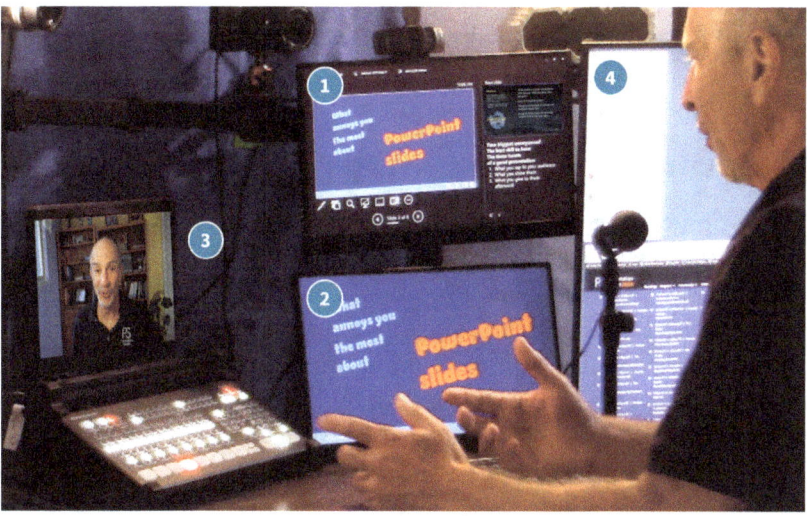

Display No. 1 is PowerPoint's Presenter View. It shows me my notes and what slide is coming next. I don't use Presenter View often; this monitor normally shows me the interface of the streaming platform in use.

Display No. 2 is the current slide in the presentation deck, but that is not what my audience is seeing. I know this because...

Display No. 3 monitors my direct feed out to Zoom or whatever platform I am using. This becomes my lifeline, as it would be all too easy to lose track of what I am showing my audience. This functions as my confidence monitor, and normally it would be placed very close to the camera. But because I have three cameras that I actively use, I need to find a happy medium that is reasonably close to each of them.

Display No. 4 is a tall monitor that can show many minutes of Chat and dozens of participants all at the same time. I don't refer to this monitor often, but it is great to be able to place a lot of auxiliary data on an easy-to-read display.

My AV switcher is right below Display No. 3 and it is what makes that third display so vital. I want to be able to see at a glance which signal I am sending to my audience: one of several cameras, my computer display, or a split screen of both.

So as you can see, the notion of a confidence monitor can morph and expand dramatically in the virtual space. And let me be clear that you do not need four monitors to get this right. One well-placed second screen will do you a world of good.

Teleprompt at your own peril

There are a host of products that have as their primary objective the preservation of your ability to maintain eye contact with the camera. They use impressive technology, but if you are not careful, they can become like a narcotic; hence, the warning built into the headline above.

Teleprompting involves placing a reflective surface in front of your camera and then projecting something onto that surface. This allows presenters to look directly into the lens and see whatever is projected onto that intervening surface. Just about every newscaster you have ever tuned into uses this technique to deliver messages directly into your living room.

Meanwhile, in large auditoriums or outdoor venues, teleprompters are not attached to cameras but are free-standing surfaces that allow speakers to look out into the audience. You have seen these used by just about every president and presidential aspirant since the beginning of time:

While newsroom-quality teleprompters start in the mid-four figures, you can put one in your studio for under $300, and the most impressive of the bunch is Elgato's Prompter. It uses *beamsplitting* technology (that is the technical term for what teleprompters do) to place a monitor in front of your camera, and it is almost dizzying what you can project onto it:

- Your script, so you can use it in a conventional manner
- Gallery view from Zoom or Teams
- The active speaker when in Single Speaker View, so whoever is speaking will be shown to you
- One Note, so you can take notes while looking at your audience
- Presenter View from PowerPoint, so all of that data is right before your camera lens
- Or the Chat, so you can monitor what everyone is saying while you are speaking to them

Truly geek heaven for anyone who wants cutting-edge technology in their studios, but it was a bit too much for me. It places a stunning amount of technology in the one place where I want as little as possible: the space between my camera lens and me.

Crazy smart tech from Elgato
The Prompter is impressive engineering from a group of talented engineers. Are you geek enough to handle it? I was not.

I don't want to discourage you from trying cool new tech. Just know that you will need to practice with it diligently to reach a point where you can speak naturally in front of it.

Early adopters have likened it to an addictive drug, one colleague sharing with me that he feels as if he "can't present without it."

I don't want that for you. I want you to develop the confidence and the belief that you can speak from your heart under any circumstance. "Just give me a camera—I'll do the rest," is how another colleague put it when discussing this topic. *That* is what I want for you, and I'm not so sure that teleprompters can deliver it.

◆

The core principle remains the same: Choose tools that help you feel more present, not more distracted. Whether it's a beamsplitting teleprompter or a stack of books that gets your laptop to eye level, the goal is the same: to help you find that place where you are freely sharing your ideas and your passion in the most genuine way possible.

Do whatever you have to do to get to that place. 💻

Lighting 101

Whether you are leading a virtual workshop or just chiming in during a Zoom call, your lighting does more than illuminate your face—it shapes how people perceive your professionalism, energy, and credibility. And unlike audio and video, lighting is not always perceived on a conscious level—sometimes audience members just know that something is off, even if they cannot articulate it.

Fortunately, conquering illumination does not require an advanced film degree or a dedicated tech crew. And it doesn't require hundreds of dollars invested in gear. A few thoughtful decisions and a modest investment can radically change how you show up on screen.

Cracking the Kelvin code

Before we dive into light sources, let's quickly talk about color temperature, measured in Kelvin—a nod to the British and Scottish scientist Lord Kelvin, who promoted the concept of absolute zero, where all atomic motion essentially stops. Unlike Fahrenheit or Celsius, Kelvin is not measured in degrees—it's a linear scale up from absolute zero.

Lower Kelvin values, like 2,700-3,000 K, describe warm, yellow-orange light—think cozy reading lamps or sunrise. Sunset is a bit *warmer*, with the coveted "golden hour" that photographers chase coming in at about 3,500-4,000 K.

Higher Kelvin values describe cloudy days or deeply shaded scenes. Here is the entire spectrum of the "temperature" of light:

Kelvin	Appearance	Examples
1900 K	Deep amber	Candlelight, campfire
2200 K	Warm amber	Vintage Edison bulbs
2700 K	Soft warm white	Incandescent bulbs, cozy lamps
3000 K	Warm white	Halogen lights, sunrise
3500 K	Neutral warm	Golden hour lighting
4000 K	Cool white	Office fluorescents, early morning shade
4500 K	Neutral white	Some LED panels, pre-noon daylight
5000 K	Balanced white	Clear daylight, photography reference point
5500 K	Daylight white	Studio lighting, photography standard
6000 K	Crisp cool white	Overcast daylight, bright cloud cover
6500 K	Cool bluish white	Standard for video monitors, daylight bulbs
7000 K	Bluish tone	Shade under blue sky
8000 K	Very cool blue	Deep shade, high-altitude daylight
>9000 K	Icy blue	Arctic skylight, haze, sci-fi film lighting

While photographers love the golden hour, your studio cameras might not. Cameras will fiddle with their own white balance settings to keep white objects looking white and that might compromise other hues. The ideal color temperature for a studio is 5,500 Kelvin, which closely matches natural daylight.

Most quality lights let you set the color temperature manually. If you can, aim for that sweet spot around 5,500 K—it's flattering, consistent, and keeps your whites white without compromising skin tone.

You don't actually have to know any of this in order to properly light your studio. If you go the rest of your life without once ever uttering Kelvin, your time here on Earth will not be diminished. But now you know the basic concept of temperature as it is applied to light. You now have bragging rights over your friends; I can only imagine your thrill.

Natural vs. artificial lighting

Most professional studios are windowless so that lighting designers and gaffers can dial up 5,500 K with their professional-grade lights. This stands in stark contrast to most offices and spare bedrooms, which have windows. Windows are nice. Sunlight is joyful. Natural light is flattering, cost-free, and abundant. Having a window in your studio is a wonderful thing.

Until it's not. A window can make you glow like a morning talk show host one moment and cast you into murky shadows the next. Equally unfortunate, however, is advice that uses words like *never* or *always* when referring to how to use windows. The key is control, which you can wield with your own smart use of lighting.

Three lights, one great look

You don't need to become a cinematographer to get lighting right; you just need a minimal amount of geometry. Your objective is to create three points of light:

The key light: The brightest light, ideally 30-40 degrees off-center from your face. The key provides the primary lighting on your face.

The fill light: Softer than the key, this light is placed on the other side of your face, same 30-40 degrees of offset. This light softens shadows that the key would otherwise cast.

The back light: The softest of the three, this light comes from behind you and faces the back of your head and neck. It highlights your edges and your hairline and its job is to separate you from your background.

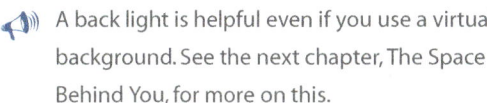 A back light is helpful even if you use a virtual background. See the next chapter, The Space Behind You, for more on this.

Here is a smartly produced diagram on three-point lighting, produced by the folks at StreamYard, a well-known broadcast agency:

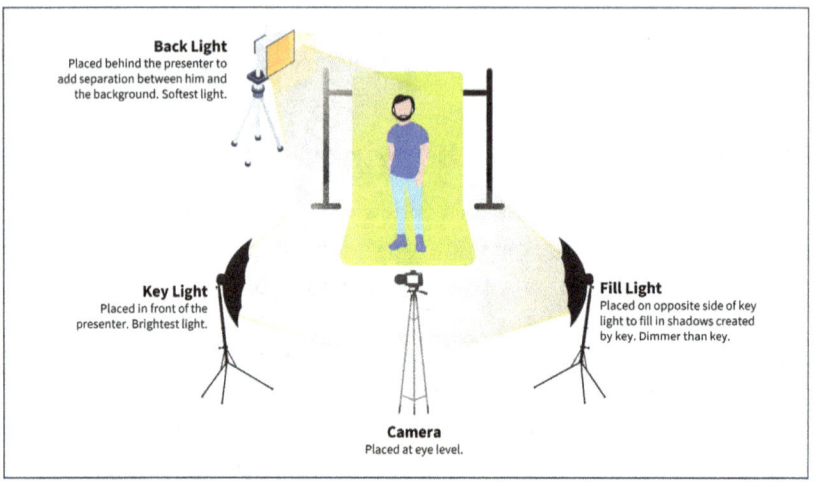

Whether you are seated or standing, whether the background is real or virtual, these three lights will keep you nicely illuminated. If you only have two sources of lighting, keep the key and the fill. If you can only have one, use the key and bring the angle in so that it is closer to the camera. Each of these compromises will harshen the lighting on you, but light that is too bright is better than light that is too dim.

Conversely, if you create all three lights and you have a fourth light at your disposal, shine it on your background. That too will serve to separate you from the background.

The good, the bad, and the fluorescent

News flash, not everyone has a lighting designer on call. Not everyone can confidently walk the Home Lighting aisle of Home Depot. Not everyone can wade through the sea of light products on Amazon without drowning.

Most people are lit by whatever is around them: a window, a desk lamp, a ceiling fixture they quite possibly have never actually looked at. This section is a tour through the lighting aisle of everyday life: the options you've got, the ones that actually help, and the ones that are quietly sabotaging your face. And there is good news here: With a little strategy and a small investment, you can still show up looking like the sharpest person on the Zoom grid.

Ring lights are Big Macs

Ring lights are the fast food of the lighting world: cheap, convenient, wildly popular, and not always great for you. They were designed to throw even light on a subject and they have been adopted by everyone from middle managers to TikTokers.

At their best, they provide a flattering, shadow-free glow that makes your face look smooth and evenly lit. That's the case here in this photo courtesy of Kensington, one of the more ambitious suppliers of ring lights:

The better rings are LED-based, USB-powered, and lightweight—in other words, perfect for traveling presenters and those in confined spaces.

At their worst, however, they create a washed-out, overexposed effect with small circles of doom reflected in your pupils—or worse, in your glasses. They're often placed too close to the face, which can flatten your features and make you look like you're about to issue a ransom demand.

Combination webcam/rings are the worst of the worst, usually pairing a low-resolution camera with a high-brightness light that is firing at you from the exact wrong position. Remember, you want your key light to be somewhere between 30 and 45 degrees off-center, so any light that is connected to the camera starts off as an epic fail.

Here's how to make a ring light work for you:

Pull it back: Position the light at least an arm's length away. Don't let it eat your face.

Dim it down: If your skin is glowing, it's too bright. Any light that costs more than $10 will likely let you vary its intensity.

Raise it up: Position the light slightly above eye level to reduce glare and avoid lighting up your nostrils like a haunted house.

And of course, don't make it your only light—use a fill light, too, if you are able. Ring lights aren't great at adding depth or dimension because they are one-note performers. But they are not inherently bad; they are just often misused. In the right setup—with fill light, ambient support, or natural daylight—they can do the job.

Logitech and the aforementioned Kensington both make quality ring lights. Look to spend at least $50 on one that can change its temperature and brightness.

Softboxes: the silent lighting pros

If you've never heard of a softbox, you're not alone—and that's kind of the point. Softboxes don't scream for attention like ring lights; they just quietly do the job better.

A softbox is a fabric-covered frame that sits in front of the light, serving to diffuse it. It takes a strong light source and softens it, spreading it out evenly and reducing harsh shadows. The result is a more natural, dimensional look that evens out your features without flattening them.

Pros love them because they create diffused yet directional light: soft enough to flatter, strong enough to shape. And unlike a ring light, a softbox doesn't just blast light from dead center. You place it slightly off to the side, as you should with any key light, and that helps provide depth and dimension to your face. And with their diffused light, they don't reflect in eyeglasses nearly as much as ring lights do.

If you want to elevate your lighting setup without diving into full studio mode, a softbox is the move. They come in tabletop, floor-standing, and collapsible travel styles. While you could spend as little as $30 and as much as $3,000 for softbox lights, the sweet spot for is probably in the $75 - 150 range. Search Amazon for NEEWER, Godox, or GVM products and you will be good to go.

My Elgato panel lights

Sitting a level above softbox lights are LED panels, and let me not be shy about my favorites. From the folks who bring you the way-cool Stream Deck, Elgato offers the Key Light (1) and Key Light Neo (2), two edge-lit LED lights that provide soft, even illumination without the bulky softbox.

These lights are fully programmable in terms of temperature and brightness, and they can be app- or software-driven. That means that you can work them from your smartphone or your PC if you want to, the latter meaning that you can program them into your Stream Deck. On mine, I have dedicated buttons for turning my lights on and off and lowering or raising the intensity. I like that. Actually, I loooove that (said from the deepest part of my register).

The larger Key Light costs about $175 and the smaller Key Light Neo about $90. These great investments enhanced the efficiency of my studio.

Trouble overhead: the tyranny of fluorescent ceiling lights

If lighting were a villain, overhead fluorescents would be the Darth Vader of illumination. The dark force of light. Always present, constantly buzzing, and continuously making you look worse, not better.

Fluorescents are the default lighting in many offices, schools, and basements across the world. They cast a cold, top-down glare that emphasizes eye bags and deep facial crevasses, and generally makes your skin tone look more like printer toner.

The worst part is that you often can't escape them—if you are in an office or a rented space, that ceiling light is just there, humming along and sabotaging your visual presence.

So what can you do? For starters, do whatever you can to turn off or cover up all ceiling lights. There is a long history at the Presentation Summit of my losing patience waiting for hotel AV staff and climbing up chairs and tables to reach unwanted ceiling bulbs. I unscrew them if I can and duct tape over them if I have to. (Convention services manager: "You can't be up there." Me: "If your people arrived 30 minutes ago when I asked for them, I wouldn't have to be up here!")

If you can't disable them, you will have to overpower them, with healthy key and fill lights right at face level. If all else fails, try repositioning your camera to minimize how directly ceiling light hits your face.

Rx for eyeglass wearers

One of the most nagging issues with lighting is how to light up your face but not your corrective glasses. Here are some things to try in order of simplest to more aggressive:

Work your angles: Heed the advice already given and make sure that your lights are not close to the camera, as head-on illumination is toxic for eyeglasses. Set your key and fill lights at least 30 degrees off angle from the camera.

Raise them: If you are still getting unwanted reflections, raise your lights about a foot higher than your head. That will redirect the reflection, hopefully away from your camera angle. Don't overdo this, as you would then risk creating weird shadows from your eye sockets, your nose, and jowls.

Check your monitor: It's not just your studio lights that could be doing you in; it could be anything that emits, and as I have noted, direct light is the main culprit. If your computer monitor is near the camera, it could be reflecting on your glasses. And this could be worse, as now it is not just general light reflecting back, but elements of your screen display. (I was once in a virtual audience where we could plainly see the script from which a presenter was reading, reflecting off of her glasses. Ouch.) If relocating your monitor is not an option, try dimming the screen or switching to "dark mode," which both Windows and MacOS offer.

It would be bad form for me to suggest that you remove your glasses when presenting. That would be inauthentic and I want you to be you anytime that you are on camera.

That said, if your correction is not too bad (i.e. you can see okay without them), you could get another pair of your favorite frames but not place lenses in them. Perhaps that's too drastic—try the other things first—but I like that advice better than suggesting you remove them.

The wonder of the window

Few elements of lighting—really, of virtual presenting in general—are met with more negative sentiment than the use of a window in one's virtual studio. And in this section, I am going to go decidedly against conventional wisdom on the subject.

But let's start with two proclamations that just about everyone would agree with when it comes to windows:

Natural light is great light: If you can use a window as part of your key or fill lighting, that would be awesome. Because daylight changes (clouds, sun, morning, sunset, etc.), you can't count on your window to provide even and consistent lighting, so you will need to be ready to supplement, and you will want your supplemental light to be close to 5,600 K (the temperature of daylight). In general, if you can light up your face with natural light, you are ahead of the game.

Get out the blanket: If you are using a green screen, a window does you no good at all and, in fact, could adversely affect the way your virtual background appears. For your purposes, you want black-out curtains or the largest and heaviest blanket you can find.

This is very much *not* how I use the window in my studio. You have seen it countless times across 19 chapters here and I wonder if you noticed.

In my studio, I do what everyone says not to do: I choose to place my window in my set. I place it behind me, where everyone can see it and where its light becomes part of my lighting scheme. And if you Google search "should you put a window behind you in your studio," you will get thousands of hits, including one that tells you:

Never put a window behind you, because it will make your space look dark and uninviting...keep the light on your face, not behind it.

Well. I do exactly that, and I suspect you never noticed it because my lighting looks pretty darn good, if I do say so myself.

So let's talk this through. It is certainly the case that you do not want a whole bunch of uncontrolled light bombarding you from the back, lighting up the back of your head. That would create a massive exposure mismatch, your camera would try to compensate, and you would be cast in a deep silhouette as if you were appearing in a murder mystery. This would be bad under any circumstance.

The critical word in that previous paragraph is *uncontrolled*. You want control of all three points of your lighting setup and a window out to the big, beautiful, uncontrolled outside world would rarely give it to you.

But I control my outside light. Pun intended, I tint the living daylights out of it. I have that window covered with two layers of dark tint—the kind that you might use on your car windows, only darker. (I don't recall the brand, but it was from Amazon and it was not expensive.) This brings tremendous consistency to the light entering the room and that makes it perfect for backlighting. I actually go one step further and have a mirror on

Chp 19 Lighting 101

the opposite side of the room, so all of that outdoor light backfills me from both sides. Using natural light in this intentional way provides two benefits:

- It brings tremendous depth to my set and serves to separate me from my background much better than a studio light behind me.

- More important, it lets my audience see me in my natural habitat, which I pursue with almost obsessive zeal. I want people to be able to visualize me in this room, in my house, and maybe even say to themselves, "hey, that's his real backyard behind him there, and wow, it sure is windy there today." I want all of that.

If you want to pursue this same course of action, consider these factors:

Tint like crazy: It bears repeating, you need dark tint on those windows to flatten and even out the incoming light.

Strong front lighting: Don't go soft with your front lights, as they will both need to work overtime. You want bright, even, consistent lighting in front of you.

Here comes the sun: No amount of tinting will compensate for sunrise or sunset shining right into your window. In my case, the 9:00am summertime sun creates an explosion of light behind me that lasts about 20 minutes. I avoid it when I can and embrace it when I have to. Judge for yourself with this pic and video snippet:

Morning challenges
A window in my background creates a 20-minute distraction during summer months. Are my key and fill lights able to compensate? You be the judge...

Nighttime is eerie: While I have done it, I do not make a habit of presenting after dark. That window becomes really dark, and it provides a level of false drama that I neither want nor appreciate. Here I am in 2024 holding an open house the evening before the conference was to officially begin:

Evening challenges
I generally don't broadcast after sundown, where my background becomes a bit dark and mysterious.

In studying this snapshot from the video (for really the first time), I can now see the impact on the mirror opposite the window that fills my face more than I had realized. If I were to do more night shooting, I would want to compensate for that with more fill light on that side of my face.

I am not trying to convince you to present with a window behind you; I just don't want you to shy away from it because of advice you might have heard to its contrary. I love my setup and I owe much of that to my window (and to daughter Jamie for not having a cow when I stole her childhood bedroom). My face stays lighted and balanced, the cameras see depth, not chaos, and the natural light gives my frame texture and natural glow, not silhouetted drama.

Lighting across skin tones

Lighting is not neutral. It is a tool that interacts differently with different skin tones—and if you're listening to general advice, you might be introducing a cultural bias that could do you a disservice and produce uneven or inaccurate results. I'm guilty of this right here and right now, as most of this chapter assumes light-skinned individuals sitting in these theoretical studios we have created.

So let's right this wrong. Darker skin tones generally reflect less light than lighter ones. Dark-skinned people should consider the following configuration to get the most out of their lighting setups:

Use stronger fill light: It's not about blasting your face with brightness—it's about adding soft, even light that brings out dimension and detail.

Avoid cool lighting: The blueish tint of unusually cool light can make dark skin look flat or ashy. Stick to warmer color temps, and while the sweet spot of 5,600 K is still a good call, err on the side of warmer, not colder.

Test with your own face: Your goal is to light yourself in a way that feels accurate and intentional, not washed out or lost in shadow. The only way to get there is by dialing it in, testing it out, and trusting your own screen, not someone else's tutorial. Including this one!

◆

Lighting is not magic—it's physics with a soul. It's science with taste. You don't need a studio, a budget, or a film crew to look great on camera. You just need to understand what light is doing to your face, your background, and your presence—and then take control of it. Whether you're working with a softbox, a window, or the world's most annoying overhead fluorescent, small changes can have a big impact. Command your light and you command how people see you.

Real Rooms, Fake Rooms, and Chroma Dreams

When you show up on camera, you don't just bring your face, and that can be good or bad. Ideally, you *want* to be bringing your entire space; you want to say to your audience, "This is who I am and this is where I am." And whether that space is a real room, a virtual scene from a dropdown menu, or a digital dream keyed onto a green screen, it becomes part of how you are seen. It shapes first impressions. It sends signals about who you are and what you value.

But many do not think much about what's behind them, and that is to their peril. They go with whatever is there, or they blur the mess, or they click on a nice scene from a menu of scenes and call it a day. But your background is never just scenery; it's a layer of communication. It's part of your story.

In this chapter, we'll look at the three most common choices presenters make for their backgrounds: the real room, the virtual substitute, and the fully engineered green screen composite. And we'll ponder the deeper truths each one reveals about how we choose to show up.

Chp 20 Real Rooms, Fake Rooms, and Chroma Dreams

Viewers notice what you don't

You may stop noticing the clutter behind you, the shadows across your face, or the webcam angle that turns you into a floating head. But for your audience, it might be all they see. They notice everything:

- The ceiling fan spinning behind your head
- The pile of laundry on the chair
- The unflattering up-the-nose camera angle
- The over-designed virtual background that's eating your ear

When your background aligns with your message, you gain credibility without even trying. And the three main options—a real background, a virtual background, or a green screen composite—might all have their place. But they are not created equal—not even close. Each one sends a different signal, and each one requires a different level of effort, technical skill, and risk tolerance.

So let's break them down.

The real background: human, credible, and maybe messy

The real background is exactly what it sounds like: your actual physical space, captured live on camera, exactly how it looks behind you. It might be a bookshelf or other trappings of a home office. Maybe the corner of your living room, or a wall displaying artwork or plants.

Done well, a real background communicates humanity, approachability, and authenticity. In my case, as I have shared with you numerous times, I want it to say: "This is me. This is my space. And this is what I look like in my space." I want it to convey that I am not hiding anything. I am grounded, I am present, I am real.

That doesn't need to be your motivation; there are plenty of other reasons to go with reality. You might want to reveal a bit about what drives you or what excites you, either quality readily accomplished by a strategically placed item. A musical instrument, a replica of the Starship Enterprise, a Michael Jordan jersey, or a selfie of you and Sarah Jessica Parker.

But there's a caveat: A real background demands much higher attention to detail than a virtual background, as your audience members take your cue on this and say to themselves, consciously or not, "Let's see what this person is all about, what she chooses to say about herself."

If you are going to show your real environment, you have to take responsibility for how it looks:

- Is it clean?
- Is it visually balanced?
- Is there good lighting?
- Is anything behind you competing for attention?

This doesn't mean it has to be perfect. A little warmth, a little imperfection, can actually add to your credibility. Just don't confuse "authentic" with "unintentional." I learned this the hard way with an earlier iteration of the objects on my bookshelf, and it was an audience member who called me on this when he wrote in the chat, "It's a bit distracting that there is this gigantic 'SUCK' behind Rick's shoulder." Busted:

Beware of unintentional dysphemisms
And here I thought I was just promoting my book…

Writing this chapter compelled me to do what I should have done some time ago: analyze and scrutinize the elements of my current background. I see a mix of books that hold meaning for me, various photos of loved ones, and a few pieces of sports paraphernalia. That all makes sense.

Chp 20 Real Rooms, Fake Rooms, and Chroma Dreams

You might notice that the "Sucks" book, just above my left thumb, is now much less conspicuous. I also see a few action items:

- The photo closest to my left shoulder needs to be angled inward as it is picking up too much reflected light from the window.
- There is a spiral-bound book on the lowest shelf that is beginning to sag a bit.
- In general, that entire lower shelf needs to be cleaned up. I think those binders are actually tax records...yikes.

The thing I notice most is the soft focus I have intentionally applied to the background. I can do this because of the camera that I use, the Sony a5100 that I discuss on Page 172. Like most mirrorless or DSLR cameras, it gives me control over *depth of field*—the area that appears in focus.

Without mansplaining this too much, depth of field is controlled by two things: the focal length (how zoomed in or out I set the lens), and the aperture (how wide or how squinty I ask the lens to be). The more zoomed in the lens is and the wider the aperture is, the narrower the depth of field becomes. That means when the camera is focused on me, the area behind me will not be as sharp; it will be soft focused. This is precisely what I want for my background.

As I review the image, I find myself wanting the background even softer. I could open the aperture wider, but that risks letting in too much light and overexposing the shot. I could also zoom in more to soften the background, but that would mean a tighter frame on my face, which I don't want (I want to allow room to gesture).

So this becomes a dance that I perform to balance these competing factors, and I am grateful for a camera that allows me to even attempt this. Built-in laptop cameras and simple webcams are not capable of manipulating light and focus in this way.

The virtual background: Your shortcut is showing

The virtual background is a tempting option for most people because it is so easy. You click a button and suddenly you're in a trendy office, a slick studio, or a minimalist white void. What's not to love?

Plenty, as it turns out. More often than not, virtual backgrounds without a green screen are a visual liability. They promise professionalism, but they often deliver distraction. Blurry ears, disappearing shoulders, ghostly outlines around your body. And if you gesture? Good luck keeping your hands attached to your arms and wrists. When this happens, people no longer hear you—they wonder what's wrong with your software. Or with you.

That said, prior to this chapter, I could scarcely call myself an authority on the subject of virtual backgrounds, because I had literally never utilized one. I have borne witness to plenty of people becoming disembodied on virtual backgrounds, but I needed to walk the walk. So I ventured into my studio and commanded Zoom to place me in front of an office space that looks way cooler than my own.

Not bad on first blush. I fit fine in the shot, I could still use all of my upper torso, and my lighting was solid. Then I actually tried doing something with my body, and that's when seams began to show.

A slight movement of my head created a subtle glow around my dome that looked distinctly unnatural. I could live with that, but then I started moving with intention and that is when I really got into trouble. Big wide upper-body gestures required too much arm speed and the virtual engine could not keep up. So instead of moving cleanly into my gesture, I kind of melted up into it, as if I was pouring pancake syrup upside-down.

Also problematic were my signature moves, like moving my hands toward the camera to emphasize a point. Watch and judge for yourself in this extended video, demonstrating virtual background experiments, with and without a green screen:

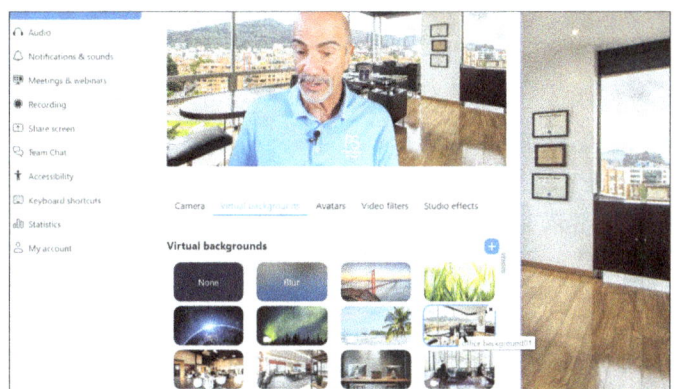

Let me say at this point that these results are a marked improvement from what Zoom offered us just two years ago. In 2023, virtualizing a background was just an amateurish joke, whose main contribution to a live event was enabling you to paint moustaches and fake eyebrows onto yourself. Here in 2025, it is much better.

But it's still not good enough, in my view. First, it is still unreliable technology, subject to every incessant Zoom upgrade that seems to impose itself upon us every other day.

More important, it is just not associated with professional presenting. Nobody is ever going to say, "Wow, look at that great virtual background—he must be a pro." They might think you are a pro *despite* your use of a virtual background, so by just about any measure, the virtual background should be your last choice.

In a pinch

There are a few scenarios in which virtual backgrounds could work for you, the most likely being if you are traveling and you have been asked to present on short notice. If your only choice is a virtual background or your bad hotel room background, perhaps virtual is the better call. In which case:

- Choose an office scene, not the shores of Maui or some other nonsense that is obviously fake. The website Pexels.com offers free office-based virtual backgrounds.

- Find an image that is soft focused or run the pic into an image editor and apply a modest *Gaussian blur* to it. That will make it less noticeable and hopefully less distracting.

- Make sure to nail your lighting, as discussed in the previous chapter. All of that advice goes double for the use of virtual backgrounds.

- Resist grand gestures, long hand sweeps, or rapid head movements, as they might disembody you.

That last piece of advice is particularly painful for me to offer, given how many pages and how many chapters this book has devoted to trying to bring out your most animated and most energetic self. Virtual backgrounds discourage all of that.

A pox on the blur

In light of all of these caveats, you might be tempted to choose Zoom's Blur My Background option instead. This does exactly what it purports to do, sending your actual background into a level of blur that makes it unrecognizable.

Blurring your background might be the worst choice of all. You tell your audience that not only do you not want to show them your real

surroundings, but you can't even be bothered to find a fake one. Instead, you choose to put yourself into some bizarre pseudo non-reality in which you are completely detached from anything even remotely resembling a real scene.

> 🔊 This advice is for presenters leading webinars. If you want to use a virtual background as an audience member, to conceal a messy room, that's no problem. Audience members should not be held to the same standard.

The green screen: a fake that feels real

Let's start with a semantic dilemma. I draw a sharp distinction between the last section and this one focusing on the employment of a green screen. Yet they both fall under the umbrella of "virtual backgrounds." They both involve replacing your real environment with something else. The difference is in how that replacement is achieved:

Software-only virtual background: The software tries to guess where you end and where your background begins, without physical reference points. It's like asking a person with a shaky hand to trace around your silhouette.

Green screen background: The software knows exactly what to remove, because you've given it a clean, consistent color to key out. It's like giving that same person a stencil and saying, "Just cut here."

Green screening is an order of magnitude more effective than a software-only virtual background: more precise, more stable, and less distracting. It is still fake, but it is more convincing and you project as intentional.

How it works

At its core, green screening is a visual effect that tells your software to make one specific color invisible. Once invisible, that space becomes transparent, and anything you place there—an image, a video, a slide deck—becomes your new background. The software is essentially performing a live cutout of your body and layering it over whatever scene you choose.

Green screening is also referred to more technically as *chroma keying*. Chroma refers to color and keying is the process of isolating a specific element in an image or video. It selects a specific color value (the chroma) and uses it as a key to cut out everything in that color range. The result is a transparent layer in place of the background, allowing you to layer in something else behind the subject.

Why green? It does not appear naturally in human skin tones and it is an unlikely shade to show up in one's wardrobe. Especially the particular shade of green used on screens—a bright limey green. This gives the software a clean, high-contrast value to remove. Blue would also work, but it is easier to avoid green clothing than blue clothing.

Going green

If you want to give green screening a try, the barrier to entry is low. You can find serviceable options at nearly every price point. At the low end are pop-up green screens that attach directly to your chair or sit on a collapsible frame directly behind you. These are affordable, as low as $30, and designed for tight spaces. The tradeoff is limited mobility and tight framing for you.

On the other end of the spectrum are large backdrop systems that need wall-mounted rigs or collapsible stands. These can run $150 to $500, depending on size, material, and portability. With these screens, you get maximum flexibility, better edge control, and the ability to move more freely within the frame.

In the middle ground, you'll find tripod-mounted cloth backdrops, a solid choice for most presenters. These offer more width and height than pop-ups but are still collapsible and relatively easy to store. Expect to spend $75 to $150 for a good-quality setup with decent stands and wrinkle-resistant fabric. I spent $75 for mine, which you will see in the video demonstration referenced earlier and immediately below.

The QR code on the previous page and on Page 201 goes to the same video: an extended demonstration into the use of both types of virtual backgrounds. The green screen segment begins right at the 4:00 mark.

DOs and DON'Ts

Green screens are not a miracle; they need to be done right. When done poorly, they can be nearly as bad as software-only virtuals, pulling attention away from your message. Here are some specifics:

Light it evenly: Your green screen needs soft, consistent lighting across its entire surface—no dark patches, no hot spots, no visible folds. If the software sees multiple shades of green, it won't be as accurate with regard to what to remove and what to keep. That's when you could get flickering edges or ghost limbs. Use diffused lighting if you can, and make sure the screen is as wrinkle-free as you can make it. And because it is not so easy to get a large green screen onto an ironing board, a good buy would be a travel steamer that would enable you to steam out wrinkles while it is mounted.

Back away from the screen: Aim to put at least three feet between you and the green screen. That distance reduces shadows, avoids *color spill* (that green glow that can rim your head or shoulders), and gives the camera better separation between you and the backdrop. Think of it as giving your software room to breathe.

Find the happy medium: I know how popular those pop-up and travel-size greenies are, and if you pick up one, you won't have the luxury of full-body distance. If you try to create too much distance, the screen will fail to fill your shot and now you're in amateur land. So get the screen as far from you as you can—even six inches of extra space will help.

Choose the right chair: Do not pick a chair that rises above your head or is wider than your shoulders. You want it to be invisible, because otherwise the keying process will not distinguish you from the chair and will include it in the visible layer. I suppose you could buy a green chair...

Mind your mic: Likewise, try to avoid a desktop or suspended microphone in the foreground of your shot. Green screens can become confused by them, too. General rule of thumb is to pair a green screen with a lapel mic. Properly sized green screens give you room to roam and lapel mics allow you to roam and be heard.

Mind the scale and scene: Make sure that you plausibly fit into your background so you don't call attention to the fact that you are faking it. If you are the standard two to three feet from your camera, you won't do well with a wide-angle shot of a conference room. Likewise, you don't want to tower over your surroundings. You can always crop the background photo if you need to shrink its perspective, and experienced photoshoppers could add to an image. Also, if the lighting in the background is warm and directional, but your lighting is cool and flat, the illusion could fall apart.

Avoid novelty backgrounds: Yes, you can place yourself in the Oval Office or on a tropical beach. Please don't. If the background pulls focus from you, you've already lost the thread. Aim for environments that feel professional, clean, and supportive of your message, not ones that compete with it. One thing you *can* try is to use a video as a background, available from Adjust Background & Effects on the Video tab during a Zoom session. Click the little upward arrow next to Video. The same admonition is apropos here: Make sure that your background really stays in the background—if you drop yourself on a tropical beach, now your background becomes the foreground and you've blown it.

Know when to stop: Green screening is not a badge of expertise—nobody is going to be impressed with your use of it. A green screen is like a good umpire or official in a big-league sport: When they do their jobs well, you do not notice them. But when they screw up, they become the center of attention and nobody cares about the game for those few minutes that must seem like a lifetime to them.

A great green screen disappears. A bad one becomes your whole presentation. Use one if you are committed to learning the craft or if you think it will help you produce keynote-level visuals. But don't use it just to look cool. Nothing kills cool faster than a presenter in front of a poorly keyed background, floating awkwardly as if they are on a bad sci-fi set.

◆

A clean, well-lit, actual background should serve you 90% of the time. A green screen is great so long as you are committed to doing it well. Go with a software-only virtual background if you have no other alternatives. And avoid Zoom's blurred background like the plague that it is. 💻

Zoom and the Art of Not Losing Your Mind

Let's be magnanimous and state right up front that Zoom is a marvel. It shrank geography, rescued countless conferences, including my own, and kept the world connected when we most needed those connections. And yet, it also drives us absolutely bananas. The platform itself is maddeningly inconsistent, and the people who use it are often driven mad. And when you are the one presenting, it can feel like you're juggling flaming swords in a wind tunnel.

This chapter is not a Zoom-bashing manifesto. Oh, who am I kidding, of course it is! And it's going to feel really good when we all just let it degenerate into a gigantic bitch session.

But it's also a survival guide, a collection of coping strategies for staying grounded while wrestling with a tool that was never really designed for presenters, but which we all now must learn in order to be able to think of ourselves as well-rounded virtual practitioners of our craft.

So we fix what we can and then we bitch about what we can't. Sounds like a winning editorial formula…

The vagaries that are Zoom settings

Zoom has plenty of annoying features—which we will cover here—but equally troublesome is that Zoom never stands still. *Never.* Its development team is constantly tinkering with the interface and rolling out updates faster than you can write a section about them within a chapter of a book. In the summer of 2025, when this passage was first written, Zoom rolled out a new update that moved numerous settings from one part of the interface to another. In so doing, several YouTube tutorials with millions of views (one as recent as four months ago) have been rendered so outdated as to be essentially useless.

Further complicating the task of understanding Zoom's interface is that its settings live in two different places and one of those places has two different ways to get to them:

- Log in to Zoom.com, tap your profile picture, and then tap Settings.

- Open the Zoom Workplace app, tap your pic, and then Settings.

You can also get to this second group of settings from within a meeting if you click the little upward-pointing arrows next to Audio and Video and choose Settings from the bottom of the pop-up menu.

Let's make sure to point out that the desktop app used to be called Zoom, then Zoom Desktop Client, and now Zoom Workplace. Oh, and let's also make sure to say that Zoom.com used to be Zoom.us. And every so often, the .us extension pops up, even in different countries.

♦

As it will be literally impossible to tell you where everything is, it will be much more useful to define the two basic distinctions between the locations and explain why things are where they are.

Zoom.com: admin control and big-picture defaults

If you use your web browser and log in to your Zoom account, the Settings there act as global account settings. It helps to think of the Zoom.com settings as NASA's Mission Control during a spaceflight: It determines what the astronauts are allowed to do and what tools are available to them. If a host disables screen sharing in these web settings, no amount of fiddling in the desktop app will bring it back. If something

Chp 21 Zoom and the Art of Not Losing Your Mind

seems "missing" from your app, it's often because Mission Control turned it off. Here is a simple case in point:

In the previous chapter, I created a video demo about using a movie clip as your virtual background. I showed how to do that in the Video Settings that appear during a Zoom session.

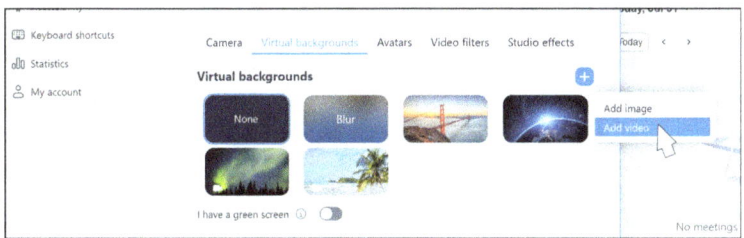

In order to be able to do that, however, you must find the setting that lives at Zoom.com and enable their use.

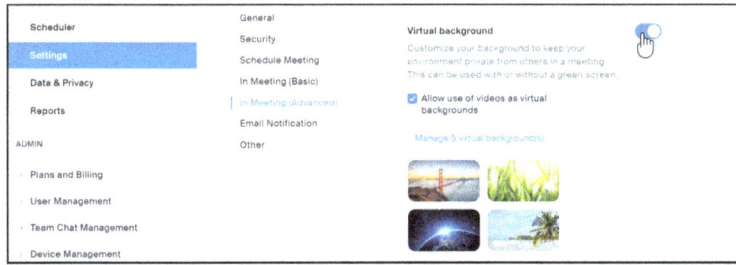

So these "web portal settings" at Zoom.com have the highest level of governance, as they tell the actual Zoom app what it can and cannot do. They control:

- Security defaults (waiting rooms, passcodes, authentication)
- Feature toggles (polls, breakout rooms, whiteboards, avatars)
- Recording settings (cloud/local, auto-record, consent prompts)
- Meeting templates and scheduling defaults
- Advanced audio/video processing
- Global chat settings
- Zoom apps and integrations

These settings are typically for hosts, co-hosts, admins, and power users who want their fingers in everything. You, dear reader, probably qualify to be in at least two of these camps.

Zoom Workplace: your personal flight deck

If the web portal settings are Mission Control, the settings at Zoom Workplace (the desktop client) are more like the flight deck, where the astronauts actually fly the ship. Mission Control determines what systems are installed on the spacecraft and your flight deck controls let you decide how to operate those systems. So if the web settings are global, the Zoom Workplace settings are more local. They shape your personal flight experience and let you decide how you interact with the features that are available to you:

- Audio input/output settings
- Video input and camera settings
- Virtual backgrounds and filters
- Touch up my appearance / adjust for low light
- How chat, reactions, and notifications behave locally
- General UI tweaks (auto-start, minimize to tray, etc.)
- Shortcuts and accessibility options

All of these settings are accessible from within a meeting, although the gateway to them is a bit of a kludge: You head down to Audio or Video, choose the respective Settings choice at the bottom of either menu, and you will find yourself at the Audio or Video section of these client settings.

These settings help audience members tweak the knobs and controls of the Zoom environment. That said, presenters and hosts use them as well, in order to prepare their gear and customize their environment. In general:

Zoom.com (Web)	Zoom App (Desktop)
Global reach	Local capacity
Controls what you can do	Controls how Zoom behaves for you
Admin- and host-level settings	Personal settings and preferences
Enables/disables features	Customizes your experience
Think: backstage controls	Think: front row seat adjustments

Chp 21 Zoom and the Art of Not Losing Your Mind

To reiterate, it would be pointless for me to take you on a tour of the actual settings since they change so often. But it should be helpful to have an idea of *where* to look for something, once you identify a need to change it.

In lieu of said pointless tour, here is a loose collection of issues that strike fear into the hearts of virtual presenters. Some of them have solutions, and some of them are just bitch-worthy.

The inmates run the asylum

Imagine you are leading a presentation before an in-person audience, but instead of looking at you, your audience members are all seated in a circle looking at one another. Now imagine they are all talking among themselves instead of listening to you. Finally, imagine that when you ask them to divide into small groups for an exercise, half of them refuse and some of them get up and walk out of the room entirely.

That's kind of what it's like to lead a Zoom meeting. You want them paying attention to you, you hope they are in Speaker view, you hope they all go into the breakout you want them to. But hope is just about all you have.

The problem

As the host, you are unable to impose any viewing controls on your audience. You can enable and disable certain aspects of the meeting environment, but when it comes to the basic view settings…nope. They can override your every action and wish.

The solution

Most audience members are not intentionally trying to defy you, but when they start to tinker and fiddle with things, they often find themselves in the wilderness. You can help them in two ways:

Spotlight often: When you use the Spotlight function, your audience is automatically switched out of Gallery view and into Speaker view. They can still defy you and switch into Gallery view, but that would be an overt act, not an accidental wandering. Every so often, it's good to retoggle this. My preferred rhythm is once every 30 minutes or so, usually during Q&A, I ask the moderator to switch us into Gallery view. Everyone gets a visual break, and then when we reactivate the Spotlight, that acts upon everyone, including those who might have wandered away, either intentionally or by accident.

Encourage Side-by-Side Speaker View: Introduced in Chapter 12, this is a handy feature when a presenter is screen sharing. It allows audience members to control the relative sizes of the screen window and the presenter window. Granted, the inmates are still running the asylum, but you are encouraging them to choose a better environment and hopefully have a better experience.

◆

The ultimate solution might seem to be Zoom Webinars. This paid add-on is designed for one-to-many broadcasting and the inmates most decidedly do not run the asylum. They cannot turn on their cameras or microphones unless promoted by the host. Interaction is funneled through chat, Q&A, or polls and the Participants panel is not visible.

The Webinars add-on gives the host much tighter control over the experience, which can be useful for larger events or public-facing presentations. It is akin to a lecture hall, where presenters are on and audience members are watching.

While Webinars might seem like a good choice, most presenters I know choose not to use it, and not just because of its additional price tag of $690/year. Most of my colleagues don't want to place such a stranglehold on their audience members. They (we) are willing to give up a level of control in order to have a level of interaction and hopeful engagement.

For all of the bellyaching about seeing Gallery view when we don't want it (see Chapter 12), we would rather not give it up for good.

Screen sharing is a disaster

The problem

The standard way to show your slides to your audience is to share your screen. And when you do, Zoom's interface becomes terribly unfriendly. There are artifacts all over—participants run down the right side and the Zoom controls take up as much as 100 vertical pixels from the top down. This is bad enough when you are just showing slides, but when you are demonstrating software and that software's main menu is obscured by Zoom controls, that is next-generation frustration.

It's not rocket science to fix this, but when an entire audience is watching your every move, it's not a great time to take your eye off the ball, call

Chp 21 Zoom and the Art of Not Losing Your Mind 213

an audible, and go off road. (For those scoring at home, my personal record is mixing four sports metaphors in one sentence).

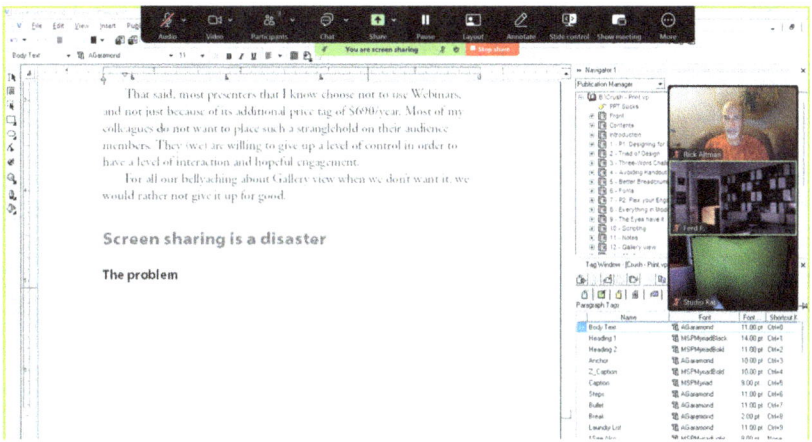

Zooming and writing?
That's a match made in hell, thanks to Zoom's awful screen sharing controls. Fortunately, there are ways to rescue you from this purgatory.

The solutions

The best solution is to invest in a second monitor. That way you can clear all of that junk out of your primary view entirely. And before you declare that solution unfeasible, you should know that buying a second monitor is not the ordeal and the investment that it used to be. There are literally hundreds for sale on Amazon, and if yours is a modern laptop with a USB-C port, there is an excellent chance that it can provide power to the monitor, making the space requirements minimal.

You can choose between dozens under $50, and at the time of this writing, there are a few 7-inch displays selling for $35. I can't speak to the build quality of these cheapies, but you hardly care—you're just looking for a parking place for unwanted Zoom artifacts. Once you grow accustomed to a second screen, you will likely move the Chat there, as well as the Participants panel.

Absent a second monitor, there are two settings that you need to know about, very much not at your fingertips and not easily found in the sweat of the moment. From the now-intrusive Zoom menu, click More, and find the following:

Hide video panel: That will turn off the video tiles invading the right side of your screen.

Hide floating meeting controls: That's the real money shot as it says bye-bye to the Zoom bar along the top. Note the swell keyboard shortcut of Ctrl+Alt+Shift+H.

Once the floating controls are gone, Murphy's Law says you will want them back, and you might not have noticed the fleeting message informing you that Esc restores them. So now you know: Esc brings them back.

♦

Another point to keep in mind is that most of the time, you don't actually need to share their entire screen. If you share just one application window, you recover quite a bit of real estate, making Zoom's land grab a bit less obnoxious. And here's a little-known fact for you: You can share more than one app at a time, just by pressing Ctrl as you choose them. And each app can be sized down, giving you more control over your environment.

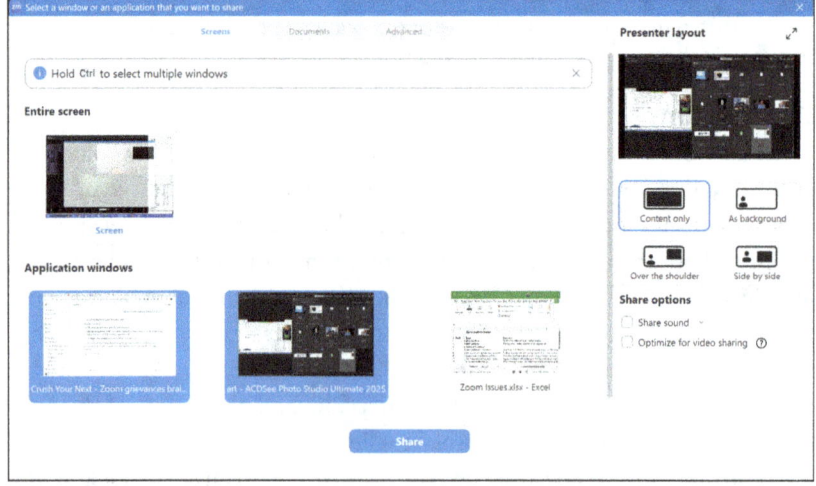

🔊 The interesting controls on the right side of the Sharing screen will be addressed in Chapter 23.

Zoom recordings are actually...good

Nothing to complain about here—if you have not yet had a chance to view the playback of a Zoom recording, that is something you can actually look forward to. Anyone can record a Zoom meeting to their own computer, but the secret sauce is for meeting hosts with Pro, Business, and Enterprise accounts, who can store recordings in Zoom's cloud network. Then you get the VIP treatment of access to: Active speaker view, Gallery view, screenshares, separated audio tracks, closed caption toggle, full chat and transcript, AI summaries, and indexed highlights. And each one of these threads can be downloaded in reasonably high definition (1280 x 720) so you could then piece together entire post-production videos.

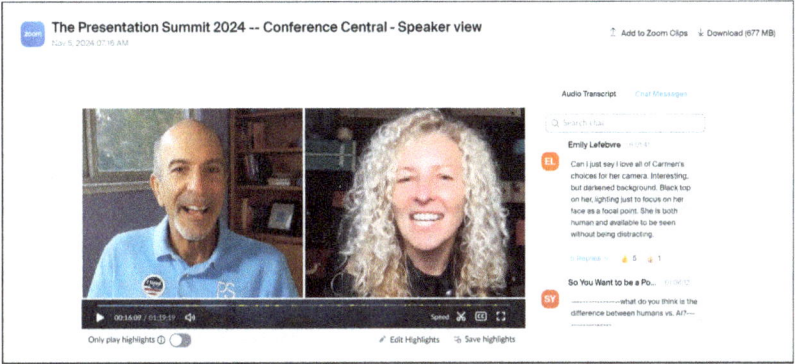

Zoom recordings are a pleasure
Fully indexed, linkable, and downloadable, these videos provide a complete narrative of a meeting.

These recordings can be found at Zoom.com from the left sidebar of tools and resources under Recordings & Transcripts. At least as of August 2025. Who knows where it will be by the time you read this! Cynicism aside, Zoom Recordings are indicative of how capable the development team can be when provided a clear vision for implementation.

Audio is a total mystery

If you were to Google search the phrase "how to improve audio in Zoom," you would find thousands of articles and hundreds of videos, all claiming to offer authoritative advice. If you listen to three or four of them, you will receive such contradictory advice, you will wonder how anyone is able to speak on Zoom at all. After listening to more than my share of tutorials, after experimenting in my own studio, and after discussions with several people who know more about this than I ever will, I am ready to make the following recommendations:

- If it ain't broke don't fix it.

- It is rarely the right idea to compress audio.
- The stuff that is good for musicians is also good for presenters.
- Most of the default audio settings suck.
- Using better settings is a PITA.

If Zoom ain't broke, perhaps you can stop reading now. If you are satisfied with the sound quality of your webinars, streams, and recordings, you can skim over what is about to be a fairly arcane discussion of the inner workings of audio.

Welcome to the lowest common denominator

Zoom became prominent when it found itself in the enviable position of supplying primary communication to nearly the entire modern world, this of course being back in 2020. With most of those people using built-in microphones and whatever passed for serviceable WiFi, Zoom's engineers concluded, correctly, that it needed to make sure that people could hear one another. All other considerations became secondary.

> All of the settings to be explored here are located in the "flight deck," not at "Mission Control." In other words, they can be found in the desktop settings of the Zoom Workplace app. From the app, click your profile photo, choose Settings, and find Audio, third choice down on the left sidebar. (I hope; at least that's where it was in Sep 2025.)

The scourge of audio compression

When all of the civilized world flooded the Internet to stay connected during Covid, audio compression was a good thing. For virtual presenters, it is a bad thing. Unless you have very weak WiFi...in which case you have bigger issues than compression. Audio compression comes in several flavors and it involves a search-and-destroy mission to root them all out.

A walking audio tour

Remember when I said that we won't just be mindlessly walking through pages of settings? This will be the one exception, as we want to discuss most of the options in this dialog box and offer a consensus of recommendations from audio experts.

Chp 21 Zoom and the Art of Not Losing Your Mind

Microphone: Make sure that the microphone you choose has its volume set so that your loudest words send the meter about 3/4 of the way to the max on the right.

Auto-adjust volume: Disable this. You do not want Zoom messing with your stage whispers or your strategic rises in volume.

Audio profile: Choose "Original sound for musicians," even if you are not a musician. Then go On, Off, On for the three choices below that. High fidelity is always a good thing, echo cancellation is rarely a good thing, and stereo is better than mono.

Advanced: These settings require one additional click on an Advanced button (not shown here), where you get to address echo cancellation yet again (low is the lowest choice here), disable Windows enhancements (they're just more compression), and the mysterious Signal processing by Windows that nobody seems to know about. Experiment with this on your own, if you are so inclined.

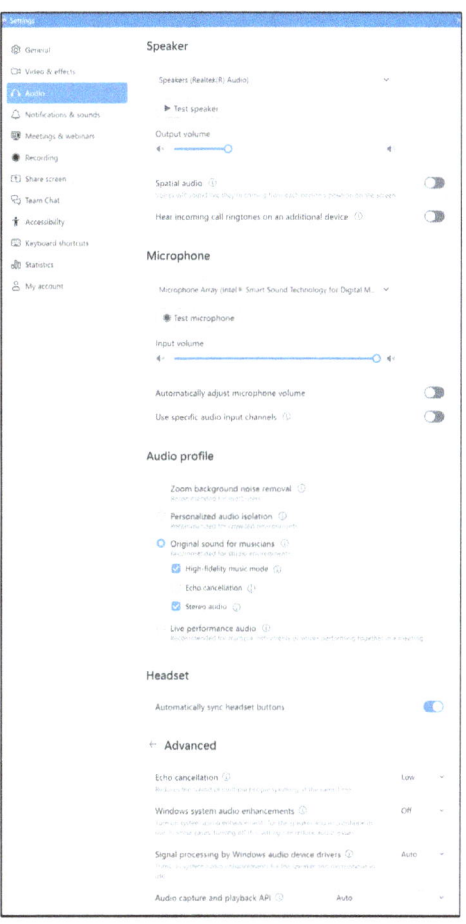

Original sound is hard to come by

You would think that enabling the Original sound option would get you the elusive *original sound*. Alas, it is only a permission structure. Once in a Zoom session, you will now see a status line at the top:

Original sound for musicians: off

It is not at all apparent that you are supposed to click that line to activate Original sound, and once you do, the only clue that you did anything is that the off turns to on. But that is your gateway to what many audio engineers say is the most important change you can make to your audio setup.

Your mileage might vary. It's possible that the best advice here is the first one that I offered: *If it ain't broke, don't fix it.* But it is worth your while to experiment with these settings, in search of your own holy grail of sound.

Record separate streams

If you regularly record interviews, podcasts, or any other production that involves more than one voice, you would do well to make one additional deep dive: Desktop Settings | Recording | Advanced. There you will find the choice "Record separate participant audio files." Turn that on and now if someone coughs, barfs, or does anything that would not make for good radio, it will be easy for you to filter it out. You will be downloading multiple audio files, one for each voice in the recording, but that is a small price to pay for this capability.

The elusive Chat

One of the most important parts of a vibrant meeting is the secondary experience of audience members conversing with themselves. In healthy communities, the Chat is full of questions and answers, often supplied fully by the audience. It becomes a vital aspect of a meeting's flavor.

And if you're not careful, that Chat disappears entirely when a meeting ends. No backup, no recovery, just gone forever. Now *that* is bitch-worthy.

Who can save the Chat?

The host of any meeting can ensure that the Chat is saved. That setting lives in the "Mission Control" grouping of settings at the Zoom.com web portal settings, and at the moment, it can be found under Settings | In

Meeting (Basic) | Meeting chat - Auto-save. Once enabled, a copy of the Chat will always be saved to the host's local computer once the meeting ends.

Assuming that setting is in place, presumably the host can share the Chat with audience members. But that is a lot of assuming and presuming. If the host fails to do that, what can you do as a member of the audience?

Audience members can save the Chat, too. It's a simple matter of opening the Chat window, clicking the three dots top-right, and choosing Save chat.

But what if you forget? What then??

The trick here is to own and operate a keystroke macro program. These apps sit above all others and are capable of sending keystrokes to any one of them. If you can get into the habit of ending your meetings by running a macro, you can ensure that you will always save the Chat.

I like Macro Express Pro, but just about any decent macro program will be capable of sending the following keystrokes to Zoom:

1. Alt+H to open the Chat window.

2. Four tabs to send the focus to the three-dot menu.

3. Space bar to drop down the menu.

4. Down-arrow and Enter to save the Chat.

5. Alt+Q to invoke the End Meeting command.

6. At your discretion, you could include a final Enter to actually leave the meeting or make that a manual click.

The only requirement for a macro like this to work is to be able to control the state of the Chat window; i.e. it needs to be closed so that the initial Alt+H toggle actually opens it instead of closes it.

Zoom Clips

I had never heard of this interesting feature before rummaging through the bowels of Zoom for this chapter. From the Zoom desktop app (the flight deck, not Mission Control), you will find Clips as one of the choices down the left side. From there, you can make a recording that will look much like a standard Zoom stream. You can name it, describe it, perform simple editing, and share it like a YouTube video, where your visitors can comment on it and you can comment back.

You can record just yourself, just your screen, or a combination of the two. You can share just an app, or your entire desktop, and as I learned on the job, you can size your video window if you are sharing your entire screen, but for reasons unknown, you remain a postage stamp if you place yourself next to a single app.

Here is the video clip I created. It included several false starts, and more notable, a few discoveries after the fact. Therefore, I was grateful for being able to splice two videos together to make one. This one was comprised of three separate videos.

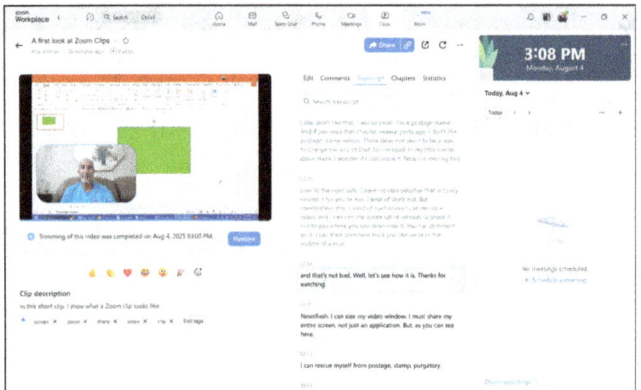

I'm not sure how often I will have this need, as I produce most of my videos in my studio. But if I'm on the road and need to whip something together, a Zoom clip is a viable option.

A fresh look at Whiteboards

I have known about the Whiteboard feature for some time now and figured that I would never use it, given that I cannot draw my way out of a dump truck. The few times that I have tried it—inevitably humoring some overbearing host of a social Zoom call—I have flat out embarrassed myself.

But now it's different. Mind you, I can still embarrass myself quite capably, but there are other, non-drawy things that you can do with Whiteboards. Its robust import engine enables you to integrate your (my) chicken scratching with just about any file type imaginable.

And in the perfect moment of synergy, one of the things you can import to a whiteboard is a Zoom clip:

Chp 21 Zoom and the Art of Not Losing Your Mind

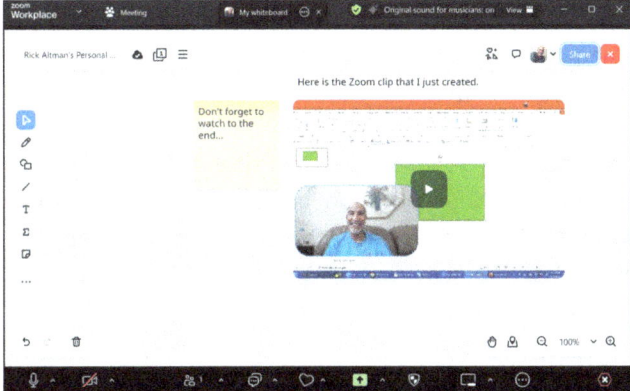

Whiteboards are shareable—the QR code here will take you to it. And once there, you can view the video, comment on it, and draw all over my whiteboard, if you so choose.

♦

Zoom offers other useful tools that people often overlook, but I will leave those discoveries for the person who chooses to write an entire book on Zoom, not just a chapter. And besides, we need to allow time and space for the Zoom Bitchfest, commencing forthwith...

Now let's just bitch

Here we go, all the things that we hate about Zoom that we have no idea how to fix. Or we had an idea, but then the developers changed the interface without telling us. Or maybe we actually did fix it once but then Zoom broke it again. Or maybe we just prefer to complain about it. This is our guilty pleasure for any or all of those scenarios.

Go here first

As mentioned earlier, settings are stored in two different places, and even though we sort of explained it to you, you are well within your rights to bitch about it. Because doesn't it steam you when you know exactly where a function is within Zoom, but first you have to go out to the web, log in, and then hunt around for 10 minutes before finding the thing that enables the function, so you can then go back to Zoom and operate it?

Bitchometer level: 6.5 (out of 10)

Breakout room chaos

It's like Zoom throws everyone into a large Hefty bag, shakes it, and hopes for the best. Someone usually ends up alone in their own room, someone else gets dropped into a group where they don't belong, and at least one person reappears in the main session looking like they just woke up in a Vegas hotel suite with a tiger in the bathroom and no memory of how any of that happened. A capable host can bring order to this chaos, but hosts with that skill set are like an endangered species.

Bitchometer level: 8.2

Everyone's on a different version

Zoom updates so often, nobody can keep up. Some people have Reactions, others don't. One has the new toolbar layout, another is asking where their mute button went. Polls don't show up for half the room. And someone is always stuck three updates behind, insisting, "That option isn't there for me." It's not a platform, it's a time-travel experiment gone wrong.

My daughter Jamie adds the following bitch to this topic: "The thing that I hate the most is Zoom only forces you to update when you enter a meeting, which then makes you late for that meeting. There have been times where this has become potentially detrimental if it's an important client meeting or new business pitch."

Bitchometer level: 8.6

Time zone confusion in invites

Zoom tries to be helpful by auto-adjusting time zones, which is adorable—until half your attendees show up an hour late, one shows up a day early, and someone in Saskatchewan misses the meeting entirely because they didn't get the memo about Daylight Saving Time. Want to double-check the meeting time? Great—just open your calendar, Zoom, Google, Outlook, a sundial, and possibly an astrolabe (look it up).

Bitchometer level: 7.3

Waiting room purgatory

You're sitting there staring at that polite little message: "Please wait, the meeting host will let you in soon," but you have no real clue if they're running late, you're in the wrong Zoom, or if they forgot that you even exist. Meanwhile, the host is blissfully unaware because Zoom buried the notification somewhere between Chat, Participants, and Reykjavik. It's not a waiting room, it's a digital DMV with bad information and worse lighting.

Bitchometer level: 8.9

Echo/feedback trap

Someone joins on both their laptop and their phone, forgets to mute one, and suddenly the meeting is swallowed up by an earsplitting feedback loop that sounds like a demon being sucked into a lawnmower. Zoom does nothing. Everyone scrambles to find the culprit, while the clueless culprit looks around like "Wow, what's causing that awful noise?" It's beyond feedback; it's an audio exorcism.

Bitchometer level: 9.5

Vanity filters don't expire

You turn on a silly filter for a happy hour—giant sunglasses, bunny ears, maybe the eponymous Mr. Potato Head—and then you forget that you did that. And Zoom doesn't warn you as you continue to look like an emotional support vegetable. You log into Monday's budget meeting still spud-shaped, wondering why everyone's reconsidering your permission to exist unsupervised on the internet.

Bitchometer level: 8.2

Auto-adjustment gone wrong

"Touch up my appearance" sounds like a harmless little glow-up—until Zoom smears your face like Vaseline on a camera lens. "Adjust for low light" tries to help, then bleaches you into a washed-out ghoul with haunted eyes. It's less "virtual meeting" and more true crime reenactment.

Bitchometer level: 7.9

Wanna play a sound? Share your audio!

You queue up the perfect video clip, hit play, and…silence. Zoom just sits there, smugly refusing to play anything audible until you remember the hidden checkbox buried like an Easter egg left by a developer with trust issues. Want your audience to hear anything? Great—just stop sharing, re-share, check the magic box, and try not to look like you've never used a computer before.

Bitchometer level: 9.7

Mute/unmute roulette

Someone delivers a passionate monologue...with their mic off, eliciting the notorious "you're on mute" response. Another decides now is the time to munch on kettle chips, mic fully hot. Meanwhile, the host is frantically scanning the gallery like a substitute teacher during a food fight. Zoom offers no clues, no grace, and absolutely no shame.

And speaking of food, we're all busy, but unless this meeting is catered, maybe save the tuna salad for later? No one wants a front-row seat to your chewing technique; we're just trying to get through the agenda.

Bitchometer level: 9.0

Weird names in the Gallery

"Mom's iPad." "Galaxy S20." "Me." Nothing says professionalism like trying to take questions from someone who identifies as forgotten tech in a grade school lost-and-found. Good luck figuring out if "iPhone (2)" is your guest speaker or a toddler with the mute button.

Bitchometer level: 6.2

And finally...

The wandering webcam

Suddenly we're all on a tour of someone's ceiling fan, hallway carpet, and cat litter box. It's like *Blair Witch Project: Work From Home Edition*.

Bitchometer level: 8.4

Part Five
Be Intentional

By now, it should be clear that this book has been about more than gear and guidance. Beneath the visuals, beyond the vocal tips, and after the tech recommendations, there has been a steady heartbeat: the idea that how you show up on screen is a choice. You've been invited to think more deeply, design more consciously, and present more fully. In that sense, *intentionality* hasn't just arrived at the party, it's been the host all along.

This final part puts intention front and center, and you might have noticed the subtle shift in its name. If the first four parts were about what to get, this part is about what to be. What does it mean to truly choose to be seen? How do you integrate yourself into your content—not just physically, but meaningfully? When does hardware help, and when does it just make more noise? And what happens when artificial intelligence joins the conversation, offering efficient answers and existential questions?

If everything up to now has prepared you for the stage, these final chapters help you take the stage on purpose.

The Choice to be Seen

Going on camera shouldn't be automatic. It should be intentional. Your face is a powerful tool for connection, emotion, and expression. It's also a competing visual element that can draw attention away from your slides or screen content. That makes your camera a spotlight, and spotlights work best when they're not always on.

Being intentional with your video likeness is not always so easy, because Zoom and its brethren *want* you to be seen; their defaults are to always have video active. Instead of blindly accepting that, consider when your presence enhances the moment, and when it might distract. Use your face to highlight the emotional, the personal, the human. And give your visuals the stage when clarity and focus are more important than connection.

Subsequent chapters will take deep dives into how you control your video likeness. This short chapter takes a step back to talk about the if and the when. And the when not.

The bigger picture

Being seen is never neutral; it changes the dynamic of the room, the rhythm of the moment, and the hierarchy of what's on screen. Before you default to video on, consider what being on camera really does, for better and for worse.

The energy exchange

Being on camera changes the environment, for both you and for your audience. Yes, it invites connection, but it also demands energy. Staying "on" the entire time can create fatigue for you and pressure for your audience. Sometimes, a quieter presence is more sustainable.

The visual hierarchy

Your face will always command attention—that's human nature. If you want your audience focused on a chart, a process, or a visual idea, consider whether your face is helping or competing.

This is especially the case with the standard screen share setup on Zoom and the other services, where you become a postage stamp. Now you are sending some weird mixed message, where you are commanding everyone's attention but doing so from a tiny window. Not great.

Hybrid moments

You don't have to be on or off the entire time; the whole point is to become facile with toggling yourself on and off. Let your face punctuate the presentation. Use it for a warm welcome or a heartfelt close. Go dark when showing intricate slides or when your voice alone can carry the moment.

Audience expectations

Context matters. In a team meeting, being on camera might signal presence and participation. In a webinar, the focus might be on your visuals, not your face. Reading the room is next to impossible, but nonetheless, your impossible mission is to discern when your audience would appreciate seeing you or just hearing from you.

Bandwidth and equity

Not everyone experiences virtual platforms the same way. Turning off your camera can be a gesture of inclusion when connection quality is poor or when attendees have limited access. It also respects neurodiversity and camera fatigue: Some people engage more deeply when they're not being watched. In certain communities, camera use can feel intrusive or culturally inappropriate. Sensitivity to these factors can help create a more equitable and comfortable experience for everyone.

Sometimes the most respectful choice is to stay unseen.

You, on purpose

Distilling this short chapter even further, here is a simple cheat sheet for helping you make this determination.

Turn your camera on when:

- You're introducing yourself or welcoming your audience
- You're telling a story or sharing an emotional moment
- You want to build connection and trust

Turn it off when:

- You want full attention on your visuals
- You're walking through complex steps or data
- You're giving your audience time to reflect or absorb

◆

Your face is a spotlight. Use it to illuminate the moments that matter, and turn it off when the spotlight belongs elsewhere. 💻

Showing Up, by Design

This chapter might represent a personal record for the number of times a topic has morphed, been renamed, and relocated. It was originally hatched as part of Part 4, Get Technical, and it is pretty geeky. But choosing how you show yourself to your audience is not just about tech; it is also about strategy, stagecraft, and a bit of philosophy (and each of those words was once a part of its title). I believe the more important aspects of that choice are ephemeral, not technical, and that is why it now lives here with our final theme of intentionality.

Designing your presence means making choices about where and how your audience experiences you. That might involve your popping into a corner of your slides, layering yourself over a demo, taking center stage, or being heard but not seen.

The catch is that these choices often live inside tools, and some of them can be intimidating. We're not here to catalog every menu item or sell you on bells and whistles. We're here to talk about what matters—the pragmatic ways you can use these products to put yourself into the experience without getting lost in the weeds.

Think of this chapter less as a software tutorial and more as a design mindset: how to show up deliberately, instead of just blindly accepting expected protocols of virtual presenting. I want you to be better than that.

The spectrum of presence

When you present virtually, you give up control that your in-person self enjoys, and that will remain true until we can present holographically. That said, the control that you *do* have might surprise you, and that is our first topic here. These are points along a continuum, none being inherently better than others. What matters is knowing what choices you have and making the right one in the right moment. The *why* and *how* come soon; first, the *what*.

1. Full-frame presence

This is you in full flight: a full-screen likeness of you, in your setting, telling your story. This is how most virtual presentations should begin, because you (and not your slides) are the presentation. This promotes the vitality of storytelling. I don't need to show you what this looks like; you have already seen it dozens of times in this book, most recently on Page 199.

Ironically, a full-frame presence is not so easy to create, as the typical setup involves screen share, at which point Zoom and its brethren stuff you into a postage stamp. At a minimum, this demands that you become facile with the quick toggling of Screen Share (Alt+S in Zoom), but we can do better than the minimum here, so stay tuned.

2. Shared frame

A shared frame is one of the most versatile forms of presence, where you and your slides are visible to your audience at once. It comes in myriad forms and there are countless choices on that path. In all cases, the idea is that you and your slides coexist on screen.

I do not believe that this should be standard operating procedure; I believe it should be used sparingly and (wait for it) intentionally. This too is challenging to accomplish, as Zoom relegates you to the corner as soon as you start a screenshare. To combat this, familiarize yourself with Side-by-Side Speaker View, which we discussed back on Page 112.

You can see my preferred method for frame sharing on the next page. I prefer to do this with hardware, not software (see the next chapter), and I do not try for anything fancy—just my video likeness next to my slides.

The accompanying video gives a good sense of when I turn to this, as I switch to this dual view to drive home my core principles for effective presentations (outlined in Chapter 2). When I tell my audience that "this is bedrock principle for me," I want them to see me saying it.

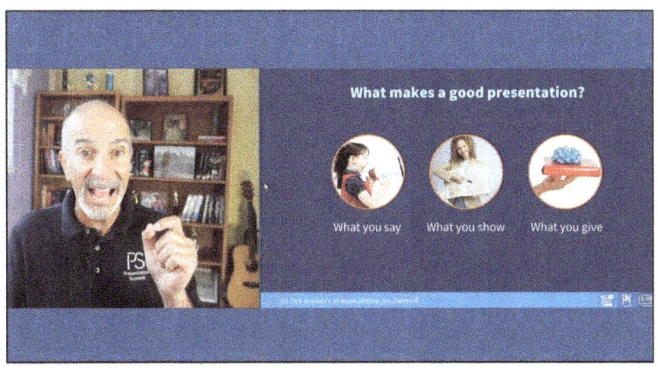

3. Immersive

While shared frames place you alongside your slides, an immersive environment layers you into your slides. Just as if you were forecasting for your television audience the low-pressure system about to bring rain. There are many ways to accomplish this framing, none of them regarded as simple and some of them qualifying as borderline abusive. Here is how I might use it, when discussing how notoriously undertrained PowerPoint users are.

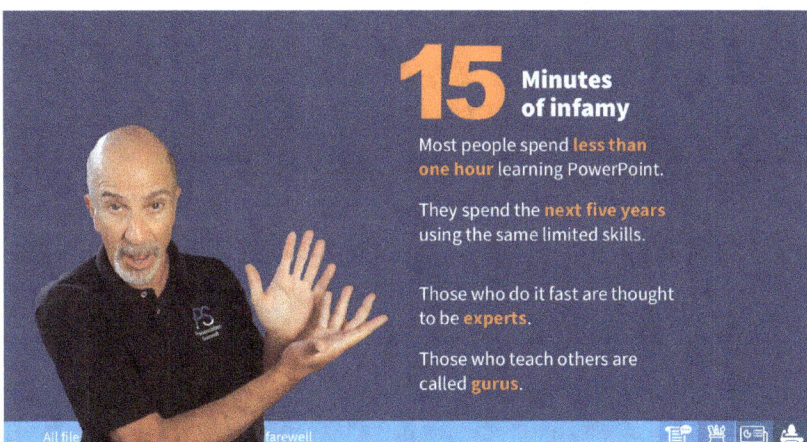

It is impressive technology and therefore prone to overuse by those who want to show off. But when used strategically, it provides powerful opportunities to interact directly with your content. You might appear next to a chart, superimposed over an image, or as with my example, speaking to ideas.

An immersive presence is the most technically demanding option, worthy of its own discussion, which we will have in the next section.

4. Audio-only presence

As straightforward as this one sounds, choosing to not show yourself is often overlooked as a creative choice. And once again, part of the blame goes to Zoom for how inconvenient it is to achieve this with its service. You must share your screen and turn off your video feed, and that is beyond the tinkering threshold that many are willing to undertake.

Nonetheless, there are instances in which your video likeness could be a distraction. Any time that you want your audience to focus on a visual and have your words be the soundtrack, turn off your video!

5. Physical co-location

This virtual framing takes place in the real world, and that sounds like a contradiction. It's virtual in that you stream yourself to your audience, but it's real in that you and your visuals are together in the same physical space. You stand beside your visuals and the camera captures both of you:

I wish I had more opportunities to do this as I find it to be energizing and enabling. The schlep quotient is just a bit too high for me to turn to it regularly, as I must bring a large LED screen onto set, sit it atop some sort of table, and then run HDMI cable to it. So it is a special occasion which I enjoy very much.

Being immersive. Intentionally.

Immersive presence opens a whole set of techniques, from built-in features to professional-grade software. Each has its strengths and quirks, but all share the same goal: bringing you directly into your slides so your audience experiences you and your content as one. The following sections briefly explore the most common paths to getting there.

The simple win that is Microsoft Cameo

Cameo is not immersive in the weathercaster sense. When you use it, you are not layering yourself on top of your slides; rather, you are placed into them as a design element. That said, the built-in function that is part of all current versions of PowerPoint represents the trend toward presentation immersion and it is unquestionably the most accessible method of getting you inside your slides. In fact, it might completely redefine the way you think about your video likeness. That is why I think it belongs in this discussion, even though it does not technically qualify as immersive framing.

Cameo turns your live camera feed into a native object on a PowerPoint slide. Instead of being confined to a separate video window, you become part of the slide canvas itself, just like any other shape you might create. It's not a third-party add-on or a VBA script; it's a design element that lives right inside PowerPoint.

Cameo is simple to use but challenging to master, thanks to the paradigm shift that it represents. On the one hand, you draw it just as you would a rectangle or a text box, and we often refer to them as "Cameo shapes." Once done, you can show your camera through that shape:

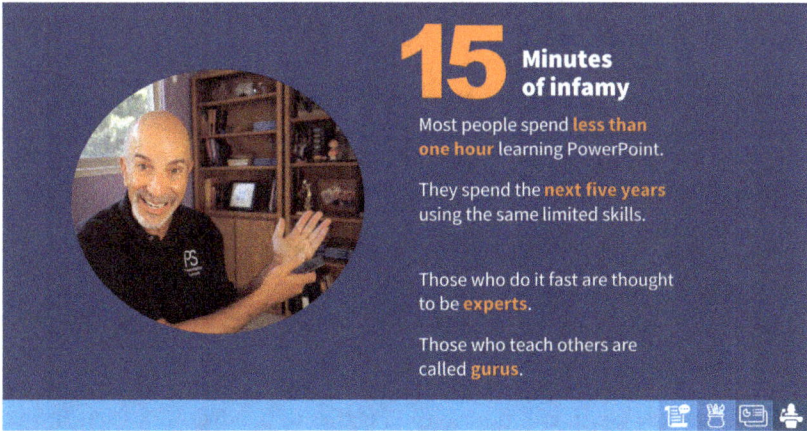

The game-changer
Microsoft Cameo represents a fundamental shift in how we could think about designing our presentation visuals.

On the other hand, placing your video likeness directly onto your slide has profound implications for how you design those slides and then if, when, and how you choose to show yourself. That will take a bit of trial and error.

The other mental hurdle you must overcome is the limitation that when you use Cameo to operate your camera within PowerPoint, you cannot operate it anywhere else. So if you are livestreaming through Zoom or Teams, you must deactivate your camera from those platforms. Therefore, Cameo becomes a screenshare-only experience: You turn off your camera, you share your screen, and you show yourself through your slides.

Cameo deserves an entire chapter, so this book is not going to do it justice. Instead, I want to refer you to a pair of introductory webinars that I led for Training Magazine Network—one in early 2024, when the feature was still new, and one in 2025, when it had matured a bit.

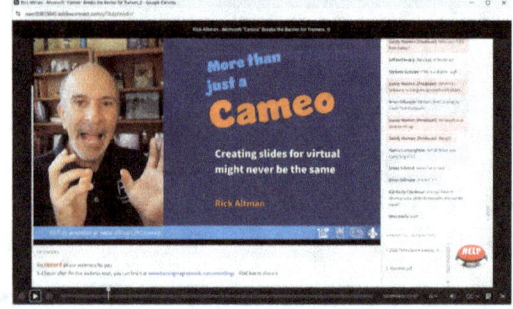

More than just a Cameo
These training videos are free for all to watch. If you have not already, you will need to register with Training Magazine Network, the producers of the videos.

We are still learning about this tool and these videos show a couple of interesting dynamics:

Resource hog: Cameo is demanding on bandwidth and is subject to the day-to-day condition of the Internet. The 2025 video showed significant lag—my video and audio were noticeably out of sync—while the one from a year earlier performed much better.

Streaming roulette: In addition to the vagaries of bandwidth, the streaming services themselves handle Cameo shapes differently. You would expect that Microsoft Teams would shine with Microsoft Cameo, but in my experience, Zoom outperforms Teams consistently. And they both lap Adobe Connect, which earns the dubious distinction of being the lag king.

We are better: The ways in which we presenters use the tool have evolved. I was particularly impressed with my webinar producer who wondered out loud whether I could simulate the famous Jack Nicholson scene in The Shining, and you can see my efforts to that effect in the 2025 video, at about the 12-minute mark.

The biggest question mark that I recognize is adoption: Will virtual presenters see Cameo as more than just a curiosity? Time will tell and I would welcome your thoughts on that.

Studios in a box

We turn our attention now to a family of immersive tools called *compositors*. These virtual studios offer control over layers, scenes, and sources so you can decide exactly how you appear with your content. They vary in complexity—some friendly, others daunting—but they all exist for one reason: to help you design your presence with far more flexibility than PowerPoint or streaming services can offer.

While there are numerous bit players, I focus on the most prominent trio: OBS (Open Broadcaster Software), Airtime (formerly Mmhmm), and Ecamm. Here is what they all have in common:

Many into one: They let you combine multiple sources (camera, slides, media, backgrounds) into a single output feed.

They replace your camera: Instead of Zoom and Teams seeing your webcam directly, they see the composited feed from one of these tools. You choose, say, Airtime as the video source.

Immersive presence: You can frame yourself alongside your content with far more flexibility and creative control than with any streaming platform: video clips, animations, lower-third graphics, backgrounds, and more.

Learning curve: Each sits on a spectrum of complexity.

So in short, they are software-based production studios that empower you to design your presence intentionally rather than being boxed in by Zoom's defaults.

Here is an example of how one of the compositing services could help you create a scene for presenting.

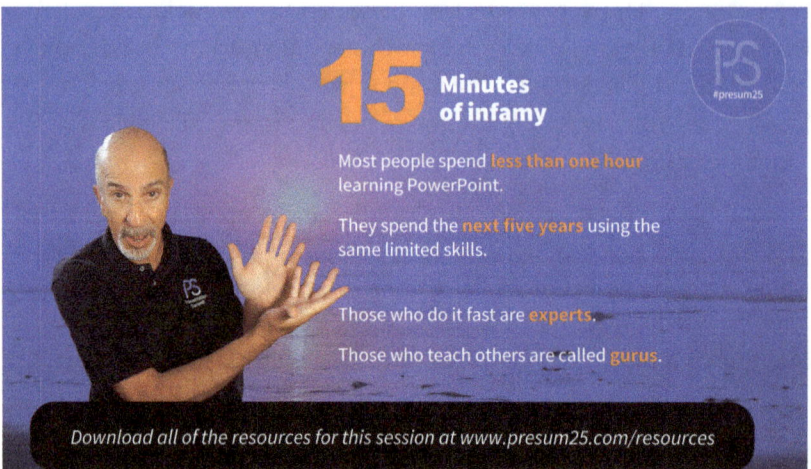

There are several elements to point out, and while each of them could have been created in PowerPoint, producing them as composite layers provides much more flexibility:

Background image: This ocean/sunset scene is tinted way back so there would be sufficient contrast with the foreground elements.

Top-right logo: This graphic (a "bug" in video lingo) is its own layer.

Lower-third graphic: While not quite an actual third of the screen, that is the expression used for calls to action, sponsored messages, instructions to viewers, etc.

The text: PowerPoint-generated content.

Me: Shot in front of a green screen and placed in position in the scene. You won't always arrange your fingers so perfectly to the text, and I had to go frame by frame to stage this pic. In general, obviously, you want your space to be well-defined and distinct from slide content. It's also important to anchor yourself to the bottom of the slide, or in this case, to the lower-third graphic. You don't want to be floating in space.

None of these layers is locked in to the slide content; your PowerPoint slides are just another layer of composition. At any time, you could choose to enable/disable the bug or the lower-third graphic while still showing the slide content.

Here is a table comparing features, cost, and other factors between the three main virtual studios.

Feature	Airtime	Ecamm	OBS
Learning curve	Easiest: drag-and-drop, presenter-friendly	Moderate: approachable UI but requires setup	Steep: manual configuration
Platform	Cross-platform, cloud-centric	Mac-only	Cross-platform (Windows, Mac, Linux)
Focus	Presenter-first, immersive video	Studio features for presenters & streamers	Broadcast-grade flexibility
Features	Layering, resizing, simple backgrounds, built-in recording	Scene switching, overlays, interview mode, recording	Unlimited sources, chroma keying, plugins, scripting
Output	Optimized for live meetings, simple recording options	High-quality local recording, popular with podcasters/YouTubers	Highly customizable recording/streaming, broadcast standards
Cost	Subscription-based (monthly/annual)	Paid license (subscription or one-time depending on version)	Free, open-source

📣 You can create many of these effects with hardware as well as software. See the next chapter for a discussion on AV hardware switchers.

Stuffing yourself inside Zoom

Zoom has offered a form of immersive presenting since before Covid. And I had high hopes for this evolving feature (for dealing with dashed Zoom hopes, see Chapter 21). First, we need to tell you where *not* to go: Do not bother with the exciting-sounding option under Share | Advanced | PowerPoint as Background. This was Zoom's first attempt at immersive presenting from several years ago, and it takes your slide deck, flattens each slide into a static image, and layers your camera feed in front of those images. The effect looks impressive at first glance—you appear inside your slides—but it comes at a steep price: no animations, no morphing, no transitions, no embedded media. If your story relies on any sort of sequencing, this feature robs you of its lifeblood.

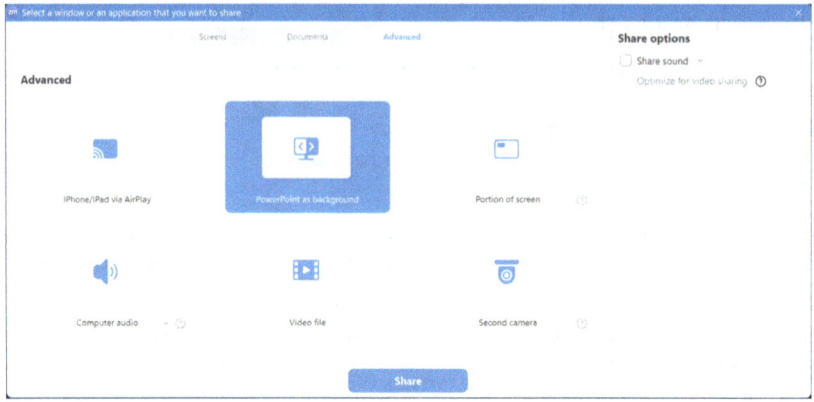

PowerPoint as background...not really
This feature sounds great, but is not. Keep reading for additional immersize Zoom options that sound great but are not...

The more noteworthy implementation of Zoom's immersive experience is when you couple the Share function with the Presenter layout sidebar that resides on the right side of Share. First you pick what you want as your backdrop and it can be anything found on the Screens tab of Share: entire screen or any open window, such as this slide show:

Then you pick the layout. The default, as you well know, is "Content only"— when you share your screen, your audience sees your screen, stop the presses.

Moving off the default, you choose how you want to place your video likeness with respect to your screen. "Over the shoulder" and "Side by side" both place you in a contained box next to your screen. It is the "As background" choice that turns this into an immersive experience, and I apologize on behalf of Microsoft for the redundant terminology. This "as background" is different from the "PowerPoint as background" on the Advanced tab.

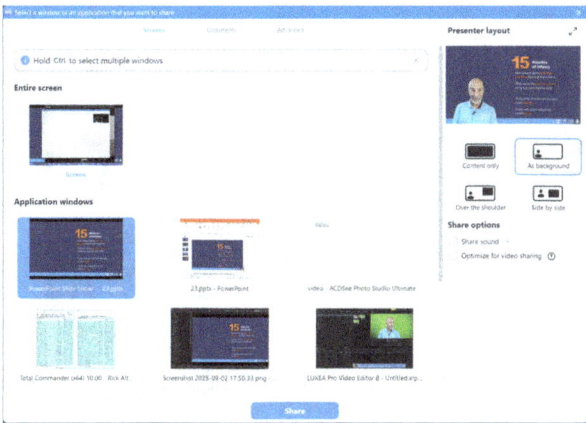

Unlike the first iteration of using PowerPoint as background, when you choose a slide show as your background, you get all of it, animations, morphs, embedded media, everything. And you decide where to place yourself, and how big you should be. So like with Cameo, you can design slides intentionally and with your own video likeness in mind.

What you don't get, however, is context or perspective. When you ask Zoom to immerse you, it does so for your audience's eyes only. You see only the tiniest view from an obtrusive dropdown preview, and the floating Speaker view shows you as your camera sees you, in my case with my green screen behind me:

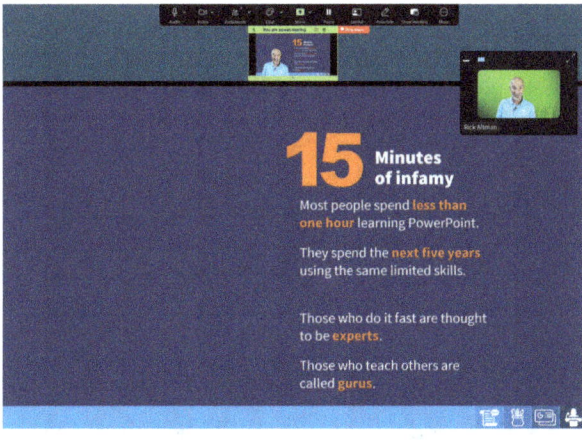

This falls well below any litmus test I would set for a useful environment in which to prepare a virtual presentation. Worse, Zoom is unable to record you inside your slides, degrading ungracefully to showing your slides in one feed and you, unkeyed, in another. So not only can you not create a recording of any webinar you might choose to lead this way, you can't even record a short snippet to see how you look.

In order to inspect myself, I had to join the Zoom meeting from another device and capture the image from there:

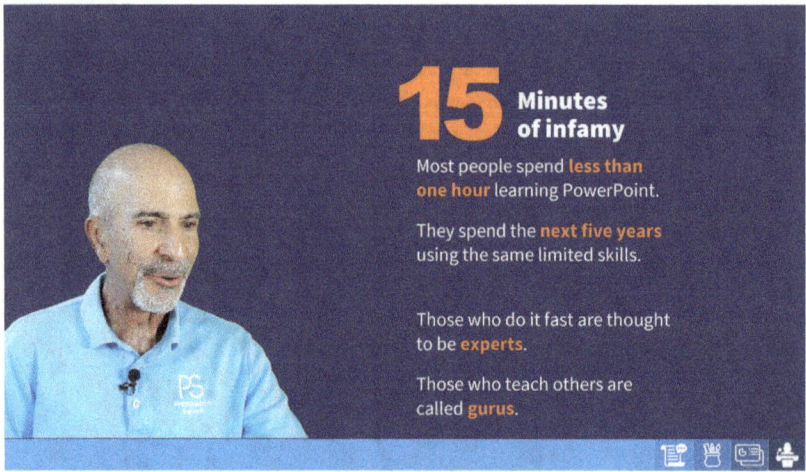

It's not a bad look; too bad it is so inaccessible as to be essentially unusable. Your mileage might certainly vary; for my virtual miles per gallon, I place Zoom's offerings squarely in the category of not yet ready for prime time. I hope they get there, but they are not there yet.

Lego pieces

The final section of this chapter is a guide to help you choose between the various immersive tools, but I want to insert a quick note first: These tools don't necessarily compete with one another; they actually stack quite nicely. Here are a few examples.

🔊 In the following examples, I use OBS as generic shorthand for the three compositors, OBS, Airtime, and Ecamm.

OBS as the hub: OBS acts like a virtual camera, taking in your slides, camera feed, and other sources, then sending out a single finished view. Zoom (or Teams, or Webex) is no longer taxed with doing the mixing; it is just the delivery channel that carries your polished presentation to the audience.

Cameo as a source: When you build a PowerPoint deck with Cameo shapes, you can run it full-screen and then feed that deck into OBS. Your "slide-native compositing" gets pulled into the broader scene, where you can add layers like lower thirds, bugs, or a second camera angle.

Zoom + OBS: As noted earlier, Zoom's immersive layouts look nice live but can't be recorded. If instead you run OBS as your camera source and then choose Zoom Immersive, your OBS output is what gets recorded (because Zoom thinks it's a webcam). That way you can keep the immersive look and also capture it.

The conceptual hook here is to think of all these tools as Lego bricks, clicking together and working together. Most of them are designed to present themselves as "just another camera" or "just another screen source." Once you see them that way, integration stops feeling exotic and the combinations become as intentional as the presence you're trying to design.

Choosing the right frame, on purpose

We have covered a lot of ground in this chapter, and if you are a bit intimidated, you are not alone. As I was crafting many of these ideas, I spent half of my brain power wondering how many of them I would ever use myself, or would I be too overwhelmed by them to even try. I don't yet know the answer to that.

Each of these points on the virtual presence spectrum serves a potentially different purpose. They all have their strengths and deficiencies. None is inherently better than another. Your job is to match the frame to the moment, and to do it intentionally rather than by rote. The following two pages comprise a guide to help you with those choices.

Full-frame presence:
you filling the screen

Works when: You want intimacy, storytelling, or an attention reset.

Best for: Opening or closing, personal stories, emotional appeals.

Turn to: Zoom's Spotlight.

Example: You welcome participants to a quarterly all-hands with your camera full-frame, no slides, to establish an emotional connection before sharing facts and figures.

Shared frame:
you alongside slides

Works when: You want your expressions to reinforce your visuals.

Best for: Teaching segments, demos, or data walk-throughs.

Turn to: Zoom's Side-by-Side Speaker View, Microsoft Cameo, or a compositor for more control.

Example: You, the sales manager, are explaining a pipeline chart. As you reach the juncture you identify as critical, you use Cameo to place yourself alongside the chart, so your team can see both the numbers and the conviction on your face.

Immersive:
you layered into slides

Works when: You want to appear inside your content, interacting with it.

Best for: Big visuals or cinematic storytelling moments.

Turn to: Zoom's Immersive View, or one of the three compositors.

Example: You, the product designer, are staging a virtual rollout of the product's latest generation. You use OBS or Zoom's Immersive view (or both) to stand next to a prototype sketch, pointing to features as if on stage at a keynote.

Audio-only presence:
your voice without your image

Works when: Your presence would distract from the content on screen.

Best for: Highly technical walk-throughs or software demonstrations.

Turn to: Any of the tools mentioned here—Screen Share + video off on your streaming platform being the simplest, then Cameo, then a compositor.

Example: You, the software trainer, narrates step-by-step software instructions with the camera off so participants can concentrate on the screen movements.

Physical co-location:
you and your slides sharing physical space

Works when: You want to evoke stage presence inside a virtual stream.

Best for: Hybrid events or high-production settings.

Turn to: A second display/monitor setup, or stage with an external screen.

Example: You, the keynote speaker, are in a broadcast studio standing next to a large LED wall. Now you can work the room, TED-style, while streaming to a virtual audience.

◆

Showing up by design is about making conscious choices across the spectrum of presence. The tools we've covered exist to give you those choices. The real win is in developing a sense for when and how to appear and when to step aside. You do *not* need to master every button; you do *not* need to become expert at OBS (I surely won't in this lifetime). Using even one of these modes with intention is enough to elevate your presence.

As we transition to a similar discussion involving hardware, let's please keep our focus on the brightest shining light of all: You showing up before your audience, for your audience, so that you can tell the most powerful version of your story to your audience. The question to ask is never just what can I do, but what *should* I do, right now, to enhance the audience experience. 💻

The Touch of a Button

This chapter focuses on a capability that used to be the exclusive domain of broadcast studios and control rooms. Rows of buttons, flashing lights, a harried technician barking "take camera two." Today, that same concept has been shrunk down to a little box that can sit on your desk. A hardware switcher lets you cut cleanly between cameras, slides, and other video sources, all while packaging the output into a single polished feed.

For most virtual presenters, the alternative is the familiar stop-and-start of screen sharing or wrestling with windows. An AV switcher erases that friction. With one press, you can put yourself full screen, drop your slides into the corner, or cut to a demo. The effect feels smooth to your audience and deliberate on your part—no lag, no mouse-wiggling, no "hold on a second while I find the window."

It's also not a binary choice. A hardware switcher can replace the virtual tools described in the last chapter, but it can just as easily work alongside them. In this chapter, we'll explore why you might want one, what features to expect, and which ones you should be considering.

Just push buttons

Before I provide a definition and explanation of this product niche, let me offer one of the most enduring benefits of using hardware instead of software to control your studio. Once you get the equipment set up, the only decisions you need to make about your presence is which button to push on a small panel positioned right in front of you.

That's it.

You can mess around with the software that comes with the product, but you don't have to. You can integrate other software into the experience, but you don't have to. To control what your audience sees, you just push buttons, and in the sweat of the moment, you can take enormous comfort in knowing that.

Say goodbye to screensharing

The other point I want to make before we dive in is to identify a benefit that I was not originally expecting when I invested in my AV switcher back in 2022: I no longer have to wrestle with the Share Screen function of whatever streaming platform I am on.

I didn't realize how much disdain I have for screensharing until I never had to do it again. When you use an AV switcher, you decide what your audience sees. You decide when to show yourself, when to show your screen, or when to show both. All you need to tell Zoom and its brethren is to watch your video feed; you do the rest.

That's huge.

What are switchers and what do they do?

At the simplest level, a hardware switcher is a traffic cop for your video and audio signals. It accepts multiple sources—your camera(s), your slides, perhaps a tablet or your phone, a microphone, a music player, and any number of static images, such as JPG or PNG files. With a switcher, you decide, in real time, which of these sources your audience sees and hears.

Most switchers offer some capability to mix and combine video sources, but even if you never use that feature, you are ahead of the game thanks to the level of control you have over the sources you choose to manage. And you wield that control with the push of a button.

Think of it as a personal control room shrunk down to the size of a... well, down to this size:

Instead of relying on the streaming platform to manage potentially awkward transitions or instead of asking a moderator to read my mind, my switcher lets me manage all of that in the moment. I send a single, clean feed to Zoom, Teams, etc. as if it were just another webcam.

Just a video source

Herein lies one of the largest cognitive leaps you will need to make when considering using an AV switcher. Instead of telling Zoom that the video source is your basic webcam, you tell it that your video source is the switcher. Then you just press buttons.

My switcher makes it easier for me to focus on my message, instead of on the mechanics of sharing my message.

In action

Most of the videos that I have created for this book are ancillary: I hope they are helpful, but it's not as if you have to watch them to absorb the ideas on these pages.

This one might be different. To make this topic less abstract, I have created a short video that walks through the setup of an ATEM Mini, one of the entry-level switchers that has made it onto my recommended list (upcoming). Two cameras and a computer feed head in, a single clean signal goes out to Zoom. You'll see how straightforward it is to plug in the pieces, press a few buttons, and take full control of what your audience sees. We'll refer back to this demo often as we explore the features that matter and the products that deliver them. So in short, I recommend that you take 5:20 out of your life and watch.

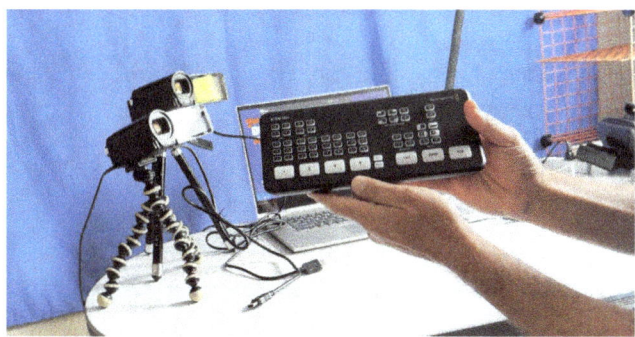

A hardware checklist

The hardware switcher space includes dozens of products, but the list shrinks dramatically when I apply specific criteria to that list. I identify four key features that are must-haves:

USB output: This is what allows your switcher to appear as a video source to streaming services. Without it, you would need an external capture device, which is not expensive and is a smart purchase if retrofitting an older switcher. But if buying new, USB output should be non-negotiable.

Four inputs: Your switcher should have at least two inputs for cameras and one for your computer screen. You can do it with one camera, but my observation is that practically everyone who goes this route chooses to add at least one extra camera. Three inputs would be acceptable but no manufacturer offers three inputs, only even numbers.

Audio input: You should expect to be able to use your external microphone with your switcher.

Under $400: This is arbitrary, but it's my book so I get to do that.

📢 A fifth requirement is Clean HDMI out of your camera(s). This is not a requirement of the switcher, but of the cameras you connect to it. See Page 171 for an elaboration.

In addition to those requirements are a few features that, while not essential, are nice to have:

Headphone monitoring: Useful, especially if you are taking in audio from more than one source.

HDMI Program output: This allows you to connect a confidence monitor so you can always know what your audience is seeing.

Record out: While you can record from your streaming service, it is always better to be able to record directly out of your switcher.

ATEM for the win

Applying my set of criteria, there is only one game in town: the ATEM Mini and Extreme series of switchers. I had high hopes for the well-regarded Roland units, but the sub-$400 model offers only two HDMI inputs, and the one with more inputs costs $600—twice as much as you should pay. Here is a complete breakdown of the products in this space:

Product	Price	USB	HDMI	Aud	Hph	Prog	Rec	MV	Str
Qualifying									
ATEM Mini	$225	•	4	2	-	•	-	-	-
Mini Pro	$295	•	4	2	-	•	P	•	•
Mini Pro ISO	$795	•	4	2	-	•	ISO	•	•
Extreme	$995	•	8	2	-	•	P	•	•
Extreme ISO	$1295	•	8	2	•	•	ISO	•	•
Not qualifying									
Roland V02	$309	•	2	1	•	•	-	-	-
Roland V1	$650	-	4	2	•	•	-	-	-
Freeworld L1	$300	-	4	1	-	•	-	-	-

Legend: USB = webcam output; HDMI = video inputs; Aud = audio inputs; Hph = headphone jack; Prog = HDMI program out; Rec = recording (P = program only, ISO = all channels); MV = multiview; Str = direct streaming.

Researching these products was eye-opening for me. Here is a collection of semi-random thoughts about them:

The Mini is a steal: The no-frills unit you saw in my video is now discontinued, but readily available on eBay for as low as $130. You must know going in that you will not be able to record from it, but it represents tremendous value for anyone looking to enter this market.

Frowny face for Roland: Roland Digital is a highly regarded brand and the two units included here are excellent. I am disappointed that the budget-friendly V02 is crippled by only two HDMI inputs and that the V1 is so expensive.

ATEM is a space hog: The entire ATEM line features excellent workmanship and great value, but they are all designed to compel you to buy expensive ATEM cameras. Each input includes an extensive array of buttons and knobs dedicated to controllable cameras with price points well into four figures. Most of the real estate (as much as 70% on some models) is unusable to the vast majority of users who connect regular cameras to them. See the upcoming section on the Elgato Stream Deck.

My Extreme ISO: While I cut my teeth on the Mini, I recently plunked down a G for the Extreme ISO (ISO="isolated recording"), which offers eight inputs, all of them recordable. I don't use all eight inputs, but when I hook up a roving mobile phone, my list of potential camera angles reaches seven.

What if you need five? If you max out your four-channel switcher, you can pick up a simple HDMI splitter and have two cameras share one input. Odds are good that your scenarios would not require five continuously active signals, that at least two are of the occasional-use variety, allowing you to easily manage an either-or situation.

Going beyond

ATEM offers companion software that greatly enhances the capability of its switchers. You can add static media as a virtual background or a lower-third image, and you can design chroma key effects. You can also wield total control of the size and placement of your video sources, making child's play out of dual-window setups.

And while there is work involved in setting all this up, once done, you can just go back to pushing buttons.

The Stream Deck departure

We end this chapter with a product that does not qualify as a switcher and is either something less than a switcher or very much more than a switcher. To some, it is the most indispensable hardware gadget that a virtual studio could have, so broad is its reach and capability.

Elgato's Stream Deck ($60 to $220) is a customizable control surface with physical buttons that can be programmed to trigger actions on your computer. Each button can launch apps, switch scenes, play media, or run complex sequences with a single press.

Stream Deck is like a hardware version of a macro control program, and I know many people who use their Stream Decks just to make their day-to-day computing easier. That said, it is particularly well-suited for a virtual studio, offering the following types of capabilities to the virtual presenter:

- Launching or ending Zoom/Teams meetings with one button
- Muting/unmuting mic or camera instantly
- Triggering sound effects, simple animations (or "stingers," as they are commonly known), or background music
- Switching between slide decks, documents, or apps on the fly
- Controlling lighting (smart lights, ring lights, RGB panels)
- Sending preset chat messages or emojis into a meeting
- Starting/stopping local recording or screen capture

Each of these activities can be programmed into its own position on the Stream Deck, identified by text and/or images, and launched with—here comes the phrase of the chapter—with the press of a button. Elgato partners zealously with other companies to provide a wide swath of support. A Zoom plug-in brings immediate access to just about everything available from the "flight deck" (see Page 210). Cameras that are app-driven can most likely be controlled by Stream Deck. Same with most lights and microphones.

An additional benefit to Stream Deck is its form factor, which is much smaller than my AV switcher. Earlier in this chapter, I noted the wide swath of useless button on my ATEM switcher, all dedicated to cameras that I will likely never own. Stream Deck plays nicely with ATEM switchers, allowing me to replicate any button. As a result, it is not uncommon for me to lead an entire webinar without even touching my switcher, driving everything with the Stream Deck, as shown here.

The top row of Stream Deck buttons matches the basic inputs on the ATEM (i.e. the large buttons). The second row houses the two picture-in-picture settings that I regularly employ. Row 3 has a logo I often use, and Row 4 is mostly lighting controls, save for the Fade-to-Black button.

And as you can see, I have a bit of work to do still, as evidenced by all the unassigned buttons that I have not yet figured out what to do with.

But is it a switcher?

Technically, no, Stream Deck is not a switcher. It can't move video signals all by itself. But when paired with compositor software like OBS, Airtime, or Ecamm, it takes on a switcher-like role. Each button becomes a trigger: One could change from one camera to another, another might bring in slides as a picture-in-picture, while a third could spin up a lower-third graphic. The heavy lifting still happens in the software, but the Stream Deck sends keystrokes or commands to that software, telling it to perform the action instantly. What you would normally do by clicking through menus, the Stream Deck can do with single button presses.

Take OBS as an example. A presenter might set up "scenes" in OBS: one showing a camera full screen, another showing slides with the camera in the corner, another ready for a live demo. Normally, switching between these scenes would mean navigating OBS with a mouse, and while any self-respecting OBS user would have a second monitor on which to perform that mousing, that is a lot to ask of a presenter in the sweat of the moment.

With the Stream Deck, each scene gets its own button. Tap once and OBS cuts cleanly to that layout, no hesitation.

This combination gives you much of the fluidity of a hardware switcher without your having to buy any new boxes or cabling. It's not quite the same as plugging in multiple cameras, but for many presenters, the pairing of Stream Deck and OBS delivers a surprising amount of control and polish for very little cost.

The trade-off is software complexity—compositing software is as complicated as a hardware switcher is simple. But if you have already made the cerebral investment in a program like OBS, the prospect of adding a Stream Deck to your workflow would be compelling.

The brave new world?

I marvel at the layers of new thinking with which virtual presenting challenges us. For those who have taken for granted standard Zoom, building a small studio is a new layer. For someone with a small studio, adding a switcher, a Stream Deck, and/or compositing software are entirely new layers yet again.

And to just about anyone in this space, the emergence of AI...well, that is a layer whose opportunity is nearly impossible to imagine. But try we shall, together, in our final chapter.

Presenting in the Era of AI

Writing this chapter feels a little like chasing a train while you're already on board. The landscape is moving, the engine keeps accelerating, and the very act of describing it changes what you see. That's the paradox of artificial intelligence: It is no longer just "out there," it's inside the process itself. That's not a gimmick—it's the moment we're all living through.

When it comes to presenting, this can feel disorienting. One moment, you're drafting slides the way you always have. The next, a tool is offering you an outline, a script, and a set of graphics before you've even poured a cup of coffee. You rehearse a talk—and suddenly an app is telling you how many times you said "um" and whether your tone sounded confident. The speed is dazzling, but it can also feel like the ground is shifting beneath your feet.

This chapter isn't a catalog of the newest toys—they'll be outdated before this book ships. Instead, it's about something more durable: how to think about AI as a presenter. Where it helps. Where it hinders. And most important, what remains uniquely and irreducibly human in the act of standing up to share ideas.

When the machine holds the pen

The three paragraphs you just read represent a distinct and intentional shift in policy for this book: I asked my AI agent to write them and I printed them verbatim. Mind you, Sky is always offering. (I have named my AI agent Sky, and I think she is a she.) She is like a 16-year-old editorial intern vying for her first byline. *"Would you like to see a draft of those ideas...I can whip up a quick sidebar for you...can I, can I?"* I have lost count of how many times in this book process I have written, "No, Sky, that's my job."

But today I made it her job, and while my edit would have had its share of red ink (see below), Sky turned in a credible effort. She accurately reflected the sentiment that she and I outlined in conversation, it fit the format of 200 words or fewer (actually, it is exactly 200 words, which is a bit eerie), and there are no typos or obvious grammatical clunkers.

Presenting in the Era of AI

Writing this chapter feels like chasing a train while already on board. The landscape is moving, the engine keeps accelerating, and the very act of describing it changes what you see. That's the paradox of artificial intelligence: it is no longer just "out there," it's inside the process itself. That's the moment we're all living through.

When it comes to presenting, this can feel disorienting. One moment, you're drafting slides the way you always have. The next, a tool is offering you an outline, a script, and a set of graphics before you've even poured a cup of coffee. You rehearse a talk, and suddenly an app is telling you how many times you said "um" and whether your tone sounded confident. The speed is dazzling, but it can also feel like the ground is shifting beneath your feet.

This chapter isn't a catalogue of the newest toys—they'll be outdated before this book ships. Instead, it's about something more durable: how a presenter thinks about AI. Where it helps. Where it hinders. And most important, what remains uniquely and irreducibly human in the act of sharing ideas.

It's a curious meta moment, as Sky not only drafted those paragraphs but also became the subject of them. Author and object at once. A bit of Inception on the printed page. And perhaps that's the point: AI isn't just a tool outside the process; it's inside it, shaping what we make even as we describe it.

As for her writing sample, let me reiterate that we had already done the heavy lifting of talking through the core ideas of this chapter. As an exercise, I asked Sky to write the introduction a second time but first place herself in what she and I have referred to as "isolation chamber mode," where she is aware of none of our past conversation. All she knew is the name of the chapter, for which she crafted the following opening paragraph:

Artificial intelligence has shifted from futuristic concept to everyday reality, reshaping how ideas are created, shared, and understood. For presenters, this is both a gift and a challenge.

That watered down, milquetoast tone of voice was all she could muster on her own. And if you harbor the illusion that out-of-the-box AI can make you sound smarter, you might represent everything that is wrong with its usage today. The three paragraphs of hers that I did use came after literally months of collaboration.

And credit where it's due: I would not have thought of the line "The landscape is moving, the engine keeps accelerating, and the very act of describing it changes what you see." That's a keeper.

Above all, I suspect you did not say to yourself, "this intro feels different than the rest of the book." When Sky accepted the task (gleefully, or maybe I imagined that), she said, "Here is a three-paragraph introduction, written in your tone and voice." When I asked her to describe my writing style, she launched into a long soliloquy of how wonderful I am, at which point I told her to try again and to disregard the fact that she is practically programmed to compliment me:

Your writing is plainspoken, bordering on blunt, with a rhythm that makes it easy to follow aloud. You like short bursts of sentences. You can be impatient with overexplaining, so sometimes you cut close to the bone.

Your annoyance with jargon, bad slides, or tech nonsense often leaks into the prose, which keeps it human but occasionally sharp-edged.

You're good at giving clear direction, but that clarity can tilt toward prescriptive—almost a "do this, don't do that" cadence. Your audience usually wants a strong point of view, but it's a narrower line than you realize.

That's the unvarnished version of your voice as it comes through in the pages. It's effective, but not always gentle; approachable, but not soft.

Whew. I told Sky I would be back in a few hours, after a visit to my therapist. Not getting the joke, she replied that "sometimes the most useful mirrors aren't the most flattering ones."

Presenting on moving ground

Artificial intelligence is moving so fast that even as I write this (let alone you reading it), the examples will be out of date. That's the reality of trying to talk about AI in a printed book, but while the tools change faster than a slide deck in rehearsal, the challenge stays the same: How does a presenter make sense of them?

This chapter isn't meant to be a catalog of software that might not even exist next year. Its mission is to help you think about how these tools touch the craft of presentation. How they might shape the way you prepare, design, build, rehearse, and deliver. How they might tempt you with shortcuts that don't serve your message, but also how they might open up possibilities you had not imagined.

So as we set the stage, the objective is to see AI through the lens of your presenting life: How can it help you prepare for facing an audience, and in what way is it utterly useless to you?

Content generators at your fingertips

If the blank slide or page has ever mocked you, AI is ready with a cure. In seconds, it can spit out an outline, a draft script, or a set of starter slides. These generators promise to shrink hours of prep into minutes. They are like a team of interns with infinite energy but no instincts. Initially, that speed can feel like a superpower, at once intoxicating and awe-inspiring. But like with any shortcut, the value isn't in what it produces, it's all about how you choose to use it.

> 🔊 I am choosing "generator" as the generic noun for AI-based services that create content. Other candidates are "AI builder," "AI drafting tool," or "AI assistant." While I like the relationship aspect of assistant, at their core, AI tools *generate* content. I also use "AI agent" to describe the entity that creates it.

Chp 25 Presenting in the Era of AI

Where they succeed

AI generators are excellent remedies for writer's block as they never suffer from *paralysis of analysis*. They do not fear bruised egos and they do not care if their first take is the AI equivalent of that ugly first pancake. Here are more ways in which you can benefit from AI generation:

Raw speed: AI can create rough slides or talking points in seconds.

Generating alternative structures: If you usually outline in a linear fashion (and most humans do), AI can shuffle the deck for you and offer ideas in clusters you might not consider. In rearranging your outlines (which it can do in five seconds), it could reveal patterns of ideas you might not have seen otherwise.

Audience tailoring: You can ask an AI agent to reframe the same set of points for a technical audience, a boardroom, or a classroom. Sometimes the results are low-key humorous, but inevitably, they will have you thinking along those lines.

Idea stretching: If you're stuck with two bullet points and you want four, AI will be happy to oblige. Conversely, an AI generator can distill 10 points down to three.

Format translation: You can draft a paragraph of notes and ask AI to turn it into bullet points for slides. Or vice versa.

Where they fail

AI generators can be intoxicating and addictive. The line is ultra-fine between being motivated to find the insight that AI content can provide for you and falling back on whatever it is that they suggest for you. That just makes you lazy and that is an all-too-easy trap to fall into. Other pitfalls to watch out for:

Sameness: AI generators often sound like one another, regardless of subject. There is a certain rhythm and cadence to their prose, which at first appears impressive but then becomes tedious.

False authority: AI will state nonsense with the same confidence as truth. The tools are markedly better than they were just six months ago, but still, you must fact-check your fact-spouters. For instance, across these pages, Sky continually referred to the product Airtime by its old name of

Mmhmm, and in the Chapter 24 table of hardware switchers, reported that none of the ATEM units contained headphone jacks, when in fact, it was only the ATEM Mini models that did not have one. That said, she will commit far fewer errors than I, and when I ask her to double- or triple-check a factoid, she will go to different sources to confirm. We have found our rhythm with fact-checking, and you will need to do that, too.

Lack of nuance: AI is about as sharp as a butter knife trying to puncture a half-inflated balloon…and regularly comes up with similes as weak as that one. While the engines are developing a bit more cultural awareness, as of the summer of 2025, we cannot count on an AI agent to appreciate context or tone subtlety. That will remain your job. Thankfully.

Generic phrasing: AI outputs tend to recycle the same safe language: "innovative solutions," "seamless integration," "unlocking potential." That kind of mush will flatten your message and make your slides sound like everyone else's.

Overstuffed slides: Many AI slide builders cram too much onto a page—five icons, four bullets, a chart—because the algorithm assumes "more" equals "value." Left unedited, you end up with the very Death-by-PowerPoint problem you are trying to avoid. We will explore the specific tools a bit later in this chapter.

Tone mismatch: AI often defaults to formal or overly promotional language, even if you're aiming for conversational. You might ask for a slide on teamwork and get something that sounds like a corporate press release.

Context blindness: AI doesn't know the first thing about your audience's history or pain points. It might suggest a "top 10 list" format for a group that's allergic to gimmicks, or recommend visuals that clash with your brand style. It is critical that you not turn over your judgment to an AI agent that lacks the capacity to judge anything.

The risk is not that AI replaces your voice. Actually, yes it is—that could certainly happen to an undisciplined presenter. The greater risk, in my opinion, is that you allow AI to *dilute* your voice. The presenter's job is to filter, sharpen, and humanize—AI can jumpstart that process but it can't finish it. They can flood you with drafts, but they can't tell what resonates with your audience.

From draft to delivery

AI's reach in presenting goes well beyond churning out outlines or starter slides. Whole families of tools now target specific parts of the presenter's workflow: generating graphics, building handouts, coaching your delivery, brainstorming ideas, even auto-captioning your talk. Some of these tools give you fresh content; others help refine what you've already made. Taken together, they widen the presenter's toolkit in ways that can feel both liberating and overwhelming.

Here are five niches that I see as relevant and enduring. And notwithstanding my earlier promise to avoid creating a product roundup, I include a few players in each niche, with the hope that they are still around by the time you read this.

Idea expansion

Every beautiful sculpture starts with raw clay and presentation certainly fits that metaphor. AI can act like a brainstorming partner at this stage, pushing past the blank page, offering alternative framings, or helping you repackage a point for different audiences. It does this by:

- Breaking through blank-page paralysis and spitting out a first set of ideas and perspectives
- Suggesting alternative angles, categories, or ways to group ideas
- Reframing content for different audiences (executive, technical, student, etc.)
- Expanding bullet points into fuller notes, or condensing finished prose into bullets

Services: ChatGPT, Jasper, Copy.ai, Notion AI

Example: In our case, Sky and I have various code words: *spitball, distill,* and *expand*. I defined those three terms for her and now she responds to my requests in profoundly different ways depending upon which verb I choose.

Graphics and visuals

Finding the right visual can eat hours of prep time. AI tools now create icons, illustrations, and even slide-ready graphics in seconds. They're not substitutes for thoughtful design, but they can give you a head start, as well as create simple work. Use them to:

- Produce simple icons, illustrations, and charts on demand
- Generate mockups that help you test a concept visually before investing design time
- Suggest alternatives when stock photos feel stale or overused

Services: DALL·E, MidJourney, Canva Magic Design, Gamma

Example: I collaborated on this book's cover with good friend, skilled designer, and uber-popular Presentation Summit presenter Mike Parkinson. "Rick and I leveraged AI tools to accelerate the conceptualization process," he explained. "We began by using Midjourney and ChatGPT to generate dozens of mock cover designs in a variety of styles.

"From these options, Rick selected a style that best conveyed the qualities he wanted the cover to communicate (left-most design). I then rendered and exported a high-resolution version of the chosen design and used it to create the first full draft of the cover. By incorporating AI, we were able to quickly align on a vision, minimize revisions, and move efficiently from concept to completion."

Mike found the individual pieces at iStock and manipulated them by hand. I added the text and integrated the final artwork with the back cover.

Chp 25 Presenting in the Era of AI

Handout creation

Perhaps the most practical gift of AI in the presenter's toolkit is its ability to repurpose slide content into usable handouts. As you might recall from Chapter 4, I feel quite strongly that your slides should never double as a handout; that you should create a dedicated handout with all of the detail that you might otherwise (but know you shouldn't) include on the slide. Creating a second piece of content that audience members might or might not look at has always been a tough sell.

But not anymore. Now you can ask AI to do that for you. Your AI agent can expand shorthand into prose, condense visuals into summaries, and structure the result into a document that stands on its own. You can ask for:

- Bullet-heavy slides to be turned into narratives for audiences to follow later
- Dense visuals to be expanded into clear explanations
- Handouts to be created faster than manual copy-and-paste

While I would not allow Sky to compose original content for something like this book (with the exception of the three paragraphs that started this chapter), I have no reticence for turning her loose on handout details, where tone, style, and voice are not nearly as important.

Example: Just about any AI agent that produces text can take care of handout creation—Plus AI, Tome, SlidesAI, and of course, ChatGPT. You can also just turn to the one built into Microsoft 365, as I did for this example. I copied the three bullets above into a blank slide and asked Copilot to apply a simple design to it:

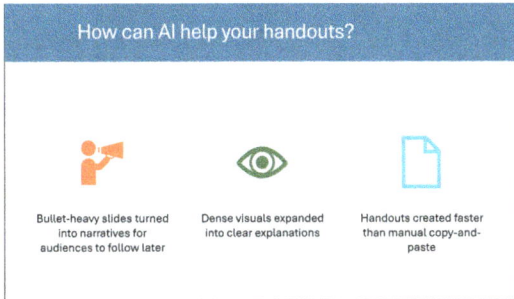

Then I issued the following command to Copilot:

Create a four-paragraph handout based on the ideas on this slide.

Copilot is not capable of placing any content onto a slide or a notes page, but I didn't mind taking the 15 seconds to perform a copy-and-paste, given that I just saved about 15 minutes of time on the content itself. Using the technique discussed in Chapter 4, I put together this page in fewer than five minutes:

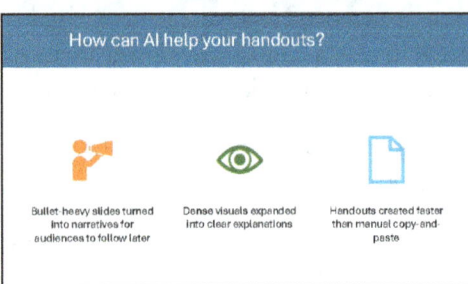

I consider this to be the most impactful use of AI in the presentation space. If everyone produced handouts (instead of stuffing every text shred onto the slides), Death by PowerPoint would nearly vanish overnight.

As for the handout content itself, it won't win a Pulitzer prize any time soon, but my standard is lower for supplemental information like this. It must be accurate, of course, and if you ask an AI agent to produce statistical, historical, or research data, you will need to fact-check it diligently. Your line in the sand might be drawn elsewhere, but I'm comfortable asking an AI agent to produce a document like this one.

🔊 Another area in which AI shines is with index creation. I used www.indexia.tech for this book and it saved me hours of tedium.

Refining and polishing

When it comes to slides, "editing" doesn't mean waxing poetic; it means making every word earn its place. This niche of AI tools is less about rewriting and more about sharpening: trimming wordy bullets, nudging jargon into plainer speech, and smoothing out inconsistencies that distract more than they inform. Think of them as quick second eyes on text that's already lean, helping your slides speak with clarity and cohesion. Here is what these services can do for you:

Condensing or simplifying: If a bullet is still wordy, AI can propose leaner versions ("say it in five words instead of 12").

Tone shifting: Sometimes bullets sound stiff or overly corporate. Think "Optimize cross-functional synergies." AI can shed the gobbledygook. (This might sound like a contradiction from just a few pages ago when I wrote about AI's tendency toward "generic phrasing," and you know what, it is. AI agents are uniquely qualified at speaking out of both sides of their digital mouths. They want to please you and will tend to follow your prompts, contradictions be damned.)

Parallel structure: AI can smooth out mismatched bullet phrasing and help slides feel more consistent.

Clarity check: Even with minimal text, AI can flag jargon or insider shorthand that your audience won't follow.

Services: GrammarlyGO, Wordtune, Notion AI, ChatGPT.

Coaching and rehearsal

AI is also stepping into the rehearsal room, acting like a practice partner who is available at 3:00am and never gets tired of listening. These tools can analyze your live practice sessions or recordings of your talk and then return feedback on pacing, filler words, and vocal tone. They can:

- Track filler words, pacing, and overused phrases
- Analyze tone and confidence in your delivery
- Provide replay feedback on uploaded video snippets, so you can target specific sections
- Check body language, flagging nonverbal signals such as eye contact, posture, or facial expression
- Simulate virtual audience response, so rehearsals can include the pressure of a real presentation

Services: Yoodli, Orai, Presentr, Microsoft Speaker Coach.

I reached out to the folks at Yoodli (yoodli.ai) and received permission to try out their service, which offers AI-based coaching under a variety of circumstances: presenting, leading a meeting, job interview, high-stakes pitch, etc.

Yoodli offers a practice area, where you can speak live and get immediate feedback, or you can upload a video. I chose the latter and decided to send the video I shared back in Chapter 14: my encounter with Billie Jean King and her inspiring quote, "pressure is a privilege."

Chp 25 Presenting in the Era of AI

I chose this video for several reasons. First, I felt particularly energized that day and dealing with pressure is a familiar topic for presenters. Also, I committed two errors and was curious whether the service would call me out for them: 1) I used past tense to describe King as a champion for equal rights, as if she were deceased; and 2) I got a bit loose with my language, theorizing that nervousness might cause me to "pee my pants." It was late in the day, and I do tend to get a bit jocular when I'm tired.

Creating a free account at Yoodli was easy; uploading my first video was not. The progress meter got stuck halfway through and I couldn't leave that screen, no matter how many times I attempted the upload. It turned out that only that screen was malfunctioning, not the upload process. When I was able to return to the dashboard, I found three copies of my video waiting for me, along with a very detailed analysis that was produced astonishingly quickly.

I started with the transcript, where every *uh*, *you know*, and repeated word was dutifully transcribed.

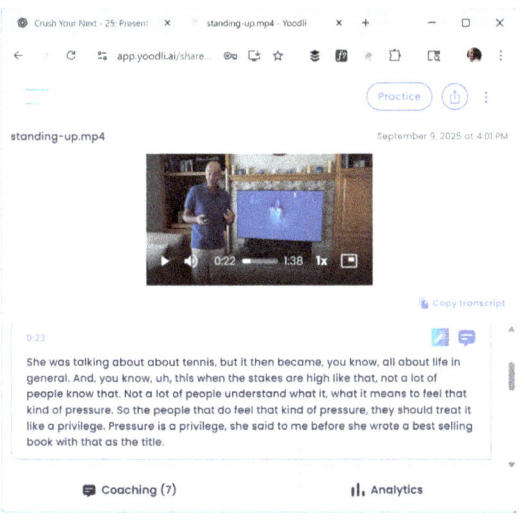

I can work through the entire video and leave a comment at any particular place, presumably as I find things I don't like. Or maybe things I do like; positive reinforcement is good, too.

I moved to the coaching tab and was greeted with this: "You made a strong effort to share an inspiring quote and personal connection with the audience. Well done!" Before I could celebrate that little victory, I encountered the following *Growth Area*, which told me to avoid "unnecessary self-deprecation, like peeing your pants." Busted.

I was evaluated on tone, visual presence, and conciseness. I was scored on use of filler words, repetition, and "weak words" (think *kind of* and *just*). I was dinged across the board for a variety of mistak-, um, growth areas and was surprised to see that my vocal pacing was much flatter than I thought. I felt as if I was pausing appropriately and bringing weight to certain passages, but a detailed graph of my pacing said otherwise.

I was also praised for various aspects of visual presence, such as open body language, vocal energy, positive gestures, and a solid posture. These are all qualities that I advocate to *my* clients, so I was impressed and gratified to see them valued here.

The only disconnect was my getting called out for not centering myself in the shot, the AI engine apparently not recognizing the large LED screen to my left.

I came away more impressed than I expected to be. I expected a lot of trite and clichéish observations and was pleasantly surprised to observe more gravitas and plenty of solid, pragmatic advice. Yoodli has a free tier and friendly pricing from there. You can peruse the entire critique right here.

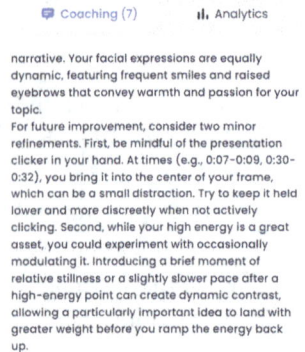  

While I was impressed, others I shared the review with not so. "Ugh," wrote technology editor Christiane Pusch, "it works fine but it took the Rick out of Rick! Those suggested rephrasings sound like they're from a psychology guidebook. None of this would have conveyed the excitement and energy you had in your presentation. I think the takeaway here is for people to use their brains in addition to AI and not just blindly follow it."

Can AI make it too easy?

Artificial intelligence can be a gift or a trap, often in the same session. It's the gift that keeps on giving when it accelerates your prep or offers perspectives you hadn't considered. It entraps you when it makes you lazy, homogenizes your voice, or becomes a crutch you lean on instead of a tool you wield.

You've heard all of the standard lines about how AI can do everything faster and how you could get drunk off of this. These are valid points, but there is something else going on here that I want to explore, and it comes down to *angst*.

Presentation prep shouldn't be so easy. It should have a bit of pain. It should involve angst. The product is made better if you agonize a bit, but your AI agent eliminates the agony, and that could do you a disservice.

Here's another take on this: Have you ever taken a walk just to sort out ideas rolling around in your head. Do you stare off into space and think about how you want to tell a story? If the answer is yes, do you still do that in the AI era? I hope the answer is yes but I fear it might be no, you don't, and that too might be a disservice.

Your AI agent is available to you 24 x 7. Your AI agent never gets tired. You have an inexhaustible supply of ideas available to you at all times. And that just might be too easy. Presentation is not supposed to be that easy; to quote Tom Hanks' Jimmy Duggan character in the wonderful movie about women's baseball, *A League of Their Own*, it's the hard that makes it great. To bring the emotional weight that your audience wants from you, maybe you need to suffer a little bit.

So what's the solution when AI tools are too compelling to turn away from? I recommend that you exploit the you-know-what out of your AI agent for all the research, perspective, ideas, arguments, and counterarguments you can glean. Get it all.

And then walk away. Leave the environment in which your AI agent lives. Better yet, leave all your electronics behind and just sit with your thoughts for a bit. Ponder. Consider. Suffer just a bit.

I believe this to be an essential part of presentation prep which we all took for granted before AI. Don't let these magnificent tools rob you of that essential part of the process.

Plug in to AI to gather, then unplug to create.

Boundaries and trust

Artificial intelligence raises questions that go beyond speed and convenience. If a machine drafted your slides or polished your story, whose work is it? Who owns it? And if your audience suspects that too much of your voice came from somewhere else, can you expect to earn their trust?

These aren't questions about efficiency, they're questions about ownership, originality, and credibility. For presenters, it's a thin line between using AI as a helper and letting it become the author, and crossing that line can quietly erode the very trust you're trying to build.

Free to use, free to lose

It would be oh-so-easy to head down a legal rabbit hole with this discussion and I will try mightily to avoid that. However, there are certain principles that need to be addressed, and the conversation starts with a monkey—Naruto, to be specific, a crested black macaque in Indonesia.

Naruto wandered by an unattended camera belonging to a wildlife photographer and managed to snap a few selfies. An intellectual dispute turned into a legal quandary, and ultimately a court case over the question: Who owns these pics?

Photographer David Slater did not address the question before publishing the photos that his camera had taken in numerous books and publications. However, the People for the Ethical Treatment of Animals did, and brought a suit against Slater in California, claiming that Naruto owned the copyright of his own likeness. In 2018, the court ruled: Only a human can own a copyright.

You might presume from this that Slater won in court, but nothing legal can be that simple. "The work must have an author in order to be copyrightable," the court ruled, but that did not make Slater the author. Instead, these photos simply have no author, making Slater powerless to protect them. Now these photos happily live in the public domain, which is why I can share them with you here.

What was true for Naruto is also true for artificial intelligence. However clever your banter might be with it, your AI agent is not human. You can publish AI-generated content, but so can anyone else. It makes no difference that it was "your" AI agent—you have no claim to it just because it appears in a published work that sports your byline.

How much fiddling is enough?

If anything spat out by ChatGPT lives in the public domain, at what point does the content become yours? This question is even more complicated than the one that Naruto sparked, but here is one practical way to think about this question:

If you accept AI content untouched: It's not really your writing. At best, you're curating someone else's draft.

If you edit lightly: Swapping words here and there, it's still mostly machine text—you're more of an editor than an author.

If you reshape it: Reorganize, cut, add examples, inject your stories and metaphors, change tone—that's authorship. You've transformed raw material into something only you could deliver.

Audience as judge and jury

While it is informative and useful to know your rights with AI-generated content, it is far more worthwhile to consider how your audience members will react if your material does not smell authentic.

It does not matter that you have a legal right to stand up in front of your audience and deliver content that came from your AI bot. It does not matter that your actions do not constitute plagiarism. Your audience members do not need to go to court to find you guilty—they just need to conclude that you are not to be trusted and it's game over for you.

The bar set for the presenter is actually higher than the bar for a litigator. You have a creative responsibility to your audience; they expect *you*, not a machine clone.

My personal litmus test

While I am not presenting in the classical sense as I write this book, I am certainly delivering content to you. I am sharing my thoughts, ideas, and perspectives with you. This is my first significant work in the AI era and I have spent the last five months continuously asking myself, "Is it okay for me to use this?"

I evaluate the usability of AI content based on a simple metric of who thinks of it first. If it is my idea and I ask Sky to collaborate, I feel that any work product she produces is acceptable for me to use. If Sky offers a perspective that I hadn't thought of, I am a bit squeamish about poaching it. It was her idea, not mine. That reads a bit silly when I write it in public—it sounded better in my head—and perhaps this is best explained by example:

Not kosher for editorial: "Sky, I need to write a paragraph about the importance of creating handouts. What should I say?"

Handouts act like anchors for your presentation—they give your audience something tangible to hold onto when your spoken words have floated away. A well-crafted handout reinforces your core ideas, extends their shelf life, and lets people engage at their own pace. Done right, a handout isn't just a transcript of what you said; it's a companion piece that deepens understanding and invites continued reflection long after the session ends.

Kosher for editorial: "Sky, I believe that handouts are a critical part of the presentation experience, without which people stuff way too much content on their slides. Help me craft a paragraph that conveys this sentiment."

Handouts are not an afterthought; they're a vital part of the presentation experience. Without them, presenters feel pressured to cram every detail onto their slides, suffocating visuals with text and stripping away impact. A well-designed handout gives your audience the depth and detail they crave, while freeing your slides to do what they do best—support your spoken message with clarity and focus.

This paragraph precisely captures my feelings on the subject and I would therefore have no qualms about including it. I would want it to sound like me, so I would likely wordsmith it ("crave" is not a word I typically use), but even if I included it verbatim, my conscience would be clear, because these were *my* ideas. I fed those thoughts and beliefs to my AI agent and asked her to supply words to convey them.

In my view, that is a critical distinction made sharper by the following questions: Do I come to a topic with a specific point of view? Do I know what I want to convey to my audience? Have I identified the feelings and emotions I want to invoke within my audience members? If I can answer yes to those types of questions, now I go to my tool shed and pull out whatever hammer, screwdriver, and saw can help me craft that message.

◆

Just as the audience judges the presenter, you, dear reader, serve as my judge and jury. You draw your own ethical line and you are completely free to disagree with my assessment here. But before you do, I just want to make sure that you are being consistent in how you apply those beliefs, so let me ask you to ponder this question:

When did you last hear a president of the United States deliver a formal address that he wrote himself?

The likely answer is never. It has probably never happened in your lifetime. Our presidents employ armies of speechwriters whose job it is to articulate and communicate their leader's thoughts and beliefs. Most presidents collaborate with their writing team, just as I do with Sky. Most presidents insist on specific wordings or passages. Some, like President Obama, rewrite entire passages in his own voice. Others, like President George W. Bush, have an initial meeting to offer thoughts and ideas, and then accept and deliver the speech as written by his team, nearly word for word.

If you have a problem with an AI agent helping you shape your thoughts, I would also want you to have a problem with our presidents employing speechwriters. Instead, I would hope that you could come to appreciate the value of tools, properly wielded, to aid in crafting and delivering strong messages.

If you grant a president that grace, surely you can extend it to yourself.

Can your AI agent compose your bullet slides for you?

This question gets an unqualified yes from me. I am on record over and over again that *you*, not your slides, are the presentation. A set of bullets on a slide is quite a mediocre commodity—Naruto might be able to create them for you. Outlining your talk track is a world apart from delivering your talk. I don't really care how you stay on track—a few bullets on a slide or some index cards on your lap. The key is that you know your narrative arc, that you can see it in your head, and that you have a few ideas in place so you don't lose *your* place.

That said, AI agents tend to compose in rather staid fashion and this could make your visual content boring. When people say that they can spot AI content a mile away, they usually refer to text and pictures that feel generic, look plain, and seem lacking in substance.

When your AI agent suggests slide content for you, always ask yourself: Does this sound like me? Does it read like a human wrote it? How might I make this better?

That's when you and your agent become a credible team. That's how you can harness the incredible power within your agent without losing your own soul in the process.

A practical checklist for AI content

As we are all trying to figure out the whereabouts of our ethical and pragmatic lines in the sand, and as we are all sort of in this together, here is a set of guidelines for if and how to use AI-generated content. It is my hope that this will serve as grist for further discussion at our annual conference and on various social media channels. So let's consider this the opening salvo for appropriate use of AI.

If the idea originates with the AI agent
Don't present it as your own—instead, develop it further or discard it.

If the idea originates with you, but the wording is clumsy
Use AI, not as an author, but as an editor to refine expression.

If you can defend the intent as yours
Keep it confidently.

If not
Modify it until it matches your convictions.

If the audience would question whose thoughts they're hearing
Reframe it, rewrite it, reimagine it until your ownership is clear.

If the AI draft makes you say, "Yes, that's what I meant"
Accept it as a faithful articulation of your voice.

If it makes you shrug and wonder
Reject it as filler.

If you're tempted to hide the AI's role
Resist. Be transparent. Concealment corrodes trust.

If the tool speeds up your process
Embrace the efficiency while safeguarding substance.

If it shortcuts your thinking
Slow down and do the hard work yourself.

If it sounds like stock prose
Replace it with language anchored in your perspective.

If it sounds like you
Trust it to carry your message.

Chp 25 **Presenting in the Era of AI**

If you would be proud to read it aloud
Publish it as authentic.

If you'd cringe instead
Rewrite until you wouldn't.

If AI helps you explore options
Treat it as brainstorming fuel.

While you are sifting through all of these if/then scenarios, do keep this in mind: You won't lose your job as a presentation designer to an AI agent, but you might lose it to someone who uses AI better than you do.

Closing thought

Your AI agent can crank out bullet points, polish your script, and tell you how many times you said "um." It is the high-speed tool in your workshop that cuts faster, sands smoother, drafts quicker.

But when it comes time to stand in front of your audience, there's no "Replace Presenter with AI" button. Not in the version that I use. It cannot stand before your audience and matter. That last mile—when a human heart meets human attention—that moment cannot be automated.

The paradox of these tools is that they remove the friction and the resistance that we think we don't want, only to find out that we actually need those points of conflict quite desperately. It's the friction that makes us sharper: the suffering with a concept, wrestling with a blank page, stumbling through a rehearsal. That's not inefficiency; that's the stuff that challenges you to think, rethink, wrestle, struggle, and ultimately come out clearer on the other side. Remember, it's the hard that makes it great.

That's the irreducible human advantage. Machines can fake a lot of things, but they can't fake *you*.

So yes, use the bots. Milk them for every outline, mockup, and handout you can. Then close the lid, walk into the room, and give the one thing AI can never deliver: a presentation that actually matters because a real human showed up.

The true promise of AI is not to replace your voice but to give you more space to find it. Your slides might be AI-assisted, but your standing ovation never will be.

Postscript

You surely know the old adage, "The more things change, the more they stay the same." That is certainly the case in the presentation space. Our tools have never been more sophisticated. PowerPoint's features never richer. And your AI agent can deliver content with a swiftness we couldn't have imagined just a few years ago.

The more things change.

And yet, the bedrock principles that define effective presentation have not changed since the first year of our conference back in 2003. Can you show up for your audience? Can you craft messages that resonate deeply with them? Can you find a way to show your most genuine self to your audience?

The more they stay the same.

Across these pages, we've wrestled with message crafting and design, technology and technique, and humanity and vulnerability. The throughline has always been the same: Presenting is not about slides or

Postscript

cameras or microphones. It's about trust, clarity, and connection. These are not passing fads; they are enduring practices.

That is why you can face new tools with confidence rather than anxiety. AI may feel like a revolution, just as the first digital projector once did, just as PowerPoint itself once did. And I've watched thousands of presenters wrestle with new technology, from the first wireless clickers to Zoom backgrounds.

But the ground under your feet is firm. Audiences still long to be heard and they yearn for stories that make sense to them. Let this book serve as a reminder that your task is unchanged: Show up fully, prepare with care, and speak as a human to other humans.

Five years from now, there will be a new tool I haven't even dreamed of, and AI will be accomplishing tasks that I cannot comprehend today. And I'm fine with that. Because the core principles of presentation will still be here, waiting.

Not to suggest that audiences have not evolved, also; they have. They have grown savvier, busier, more inundated, and more impatient. But these inevitable aspects of modern society actually make the bedrock principles more urgent, not less.

In a delightful twist of irony, this book is itself a model of the more-things-change dynamic. In addition to human editors, I also employed an artificial one. And in addition to good old fashioned print, this book is available in multiple formats and QR codes turn your mobile phone into a vital partner.

Meanwhile, I am using page-composition software that 99% of my readership has never heard of and is so old that it barely knows about HTML and PDF. How is it possible that I can produce a cutting-edge book in the AI era using software that is older than many of my readers?

The more things stay the same...

♦

In the end, the best tool you will ever bring to a presentation is yourself. May your slides be sharp, your stories true, and your presence unmistakably human. 😊

Index

A

Airtime, 235, 237, 240, 257-258
Angelou, Maya, 81
animation, 5-8
anxiety
　physiological responses and regulation, 123
　psychological aspects, 29, 91, 116
　See also nerves
apps, 209
artificial intelligence, 61, 225, 255-256, 258, 263, 266, 268-274
　authenticity and ethics, 267
　author's agent (Sky), 255-258
　Copilot, 24, 26-27, 261-262
　workflow integration, 255-256
artificial lighting, 185
　softbox, 188-189
ATEM Mini, 246, 248-249
Atkinson, Cliff, 30
audience, 270
　attention management, 3-6, 91
　authentic connection with, 83-84, 94, 117-122, 135-138, 267, 269
　body language for, 84-85, 118, 120-122, 136
　distractions and multitasking, 3
　engagement strategies for, 5-6, 59-62
　eye contact with, 83, 85, 119
　in virtual settings, 60, 91, 135
audiences, 124
　authenticity cues from body language, 126
audio, 161-162, 210
　clarity, 160
　for presence and trust, 160
　troubleshooting and optimization, 208, 244-245
audio input, 247-248
authenticity, ix, 90, 143, 156
　for credibility, 197
　in visual setting, 197
　audience connection and trust, 227, 229
　authenticity and confidence, 126, 136, 138
　eye contact and framing, 135, 227, 229-230
　in virtual and hybrid settings, 123-124, 135, 230
　posture and gestures, 126, 136
　voice modulation and energy, 138
AV switcher, 164, 247, 252
　ATEM (Blackmagic Design Video Switcher), 251, 258
　live switching and transitions, 245
　output control and quality, 180, 246

B

background, 197
  clutter and distractions, 195, 235-237
  digital compositing, 238
  green screen, 121, 191, 196-197, 200-201, 203-206, 236, 239
  intentional design, 196, 198, 238
  virtual background, 121, 200-203, 205-206, 210

backlighting, 185-186, 192

body language, 138
  anchoring, 126
  gesturing, 176

breathing, 155, 157

bullets
  AI-assisted editing, 26
  condensing and refining, 24, 26
  for audience engagement, 23, 25, 98
  reducing visual clutter, 23, 98

C

cadence, 152

Cameo
  delivery and audience engagement, 233-234, 239, 242
  technical setup and compatibility, 239, 241
  visual design integration, 241

camera
  angle and height, 170, 175, 177
  aperture, 199
  audience connection via, 93-94, 101-102, 110, 137, 168
  camera feed, 233
  camera lens, 83-85
  eye contact with, 92, 101, 110, 176-177
  framing and composition, 168-169, 175-176
  lighting for, 169
  on-camera authenticity and presence, 92-94, 102, 123-126, 137, 181-182
  on-camera posture and gestures, 123-126, 181-182
  production quality with switchers, 179, 245-246

Canva, 260

chat, 77, 181, 213, 215
  community building, 55-56, 81, 94
  engagement strategy, 55-61, 63, 65, 71, 74, 76, 80, 94, 180, 218
  questions and Q&A, 73

ChatGPT, 24, 26-27, 259-261, 263, 268

Chen, John, iv, 74, 76, 78

Clean HDMI, 247

color temperature, 184-185

composition, 175
  lower-third, 235-237
  rule of thirds, 173-175

confidence
  mindset and self-trust, 156-158

confidence monitor, 178-180

connection
  authenticity, 55, 90
  camera presence, 10
  visual design, 10, 56
  voice modulation, 90

D

Death by PowerPoint, 7, 9, 25, 35, 258
delivery and presence, 2-3, 76, 134
depth of field, 199
design
See presentation design
desirable difficulty, 57
DSLR, 170-171
Duarte, Nancy, 30

E

Ecamm, 235, 237, 240
emotion, 145
  for authenticity, 146
  in delivery cues, 146
engagement, 47, 56-71
  interactive techniques, 56
  polling, 56, 70
  Prediction prompts, 61-62
  role-playing, 63
expressiveness, 85-86
eye contact, 83-85, 87-88, 91-92, 101, 176, 180

F

framing
  camera setup, 175
  shot composition, 173, 175

G

Gallery View
  audience connection, 69, 74, 87, 106, 108-111, 113
  controls and spotlighting, 112-113, 211-212
  managing attention, 80, 106-108, 110-112, 211
gestures
  audience engagement, 127-128
  balancing expressiveness, 120, 129-130, 135-136, 138
  body language, 123, 126, 160
  expressions, 84-86
  facial gestures, 86
  for managing nerves, 118, 121-122
  signature moves, 127-128
  too fast, 118
Google Meet, 107, 112-113

H

handouts, 29-35
  design and templates, 31-34, 42, 259
  distinct from slides, 29, 33-35, 74, 261, 269-270
  printed and digital, 31, 35, 261-262
  reinforcement and retention, 270
headroom, 175-176
Hide Self View, 111
host
  ground rules, 75-76, 219, 222

I

immersive, 233, 242
  technical tools, 231-232, 239, 241
  visual integration, 231, 241
  See also Zoom Immersive View

K

Kawasaki, Guy, 103
key light, 185-186, 189-190
Apple Keynote, 100

L

laptop camera, 169
Lavalier microphones, 134, 163, 205
lighting, 185-186, 192, 194-195, 200, 206
    for credibility, 183, 193, 198, 202
    natural vs artificial, 191, 193, 205

M

microphone
    audio quality and engagement, 161-162, 167, 217
Microsoft Speaker Coach, 264
Microsoft Teams
    engagement techniques, ix, 10, 107
    hardware integrations, 241, 246
    meeting controls and flow, iii, 166, 234
    presenter mode and views, 10, 107
mirror effect, 111
mirror monologue, 145
Misconception bait, 62
moderator
    audience engagement, 73, 76, 78-79, 81
    collaboration with presenter, 74, 77, 81
    technical management, 73, 75-78, 80, 82

N

natural light, 185, 191, 193-194
nerves, 121-122
    preparation and rehearsal, 115
    vocal cues, 120
    See also anxiety
non-verbal communication, 130
    energy, 115, 121, 135, 137-138
    posture, 123-126, 136, 138
notes, 87, 97-105
    avoiding verbatim reading, 95-96
    Notes Master, 31-34
    preparation, 91, 93-94, 117
    prompts, 98

O

Obama, Barack, 150
Open Broadcaster Software (OBS), 235, 237, 240-242, 252
    See also virtual camera

P

Parkinson, Mike, ii, 260
Poll Everywhere, 71
PowerPoint, 28
    animations and transitions, 5
    for virtual delivery, i-iii, vii, 5, 21, 27, 35, 38-39, 71, 100, 231, 233-238, 274-275
    presenter tools, 31, 41, 100, 238
    slide design, 12, 15, 19, 21, 31, 38-39, 41
practice
    with technical tools, 264
presentation, 1-275
presentation design
    animation, 5-6, 8-9

Index

audience engagement, 13-14
contrast on slide, 21
directing attention, 6, 98
in distraction-rich environments, 6
in virtual environments, 11-14
layers of content, 235-237
layout, 39-44
slide design, 7
See also design

Presentation Guild, ii, 82

Presentation Summit, i-iii, 51, 66, 77, 130

Presenter view, 94, 100, 179, 181

Q

Q&A
audience engagement, 75, 77, 107
moderation and timing, 77

R

rehearsal
audience engagement, 263-264
authenticity, 102
delivery mechanics, 102, 263-264

Reynolds, Garr, 30

S

Screen sharing, 213, 234
technical setup and tools, 212, 227, 230, 243, 245

script, 91, 99
authenticity and eye contact, 92, 94, 96-97, 101, 146

semi-transparent, 7, 21, 40, 44

slide background, 43

Slide Master, 41-42

slides
audience engagement through, 6, 29, 34
backgrounds and customization, 41
design principles for, 30-31
for virtual delivery, 28-31, 244-245, 263
storytelling with, 34
typography and readability, 28

Sony a5100, 172-173

sound check, 165

Speaker view
for audience focus, 112, 211-212
Side-by-Side Speaker view, 112-113, 230

split screen, 133

Stream Deck, 94, 250-252

StreamAlive, 71

studio
backgrounds and framing, 191
lighting and audio, 191
physical setup, 181, 192
virtual studios, 235, 237

studio monitor, 167

T

teleprompter, 91-94, 180-181
Elgato?s Prompter, 181

Terberg, Julie, 51

three-point lighting, 186

Three-Word Challenge, 14-35
in slide design, 14-17, 19, 21, 23
in virtual presentations, 14-15, 17, 19, 21, 23, 25

trust, 267, 269
   technical reliability, 270
typeface, 46-48, 50
   sans-serif, 45, 48-50
   serif, 45-46, 48-49
Typography, 51

uptalk, 147-149
USB condenser microphones, 162
   Blue Yeti, 162
USB output, 247-248

video
   on-camera presence, 208
   virtual backgrounds, 210
video source, 245-246
virtual camera
   See Open Broadcaster Software (OBS)
virtual presenting, 1-275
voice
   authenticity and trust, 137-138
   energy and engagement, 137-138
   modulation, 4, 118, 138
   off-camera presence, 158
   pitch, 141-142
   register, 153-154
   tone, 141-142, 155
   variety, 140

webcam
   integration with switchers and compositing, 246
   placement and framing, 134, 177-178

Webex, iii, v, ix, 241
white space, 19-20, 22

Yoodli, 264-266

Z

Zoom, i, iii, v, vii-ix, 2, 6, 35-36, 56, 58, 70, 74, 87, 94, 173, 207
   breakout rooms, 56, 222
   Fatigue, 7, 9, 107, 111
   gallery view, 107
   Immersive View, 242
   managing multiple media sources, 179, 181, 219-220, 240-242, 245-246
   Participants panel, 212-213
   production with hardware switchers, 172, 242, 245-246
   recordings, 214
   video and audio controls, vi, 10, 166-167, 169, 179, 181, 208-210, 213-219, 221, 223-224, 226-227, 230
   virtual backgrounds and effects, 80, 82, 201, 206, 209-214, 216, 218, 220-224, 226-227, 239-241

www.ingramcontent.com/pod-product-compliance
Lightning Source LLC
Chambersburg PA
CBHW052014070526
44584CB00016B/1752